Psychotherapy and the Human Predicament

Psychotherapy and the Human Predicament

A Psychosocial Approach

Jerome D. Frank

Edited by Park Elliott Dietz

SCHOCKEN BOOKS • NEW YORK

First published by SCHOCKEN BOOKS 1978

10 9 8 7 6 5 4 3 2 1   78 79 80 81

Copyright © 1978 by Schocken Books Inc.

Library of Congress Cataloging in Publication Data

Frank, Jerome David, 1909–
Psychotherapy and the human predicament.

Bibliography: p.
1. Psychotherapy—Philosophy.   2. Personality
and culture.   3. Psychiatry and religion.
I. Dietz, Park Elliott.   II. Title.

RC480.5.F68   616.8'914   78–54396

Manufactured in the United States of America

ACKNOWLEDGMENTS

The material in "Psychotherapy: An Overview" originally appeared in: An Overview of Psychotherapy, ch. 1, pp. 3–21, in Usdin, G., ed., *Overview of the Psychotherapies* (New York: Brunner/Mazel, 1975); pp. 352–53 of Therapeutic Factors in Psychotherapy, *Am J. Psychotherapy* 25:350–61, 1971; and pp. 31–34 of The Bewildering World of Psychotherapy. *J. Social Issues* 28:27–43, 1972.

"The Dynamics of the Psychotherapeutic Relationship" is reprinted with minor changes from: The Dynamics of the Psychotherapeutic Relationship: Determinants and Effects of the Therapist's Influence, *Psychiat.* 22:17–39, 1959.

"Treatment of the Focal Symptom" is reprinted with minor changes from: Treatment of the Focal Symptom: An Adaptational Approach, *Am. J. Psychotherapy* 20:564–75, 1966.

"On Illness and Healing in Nonindustrialized Societies" is reprinted with minor changes from: Foreword, pp. vii–xii, to Kiev, A., ed., *Magic, Faith, and Healing: Studies in Primitive Psychiatry Today* (New York: Free Press, 1964).

"*The Two Faces of Psychotherapy*" is reprinted with minor changes from: The Two Faces of Psychotherapy, *J. Nerv. Ment. Dis.* 164:3–7, 1977.

"Conflict in Therapeutic Groups" is reprinted with minor changes from: Some Values of Conflict in Therapeutic Groups, *Group Psychotherapy* 8:142–51, 1955.

"Cohesiveness in Therapeutic Groups" is reprinted with minor changes from: Some Determinants, Manifestations, and Effects of Cohesiveness in Therapy Groups, *Int. J. Group Psychotherapy* 7:53–63, 1957.

"Emotional Reactions to an Unfamiliar Disease" is reprinted with minor changes from: Emotional Reactions of American Soldiers to an Unfamiliar Disease, *Am. J. Psychiat.* 102:631–40, 1946.

The material in "Psychosomatic Aspects of Illness and Healing" originally appeared in: Psychotherapy of Bodily Disease: An Overview, *Psychotherapy and Psychosomatics* 26:192–202, 1975; pp. 48–49, 52–55, and 57 of Mind-Body Relationships in Illness and Healing, *J. Int. Acad. Preventive Med.* 2:46–59, 1975; and pp. 128–29 of The Faith That Heals, *Johns Hopkins Med. J.* 137:127–31, 1975.

"Galloping Technology as a Social Disease" is reprinted with minor changes from: Galloping Technology: A New Social Disease, *J. Social Issues* 22:1–14, 1966.

"Psychological Challenges of the Nuclear Age" is reprinted with minor changes from: Breaking the Thought Barrier: Psychological Challenges of the Nuclear Age, *Psychiat.* 23:245–66, 1960.

"Psychologic Aspects of International Negotiations" is reprinted with minor changes from: Psychologic Aspects of International Negotiations, *Am. J. Psychotherapy*, 23:572–83, 1969.

The material in "Behavioral Scientists and International Affairs" originally appeared in: Psychiatrists and International Affairs: Pitfalls and Possibilities, *Int. J. Social Psychiat.* 18:235–38, 1972/73; and pp. 283–84 of Contributions of Behavioral Scientists Toward a World Without War, *Compreh. Psychiat.* 5:283–93, 1964.

"Deterrence—For How Long?" is reprinted with minor changes from: Deterrence—For How Long? *War/Peace Report*, 8:3–7, 1968.

"Religion and Psychiatry" is reprinted with minor changes from: A Psychiatrist Looks at Religion and Psychiatry, *Ethical Religion Speaks*, American Ethical Union Talk of the Month, 1957.

"Sources and Functions of Belief Systems" is reprinted with minor changes from: Sources and Functions of Belief Systems, *Am. Psychologist* 32:555–59, 1977.

"Conscience and Moral Law" is reprinted with minor changes from: Conscience and Moral Law, *The Standard*, pp. 4–8, January–February, 1955.

"The Challenge of Nuclear Death" is reprinted with minor changes from: Nuclear Death—The Challenge to Ethical Religion, *The Ethical Platform*, pp. 1–10, April 29, 1962.

To Liza

Life is not a spectacle or a feast: it is a predicament.

—GEORGE SANTAYANA

Contents

Foreword

JEROME D. FRANK has had an important influence on a generation of psychotherapists in the English-speaking world, on several generations of medical students and psychiatry residents at Johns Hopkins, on the methods used to study and evaluate psychotherapy, and on some of our nation's leading statesmen. This influence has been exerted through his tireless writing and teaching, both of which reflect uncommon clarity and wisdom.

Three themes run throughout Frank's work, from his early psychological experiments on level of aspiration to his most recent reflective essays. The first is that people react to the world as they perceive it to be, not as it is. The second is that many of the predicaments of individuals and of groups constitute maladaptive reactions to distorted interpersonal perceptions. The third is that the resolution of many predicaments lies in the correction of these distortions through changes in attitudes and beliefs, particularly expectations.

This book brings together Frank's most important nontechnical papers and makes them available to a wider audience than has seen them previously. The book continues some of the explorations begun in *Persuasion and Healing* and *Sanity and Survival* and introduces new ones. As a compendium of Frank's nontechnical writings, it complements a technical volume on the work of the Psychotherapy Research Unit of the Henry Phipps Psychiatric Clinic, Johns Hopkins Hospital, which he

directed. The present volume is organized into five parts,
though the boundaries between them are fluid, and the reader
will find evidence in each part of the three themes mentioned
above.

The first part of this volume, "On Psychotherapy," presents
Frank's conception of the shared features of psychotherapies.
His view emphasizes the characteristics that are common to all
healer-patient relationships. These relationships take divers
forms and occur in all cultures, but those that persist do so by
virtue of their success in combating demoralization and relieving those specific adaptational failures that we identify as
symptoms. This broad view is the keystone of a unified theory
of suffering and healing that is more fully articulated in the
essay on "Psychosomatic Aspects of Illness and Healing" in the
third part.

Therapists in training typically devote considerable effort to
mastering the formal ideology and informal rules of one or more
therapeutic techniques and diagnostic schemes. In most circumstances they are also compelled to learn something of other
approaches and are, however subtly, indoctrinated with dis-
crediting information and disapproving attitudes toward the
approaches that compete with those of their teachers. In being
socialized into one group of healers, only the rare trainee can
maintain a broader vision of suffering and healing.

Although Frank repeatedly acknowledges the importance of
therapists' believing strongly in the techniques that they use,
his analysis suggests a growing integration of religio-magical
and scientific approaches to healing. As this occurs, it is all the
more essential that we have a unified theory, for without it the
erosion of apparent boundaries between techniques will lead to
loss of faith in the techniques, which will no longer appear
unique. Therapeutic anomie, or the demoralization of therapists,
would be detrimental to patients, whose success in treatment
depends to an important degree on their therapists' faith in the
techniques employed.

The second part, "On Group Therapy," explores the functions of conflict and of cohesiveness in therapeutic groups regardless of the schools they represent. In cohesive groups in
which the members take each other seriously and continue

communicating despite hostility, conflict situations can help enhance self-confidence and communication skills. Moreover, group cohesiveness, or the attraction the group holds for its members, is an important determinant of the degree to which group standards induce change in the group members. These principles illustrate Frank's thesis that "interactions of members of a therapy group may be understood in part as manifestations of properties of the group per se rather than as exclusively determined by personal characteristics of the members." That it should be necessary to suggest this as a "thesis" testifies to the depth of our Western belief in the supremacy of individual consciousness. Durkheim's proposition that social groups comprise more than the sum of their individual members elicited vehement debate in the final years of the nineteenth century, and the issue is not yet settled.

The third part, "On Psychosomatics," juxtaposes two formulations that were written three decades apart. The account of Frank's original observations on the importance of expectations in determining the progress of healing shows the origins of much of his later work, and the essay that follows is the most comprehensive statement available of his holistic approach. Taken together with the material in the first part, this forms the basis for what I have called a unified theory of suffering and healing.

Although Frank speaks of the need for a paradigm shift in medicine, he does not claim to have provided a unified theory that can accomplish this shift. Nonetheless, his essay on the holistic approach does point the way, and by focusing on lacunae in the dualistic view of man, it documents the need.

The papers in the fourth part transcend the concern with the well-being of individuals and groups that characterize the rest of the volume. Here the focus is on threats to civilization on a global level. Frank takes a risk as he tackles issues that are outside his areas of official expertise, and the result is not flawless. But without such risk-taking the development of interdisciplinary views would be considerably delayed, and the urgency of the issues tackled here compelled Frank to treat them as best he could. The enduring value of these papers, I believe, lies in their creative application of social psychological principles to problems that are too often formulated in terms that preclude their solution and in their emphasis on the importance of the behavior of individual decision makers who hold the fate of millions in their hands.

Finally, in the fifth part, Frank discusses the functions of the belief systems that humanity has constructed and used to maintain morale and alleviate despair. The analysis takes several turns, but is consistently synthetic. Even as he compares and contrasts belief systems, Frank enhances their integration. For some readers these papers will provide new options, and a few may even find solutions to their individual predicaments. All, however, should be left with a heightened sense of community, which, if Frank is correct, is itself therapeutic.

Theories of behavior, like theories of psychotherapy, share common features, such as a recognition of the reinforcing properties of individual gratification, but differ so widely in emphasis that they can appear incompatible. Thus, at first glance, psychoanalysis, behaviorism, symbolic interactionism, the structural and functional schools of social theory, and the ideologies of the great religions appear worlds apart. But the rarity of critical experiments that pit one theory against another in a definitive test suggests that the explanatory and predictive powers of many theories may be equivalent. Like the proponents of psychotherapeutic schools, the proponents of various theories of human behavior tend to be socialized into the ideology of one or a very few schools of thought, to associate selectively with those of like mind, and to seek out only the evidence that supports their views. This contributes to the cumulative development of each school and helps to maintain the faith of believers.

Frank vindicates psychotherapeutic isolationism by emphasizing the importance of the therapist's and patient's faith in the treatment. I wonder whether the faith of theorists of human behavior and their followers, including those in both the scientific and the religious traditions, does not contribute to the morale of all concerned. If so, the importance of a unified theory of human behavior cannot be overemphasized, for the erosion of boundaries among our current theories threatens the morale of all who dare look beyond the ideologies into which they are socialized.

In his Foreword to the first edition of *Persuasion and Healing*, John C. Whitehorn wrote that Jerome Frank "has kept within his range of vision much more than the minutiae of method or of doctrine." The reader of the papers collected here will agree that this has remained a hallmark of Frank's writings, for he has a synthetic touch. I am inclined to believe that the tendency of so many of us to subdivide, to classify, and to polarize is the source of much bigotry and despair. We are indeed fortunate that there are some among us who, like Frank, maintain the broader vision and link us together.

I helped to initiate and organize this volume while Dr. Frank was my psychotherapy supervisor at Johns Hopkins. Although others had encouraged him to produce something of this kind, he had been reluctant to do so. I attributed his reluctance to modesty and set about convincing him of the feasibility and worth of the project by asking him to prepare a list of his writings that would help guide my reading. In doing so, he sorted his writings into thematic categories and reminded himself of the scope of his work. As we discussed the writings, I made notes on linkages, overlap, repetition, the appeal that each paper might have for a general audience, and, most importantly, Dr. Frank's appraisal of the paper. Through this process, we eventually selected the papers to be included. By the time this was accomplished, there was open acknowledgment that a book was being prepared, and Dr. Frank undertook the task of collating the materials from small clusters of closely related papers into cohesive essays in the several instances in which this was necessary. Moreover, it was Dr. Frank who updated and made minor revisions in reprinted papers.

Dr. Frank's brief autobiographical Preface was written for this volume, and Chapter 10 and his bibliography have not been previously published. Three selections are reprinted from periodicals issued by the American Ethical Union and one from *War/Peace Report*, all of which are difficult to obtain. The remaining fourteen selections contain material reprinted from nineteen professional publications, some of which are widely read by psychiatrists and psychologists, but none of which has a large general readership.

We have deleted a number of passages from reprinted papers, primarily to reduce repetition. The sites of deletions are purposely not noted in the text, for Dr. Frank characteristically disavowed the presumption that such detail would be of scholarly interest to anyone else. I am grateful to Dr. Frank for permitting me to play a part in the development of this volume.

Miss Frances Partlow, Dr. Frank's secretary, has been invaluable in the production of nearly all of the manuscripts that comprise this volume, and it is through her that there were reprints and a bibliography from which it could be produced. My participation was possible by virtue of a grant from the Robert Wood Johnson Foundation, Princeton, New Jersey, and I was helped in my tasks by Beverly Atkins, Tracey Elliot Young, and my secretary, Joanne Henderson.

Park Elliott Dietz, M.D., M.P.H.
April 1978

Preface

In perusing a collection of papers on a wide range of topics written over a period of some thirty years, the reader may be curious as to what, if anything, links them together. A brief account of the writer's intellectual history, as he perceives it, may suggest some linkages. Accordingly, this Preface briefly sketches the major influences that have shaped my interests and orientation.

The papers have been grouped into five sections. Three—psychotherapy, group psychotherapy, and psychosomatics—are within my professional purview. The section on the future of civilization focuses on new menaces to survival—nuclear weapons and pollution of the biosphere. The one on belief systems and the human condition reflects the shift from detailed studies of specific phenomena to general speculations about broader issues, so characteristic of maturing—or should one say aging?—minds.

The roots of a career in psychiatry and an interest in psychosomatic medicine are to be found in a proneness to anxiety and susceptibility to repeated minor illnesses throughout childhood. In retrospect, I believe the latter to have been triggered by emotional states. They fostered a preoccupation with the functioning of the body, and by early adolescence I had determined to become a physician specializing in psychosomatic disorders. I chose psychology as a field of concentration in college because it enabled me to satisfy premedical requirements while taking a minimum number of courses in physics and chemistry, which were too quantitative for my taste.

The department of psychology at Harvard in undergraduate years showed no interest in the functioning of persons, but rather was preoccupied with sensation, perception, memory, and the quantitative relationship between stimuli and sensations. Fortunately, I was rescued from these arid pursuits by my tutor, Dr. J. G. Beebe-Center. An independently wealthy "Boston Brahmin," he had no ambitions for wide recognition or academic rank, and so remained obscure, but was a superb teacher with a lively intellect and wide interests.

He steered me to the writings of the psychologist Kurt Lewin. Here was a man who dared to devise psychological experiments that had direct relevance to human motivation! He and his students, under his close supervision, conducted experiments on memory, anger, success and failure, and similar topics that were reported not only with extraordinary clarity but with a sense of intellectual excitement. I fell completely under his spell, postponed entering medical school, and went to Berlin to study with him for a year. He proved to be a cheerful, energetic little man with an informal, friendly manner sharply contrasting to that of most German professors. He was overflowing with ideas and proved to be even more fascinating in person than in print. As a result, I switched temporarily from medicine to psychology and wrote a Ph.D. thesis on one of his interests, the level of aspiration. By its completion, he had come to the United States, and I spent another year with him at Cornell doing experiments on personal pressure and resistance.

Two of Lewin's conceptualizations strongly influenced my thinking. The first was that behavior is determined by the interaction of the person with his current environment. Past life experiences are relevant only to the extent that they affect the person's present perceptions of himself and others. By focusing on current determinants of behavior, this view facilitates formulation of experimentally testable hypotheses. The second influential concept was that of "action research," namely that the best way to study a phenomenon is to try to change it. Psychotherapy, aimed at producing change, appeared to be an ideal candidate for this approach.

Lewin applied these concepts to analysis of social issues and was an active Zionist. Thus both as a teacher and a model, he reinforced a concern with social problems, to be described presently.

After five years in psychology, the urge to become a physician reasserted itself, so I entered medical school, during which my interest in psychosomatic problems was reawakened. After a year's medical internship, I obtained a psychiatric residency at Johns Hopkins Hospital during the last year of the tenure of the legendary Adolf Meyer, the dominant academic psychiatrist of his time. As a theoretician of "psychobiology," he provided an integrated conception of human functioning based on a remarkably extensive knowledge of psychiatry and neurology. As a clinician, he took a broad view of both historical and current sources of patients' symptoms and problems in living, while at the same time focusing sharply on central issues. His successor, John C. Whitehorn, trained as a biochemist, reinforced the nondogmatic approach to psychiatric problems and, as a psychotherapist, sought chiefly to help the patient to deal with current interpersonal difficulties.

After two and a half years of military service in the Southwest Pacific, I became the principal assistant for a research project in group therapy for the Veterans Administration. This form of treatment highlights the importance of a person's current perceptions and behavior in determining his adjustment to life.

A psychoanalysis in graduate school, while helpful, left me unconvinced as to the validity of the theory underlying it, but I decided to give it another try and became a candidate at the Washington-Baltimore Institute of Psychoanalysis, then dominated by Harry Stack Sullivan, who defined psychiatry as the study of interpersonal relations. I was assigned for training analysis to a highly unorthodox analyst, who strongly emphasized one's current adjustment. The influences of Lewin, Meyer, Whitehorn, and Sullivan strengthened my reserve about orthodox analytic theory, as well as psychoanalysis as a form of therapy.

On returning to Hopkins, my background in academic psychology and experience in research on group psychotherapy virtually guaranteed that my research interest would be

psychotherapy, first group and then individual. The conceptualization of psychotherapy that emerged from this research
and my earlier experiences is presented in the papers in the
first two sections.

Our research findings seemed most compatible with the view
that features shared by all schools of psychotherapy in the
United States accounted for much of their effectiveness. This
led to a search for similar features of healing ceremonies in other
cultures, an interest stimulated by a fellowship at the Center for
Advanced Study in the Behavioral Sciences, where I was fortunate to be thrown in with some outstanding cultural anthropologists, who took pity on my ignorance. From them I
learned that healing ceremonies in most of the world are based
on a view of humans as integrated, open systems interacting
with their environment at both psychological and biological
levels. Disease is evidence that the person has fallen out of
harmony within himself and with his environment, and healing
seeks to restore this harmony.

Exposure to this orientation, coupled with an observation
during military service that delayed convalescence from a tropical disease, schistosomiasis, was related to noxious psychological forces in the hospital ward, revived an interest in mind-
body relationships, represented by papers in the third section
of this volume.

Ethical and social concerns, like professional interests, also
have a lifelong history. A beloved aunt, who was deeply interested in promoting human welfare, involved me in political
discussions from an early age and gave me liberal magazines to
read. Problems of social justice became more salient in early
adolescence as the result of having as a summer tutor Algernon
D. Black, then a magnetic, idealistic college sophomore already
involved in social work, who went on to become a major figure
in the American Ethical Union, a group that views the essence
of religion as the striving to raise the ethical level of human
relations. We have remained lifelong friends and years later, at
his instigation, I helped found the Baltimore Ethical Society
and was active in it for many years.

As mentioned earlier, Lewin reinforced my interest in social
problems. In addition, during the year I spent in Germany with

him the Nazi party rocketed from obscurity to the threshold of power. Since I had naively believed that World War I had indeed made the world safe for democracy, the rapid collapse of a democratic society before my eyes was a strong shock which left a permanent impression.

A final event with a profound effect was the atomic bombing of Hiroshima and Nagasaki. I was stationed in the Philippines at the time, and my immediate reaction to the news was that the emergence of nuclear weapons demanded the eventual abolition of war as the price of human survival, a conviction that has grown stronger with the mushroom proliferation of these weapons. This has stimulated me to attempt to contribute psychological and psychiatric insights toward the resolution of this menace and its corollary, the threatened suicide of humanity through poisoning of the environment. Papers on this topic constitute the fourth section.

The final set of papers on belief systems and the human condition reflects efforts to grapple with aspects of the meaning of human existence, a problem that has to be faced sooner or later by all thinking persons.

A character trait that underlies all these papers but that is obscured by the variety of their contents is reluctance to become fully committed to any group, reflected at the intellectual level by a distrust of all group ideologies. This characteristic, too, goes back to early life. In high school I wrote a satiric letter to the school paper about school spirit; in college I joined only the liberal club; and in graduate school refused to be confined in the intellectual straitjacket of the psychology department.

As a member of quite a few professional and peace organizations, I have often found myself in the role of loyal opposition. While office has sometimes been thrust upon me, it has never been sought. Professionally qualified in both psychology and psychiatry, I have stayed aloof from the power struggles of the professional societies in these disciplines.

Trained in the dominant Western view of medicine as the diagnosis and treatment of diseased or injured bodies rather than disturbed persons, I have remained open to holistic concepts of illness and healing, not excluding the possible roles of paranormal influences. In politics, my views have been shared by only a small minority, and, consistent with the orientation of the Ethical movement, I am uncommitted to any religious belief, whether transcendental or humanistic. To me, it is the height of arrogance to suppose that our finite, ephemeral human minds can hope to comprehend more than a tiny fraction of the mysteries of the universe.

Nor has any school of psychotherapy secured my full allegiance. Recognition that all possess some validity probably was the main determinant for focusing research interests on the features all schools share. Fortunately, this avoidance of formal group identification has not prevented the establishment of close and rewarding informal relationships. At the same time, it has enabled me to remain dispassionate while exploring issues that frequently arouse strong feelings. Whether this detachment adds or detracts from the interest of my writings, the reader will judge.

JEROME D. FRANK, Ph.D., M.D.

ON PSYCHOTHERAPY

1. *Psychotherapy: An Overview*

THE PROSPECT OF preparing an overview of psychotherapy in America today is enough to make the most stout-hearted quail. Gone are the days when the scene could be encompassed by Freud, Jung, and Adler, with side glances at Rank, Horney, and Rogers. In the last two decades, psychotherapy has been undergoing a continuous explosion, and the end is not in sight. Its targets have spread from individuals to families and groups, and now whole neighborhoods. Methods range from traditional interviews to tickling, nude marathons, and elaborate rituals of meditation; practitioners have broken the bounds of the traditional disciplines and now include many whose only training is having undergone the therapy they offer to others, or who are simply fellow sufferers. The settings in which therapy is conducted have burst out of hospitals and offices to living rooms, motels, and resorts, and new psychotherapies spring up almost overnight.

This lush overgrowth, of course, is in response to public demand, which seems insatiable. Persons are not only flocking to psychotherapies in droves, but are frantically searching for solutions to their personal problems in self-help books, which repeatedly make best-seller lists. Two recent front runners were *I'm O.K., You're O.K.* and *How To Be Your Own Best Friend.*[1]

Actually, the situation may not be as chaotic as it appears. Much of the apparent confusion results from the understand-

1

able insistence by proponents of each therapy that their particular brand is uniquely different from its rivals. Similarly, although the consumers of psychotherapies seem superficially
extremely diverse, the sources of distress for which they seek
relief have much in common. All reflect disturbances in the
person's communicative and symbolic functions, including his
image of himself, of people close to him, and, sometimes, of his
place in the cosmos, as well as his social behavior. Underneath
the diverse superficial manifestations of these disturbances, all
candidates for psychotherapy suffer from dysphoric affects, particularly anxiety, depression, resentment, and sense of alienation. Moreover, the patient and often those about him seek
psychotherapy for him primarily because they despair of his
being able to gain his emotional equilibrium and self-control
without outside help. In short, and as I shall develop more fully
below, I believe that persons seek psychotherapy chiefly because they are demoralized, and that the shared features of different psychotherapies, in which lie their main therapeutic efficacy, combat this state of mind.[2]

Furthermore, since the determinants of the patients' demoralization include early interactions with his family—the
society's major agent of acculturation—as well as conflicts with
the values and codes of conduct of his contemporaries, the patient's culture largely determines the nature of the stresses that
have demoralized him and the ways in which he manifests this
state of mind. Since psychotherapists are products of the same
culture and derive their power and prestige from it,
psychotherapeutic concepts and methods also are largely determined by features of the society that spawns them.

In this presentation, therefore, rather than attempting the
almost impossible tasks of making a systematic survey of the
panoply of contemporary schools and methods of psychotherapy, I shall attempt to relate psychotherapy in a generic
sense to forces in contemporary American society, consider the
effects of these forces on both practitioners and patients, describe features shared by all forms of psychotherapy, and, finally, very briefly consider some implications for classification
of patients and training of therapists.

PSYCHOTHERAPY AND CONTEMPORARY AMERICAN SOCIETY

Let me approach the relationship of psychotherapy to society through an examination of some of the reasons for its extraordinary popularity and diversity in America today. In order to be psychologically comfortable, a person has to have confidence in his bodily health, feel that his life has significance, and have confidence that he can love and be loved by others.[3] Modern society has proved deficient in meeting these last two needs.

The triumphs of medical science have alleviated many forms of suffering and prolonged many lives, but have not changed the fact that there will always be ten leading causes of death. To cope with this existential reality, humans have turned to religion for reassurance that their brief sojourn on earth has made a difference, if only to God. However, as a result of the challenges of scientific findings to many traditional religious beliefs, the power of traditional religions to give meaning to life has been seriously eroded. For a while it seemed as if the search for truth, as defined by science, might afford a sufficient substitute, especially in view of science's ability to bring so many betterments in the human lot. With the advent of nuclear weapons and the increasingly menacing pollution of the biosphere, however, science begins to look less like a savior and more like a Pied Piper leading mankind to destruction through the promise of endless goodies.

That psychotherapy can perform some of the same functions as religion is evidenced today by the blurring of the lines between psychotherapeutic schools and religious sects. Scientology, an outgrowth of Dianetics, has officially become a religion, and the messianic zeal of adherents to Transactional Analysis and Reevaluation Counseling, to mention only two, is indistinguishable from that of members of proselytizing religions. Furthermore, many currently flourishing religio-mystical cults, while not aimed at relieving specific symptoms, offer their acolytes the hope of achieving inner peace by the practice of rituals believed to enable them to escape from the tyranny of the individual ego and achieve union with the cosmic consciousness. Foreshadowed by Christian Science, such movements as Oscar Ichazo's Arica Institute, Maharishi Mahesh's Transcendental Meditation, and the Divine Light Mission of Guru Maharaj Ji are attracting thousands of suffering persons who in the past have turned to naturalistic forms of psychotherapy. While these religious movements share many features with schools of psychotherapy in the narrower sense, to keep this review from becoming impossibly complex I shall not consider them further.

The rush to psychotherapy has been stimulated not only by the decline of traditional religions but also by psychological insecurities resulting from unprecedentedly rapid changes in the conditions of life. This leads to questioning of traditional ethical values that offered guidelines for conduct. Consider, for example, what has happened to chastity and thrift in recent years. Since new values cannot achieve the acceptability and power of old, discredited ones until society has settled down, members of a changing society tend to lose their sense of direction.

The speed of social change has also disrupted the close, mutually supportive, enduring relationships so essential to our sense of well-being. It has especially undermined the ties of kinship, especially between generations, and substituted the shallow, self-serving affability of the housing development, the office, and the club.

Gregariousness has always existed along with, and to some extent has ameliorated, the American stress on competitiveness and individualism. The isolation and hardships of frontier life were periodically relieved by religious revival meetings, characterized by intense emotional outbursts, public confession of sins, and, for many participants, intimate sexual activities.

American sociability, however, too often is the servant of competitiveness rather than a genuine expression of liking for others. While nineteenth-century Western man had to maintain a mask of righteousness, his modern counterpart, at least in America, feels impelled to wear one of affability, behind which may lurk considerable hostility and suspiciousness. To get ahead, one must be likable; so the need to be liked has replaced the need to appear righteous as an important source of inner conflicts.

Role relationships in which people use each other as objects are increasingly encroaching upon feeling relationships, which are sources of psychological support.[4] As we seek to manipulate rather than care for each other, we have developed increasingly subtle techniques for concealing our intentions. Restlessness and deceptiveness are hidden behind masks of friendliness, warmth, and sincerity. It becomes increasingly difficult to distinguish the liar from the honest man. So, in addition to being uncertain about why he is alive, modern man suffers from feelings of alienation and mistrust.

Finally, too many people today have too much money and not enough to do, and they turn to psychotherapy to combat the resulting boredom. It supplies novelty, excitement, and, as a means of self-improvement, a legitimate way of spending money. Today hosts of persons seek psychotherapy for discomforts that a less affluent society would regard as trivial.

Rapid changes in conditions of life, too much leisure and money, and the substitution of role relationships for feeling relationships may help account for the popularity of psychotherapy. To explain its extraordinary diversity, however, one must invoke other aspects of American society.

In monolithic societies one form of psychotherapy dominates, such as exorcism in the Middle Ages. Societies like ours, which contain a wide variety of subcultures, each with its own values and approved behaviors, tolerate a wide range of psychotherapies, all sharing some common values to be mentioned presently, but having special appeals to members of different subgroups. Diversity is further encouraged by our competitiveness, the high value we place on entrepreneurship, and our thirst for novelty. For us, the new is always better than the familiar until proved otherwise.

The psychological health of members of a society depends on their sharing common goals and having faith in their leaders and each other. When conditions of life such as those I have just reviewed weaken these cohesive forces and the institutions supporting them, its members become demoralized; that is, they lose a sense of purpose and feel alienated from each other. At this point many seek to recover common goals and trusting human relationships by clumping into groups of the like-minded who offer each other mutual support. The psycho-therapeutic dyad or therapeutic group is one such supportive arrangement for combating demoralization. Psychotherapy can be viewed as a social institution created to fill the gap left by the decay of other institutions that gave meaning to life and a feeling of connectedness to others.

As institutions of American society, all psychotherapies, de-spite their diversity, share a value system that accords primacy to individual self-fullfillment or self-actualization. This in-cludes maximum self-awareness, unlimited access to one's own feelings, increased autonomy and creativity. The individual is seen as the center of his moral universe, and concern for others is believed to follow from his own self-realization. Thus, psychotherapies assume that an individual can truly realize his full potentialities only to the extent that he permits and encour-ages those about him to do the same.

Self-realization is antithetical to the values of many reli-gions, which seek destruction, not glorification, of the ego, but American psychotherapy also downgrades or omits many sec-ular values that rank high in other cultures. Our psycho-therapeutic literature has contained precious little on the re-demptive power of suffering, acceptance of one's lot in life, filial piety, adherence to tradition, self-restraint and modera-tion.

The primacy of individual self-fulfillment is well suited to a fluid, underpopulated society with plenty of space and unlim-ited resources, as America was during the first centuries of its existence. In such a society, the efforts of every individual to enhance himself advance the general welfare. An individual-centered value system, however, may be incompatible with survival in today's overcrowded America faced with shrinking resources and progressive destruction of the biosphere. Be that as it may, such a value system, which has its modern roots in Jefferson's dictum that man possesses an inalienable right to the pursuit of happiness, can easily become a source of misery in itself. For this has become, in the minds of most Americans, the right to be happy; so when they are not, which is inevitable at times, they suffer an additional burden of resentment and anger.

Moreover, the goal of self-realization can become caricatured as justifying exaltation of feelings at the expense of intellect, and disregard for the needs of others. This is exemplified by some encounter groups, which seek to foster ecstatic experiences through intimate, highly charged emotional interactions.[5]

While such groups pay lip service to mutual concern, it stops abruptly at the group's edge. Within the group itself the leader, under the cloak of respect for the members' autonomy, disclaims responsibility for the effects of his actions. Following his example, each member feels free to use the others to serve his own needs. Thus, such groups can easily become exercises in mutual exploitation and can seriously damage some participants.[6] It is well to keep in mind that the true opposite of dependence, regarded as the ultimate evil by many American psychotherapeutic schools, is not autonomy but responsibility. In this connection, it has been pointed out that American psychotherapies are ineffective or even destructive in cultures such as the Hindu, which stress dependence and mutual responsibility.[7]

Turning from the values of psychotherapy to the psychotherapist, his power derives from his socially sanctioned role as a healer, which he achieves by undergoing special training. Together with his personal qualities, this enables the patient to form a trusting, emotionally charged relationship with him. An American value from which the legitimacy of most psychotherapists springs is the continuing, if eroding, belief in science as the wellspring of human welfare. As a result, most psychotherapists derive their power from their scientific training. Of these, physicians have enjoyed a brief period of supremacy. Although physicians have always employed methods of psychological healing, often unawares, until the last century treatment of mental illness was primarily in the hands of priests. Freud was one of the first to assert the physician's claim to treat psychologically caused symptoms and disabilities by scientifically derived psychological methods. To make this possible, he assimilated mental illness to medical illness. The detailed exploration of a person's inner life, however, has no resemblance to any other form of medical treatment.

The dominance of physicians as practitioners of psychotherapy was not shaken until World War II created a demand that psychiatrists could not meet. They called upon members of two other professions for help, psychiatric social workers and clinical psychologists. Social workers have, for the most part, continued to work under the aegis of psychiatrists and to use their methods. Not so psychologists, who soon asserted their independence.

At first the therapies of psychologists were dominated by Carl Rogers, whose approach was an outgrowth of psychoanalysis, but in recent years behavior therapies with greater claims to scientific objectivity have gained ascendance. Just as Freud is the intellectual godfather of psychiatric psychotherapists, so behavior therapists look to the work of Pavlov, Thorndike, Hull, and Skinner for validation of their theories and methods. Consistent with this intellectual ancestry, psychologists conceive mental illnesses to be disorders of learning rather than disease syndromes.

The entrance of psychologists into psychotherapy has led to a desirable increase in efforts to describe psychotherapies and their results in objectively measurable, verifiable terms. Without this kind of information, the field cannot advance. Nevertheless, despite mountains of graphs, charts, and statistical tables, the fact remains that the connection between behavior therapies and laboratory findings on which they claim to be based remains questionable, and in actuality most deal with patients' fantasies and reports of inner experiences. (Behavior therapists solve this conceptual dilemma by calling these implicit behaviors.) Since most behavioral methods are relatively brief, however, and seem no less effective than analytically based ones for most patients, their share of the psychotherapeutic field will probably continue to increase.

A final group of professional therapists, who see more troubled people than psychiatrists, psychologists, or social workers, look not to science but to religion to sanction their healing efforts. These are ministers of religion, ranging from Christian

Science healers to pastoral counselors, most of whom derive their methods from Freudian, Rogerian, or existential-humanist traditions.

To complete the picture, we must note that the enormous demand for psychotherapy, in conjunction with the declining prestige of both science and religion, has resulted in the emergence of masses of therapists with only tenuous claims to legitimacy. Many are trained in independent institutes; others claim competence in a particular type of therapy through having themselves undergone it; and some, like L. Ron Hubbard of Scientology and Harvey Jackins, the founder of Reevaluation Counseling, have attracted large followings primarily through personal charisma.

Finally, we are witnessing the multiplication of peer self-help psychotherapy groups. A few, like Alcoholics Anonymous, have been originated by fellow sufferers, but most trace their credentials to a healer who was trained as a physician or psychologist, and they continue to seek guidance from the writings of their founder. Outstanding current examples are Transactional Analysis, founded by Eric Berne, and Recovery Incorporated, created by Abraham Low.[8]

In short, practitioners of psychotherapy now come from so many sources, while performing essentially the same social role, that perhaps they should be viewed as a new profession whose members function to various degrees as healers, teachers, spiritual guides, and sympathetic friends.[9]

Certain attitudes and personal qualities of the therapist seem related to his or her success regardless of the therapeutic procedure. These have been characterized by such terms as capacity for active personal participation, warmth, genuineness, empathy, and therapeutic zeal. The last is displayed by practitioners of every new therapy, which may largely account for the fact that all seem to work best when first introduced.

Social forces largely determine not only who become psychotherapists but also who become patients. It is customary to speak of certain persons as needing psychotherapy, but this is already a culturally determined judgment. Very few persons indeed need psychotherapy in the sense that their survival depends on it. Rather the term "need" is applied to those whose suffering and disability are viewed by common consent as amenable to this type of treatment.

THE DEMORALIZATION HYPOTHESIS

Despite the diversity of their complaints, most persons who seek or are brought to psychotherapy suffer from a single condition that assumes protean forms, and all psychotherapies contain components that counteract this condition. As a first approximation, this condition may be termed demoralization, and the effectiveness of all forms of psychotherapy depends primarily on ingredients that combat this state of mind.

Demoralization ensues when a person is unable to cope with a life situation that he and those about him expect him to be able to handle. His failure produces a syndrome with a variety of manifestations. His life space becomes constricted in that he becomes self-absorbed and preoccupied with trying to cope with the threats posed by the environment. He typically experiences depression, self-blame, guilt, and shame. The sense that he has lost control of the situation frequently gives rise to fear of insanity. Since the environment has become menacing, he often feels anxious and resentful toward those whom he expects to help him but who seem unable or unwilling to do so and who, in addition, are often aggravated by his behavior. As a result, he feels alienated from his associates. His distress may be heightened by loss of faith in the belief system he shared with them, which had provided a sense of security and significance.

Demoralization varies widely in severity and duration. It may be no more than a brief period of uneasiness caused by a problem that is rapidly solved, or it may be so severe that the patient's state requires him to be hospitalized. Acute, severe demoralization has been termed a crisis response; chronic demoralization, the social breakdown syndrome.[10]

The central point is that persons do not seek therapy *solely* because of their symptoms. They do not come to psychotherapists only because they fear snakes or hear voices or drink too much, much less because they have an hysterical personality. The world is full of persons with these and other so-called psychopathological symptoms who go about their daily lives. According to the hypothesis offered here, what actually brings patients to treatment is demoralization—their own or that of persons who control their lives—and whatever else psychotherapy does, it fails if it does not restore the patient's morale.

Relief of specific symptoms helps to do this, but, more significantly, overcoming of demoralization by whatever means leads to a diminution of those symptoms that either express it or are attempts to cope with it. Sometimes patients feel no need for further therapy despite persistence of symptoms once they have recovered their morale.[11] Thus psychotherapeutic procedures perform two interrelated functions: combating the patient's demoralization and overcoming his specific symptoms.

Although all persons in psychotherapy suffer from demoralization, in America they can be roughly grouped into five categories, which may be termed the *psychotic*, the *neurotic*, the *shaken*, the *unruly*, and the *discontented.*

Genetic-organic determinants clearly play a significant role in psychoses, although their exact nature is still to be determined. After years of dedicated psychotherapeutic efforts, it now seems clear that psychotherapy cannot cure psychoses.[12] Since psychologically induced emotional states can aggravate organic vulnerabilities, however, psychotherapy can significantly ameliorate the distress of psychotics and help them to function better. Psychotherapy can play a similar role for patients with diabetes, heart disease, arthritis, and other chronic organically based ailments.

Psychotherapy is the treatment of choice for the remaining categories, in all of which the sources of difficulty are primarily psychological. Among these, neurotics suffer from symptoms that are persistent faulty strategies for coping with life, presumably resulting from deprivations or traumata in early life, which distorted the normal process of maturation and learning. This group seems to evoke the most intense competition between proponents of dynamic and behavioral psychotherapies.

The third category, the psychologically shaken, consists of persons unable to cope with aspects of their immediate life situations, including marital disharmonies, misbehaving children, and crises that temporarily overtax their adaptive capacities. Relatively brief interventions usually suffice to restore them to emotional equilibrium. Since persons shaken by current life stresses can manifest the entire gamut of neurotic and psychotic symptoms,[13] and since all respond gratifyingly to any form of psychotherapy, they fan the competitiveness between different therapeutic schools.

The behavior of the unruly, who constitute the fourth category, disturbs those about them, but is attributed to psychological causes rather than to wickedness. Here belong "acting-out" children and adolescents, husbands or wives whose spouses cannot stand their behavior, and, of course, addicts and antisocial personalities. Some of these merge with the preceding category. The difference lies in the chronicity and severity of the disturbance and the motivation for help. The shaken seek treatment themselves; the unruly are brought to treatment by others. In any case, they are poor candidates for psychotherapy.

The fifth category, the discontented, consists of members of the leisured and educated classes who suffer from ennui or struggle with philosophical issues of existence. They shun behavior therapies and gravitate instead to psychotherapies with well-articulated, strongly held values, such as Freudian and Jungian psychoanalysis and logotherapy. They also flock to the quasi-religious movements mentioned earlier.

For the sake of completeness, mention must be made of two small groups who undergo psychotherapy for extraneous reasons. One consists of trainees whose training includes exposure to the type of therapy they are learning; the other, college students with minor symptoms who volunteer as subjects in experiments on psychotherapy in return for such inducements as small financial payments or being excused from an examination.

SHARED CONCEPTUALIZATIONS AND
PROCEDURES OF AMERICAN PSYCHOTHERAPIES

Beneath the din of conflicting claims and the kaleidoscopic panorama of activities, it is possible to discern certain characteristics that all schools of psychopathology share. That these may account for more of their effectiveness than the features that distinguish them is suggested by the persistent difficulty in demonstrating significant differences in their outcomes.[14] All therapies attract a loyal following, and I have yet to hear of a school that has disbanded because it became convinced of the superiority of its rivals.

To be sure, behavioral modification techniques seem more effective than open-ended interview therapies in relieving certain circumscribed phobias,[15] but these account for less than five percent of persons seen by psychotherapists.[16] Many schools of therapy claim to reconstruct the patient's personality, although recent data from the Menninger psychotherapy research study suggest that this rarely occurs, even after extensive psychoanalysis.[17] It probably happens occasionally, but its frequency is probably no greater than that of religious conversions, which have similar effects.

In any case, the least common denominator of all therapies, and the one on which their claims to success must depend, is their ability to help the patient reduce his suffering, smooth his social relationships, and improve his performance. All aim to achieve these ends through patterned communications, which seek to foster changes in the patient's cognitions, feelings, and behavior. A brief review of the features shared by all psychotherapies that contribute to this goal may help to clarify my view of the field.

The success of all therapies depends in the first instance on the so-called therapeutic relationship or therapeutic alliance, in which the patient accepts some dependence on the therapist, based on his confidence in the therapist's competence and good intentions. The therapist uses his power to achieve three aims. The first is to enable the patient to discover new information about himself, both cognitively and experientially; the second is to arouse him emotionally, since emotions supply the motive power for change; and the third is to encourage him to change his behavior in the light of what he has learned and to practice the new patterns.

Schools of psychotherapy differ, in theory and in fact, in the relative emphasis they place on these components, but all exist in all therapies. Each of these areas will now be briefly considered.

The therapeutic relationship gains support from the therapist's training, his locale, such as a prestigious clinic, and the congruence of his approach with the patient's expectations. These expectations sometimes may be greatly enhanced by the patient's knowledge that the therapist has faced and overcome problems similar to his own. This is the main source of mutual influence in peer self-help psychotherapy groups.

While these attributes determine the therapist's ascendancy even before the patient meets him, after they are face to face, the main source of the therapist's power soon becomes his personal qualities, especially his ability to convince the patient that he can understand and help him. A successful therapeutic relationship in itself inspires the patient's hope, which not only keeps him coming through periods of apparent lack of progress or even of increased distress, but also is a powerful healing emotion in itself. His ability to establish a bond of mutual trust and confidence with his therapist also encourages the patient to try to move closer to others, thereby combating his sense of isolation.

For Rogerian and existentialist therapists, the therapeutic relationship is the therapy; it is both a necessary and a sufficient cause of the patient's progress. They leave the patient free to structure it as he wishes and confine their own activities to facilitating his exploration and expression of his feelings, to which the therapist responds by freely revealing his own reactions. Such encounters are believed to promote personal growth, the ultimate aim of therapy. Therapies in the psychoanalytic tradition also foster openness by the patient but make the therapeutic relationship itself an object of scrutiny. To this end, the therapist does not reveal himself, since to do so would interfere with the emergence and analysis of transference reactions. Behavior therapists, by contrast, while making a strong effort to mobilize the patient's expectations at the start,[18] regard the relationship simply as a means for persuading the patient to cooperate in the techniques of behavior modification on which they believe their success depends.

In any event, the relationship enables the therapist to indoctrinate the patient into his particular conceptual framework and to teach him the procedures based on it. In conjunction, conceptual scheme and procedure have several crucial therapeutic functions. First, they provide a cognitive structure that enables the patient to name his symptoms and fit them into a causal scheme. Since major sources of anxiety are ambiguity and fear of the unknown, this, in itself, can powerfully reduce the patient's anxiety and enhance his self-confidence.

Conceptualizations of different schools differ in their views of causation. Since man is a time-binding creature who lives simultaneously in the past, present, and future, all three perspectives are relevant. Analytically oriented therapies, however, place the main emphasis on historical causes. They search for past experiences that set in train developments leading to the patient's present difficulties, on the assumption that these will be relieved if he can rediscover and re-experience their origins. Behavior therapies, by contrast, stress the present. Although using a wide variety of techniques such as modeling, progressive desensitization, and emotional flooding, all try to smoke out and modify the immediate antecedents and consequences of the patient's symptoms or problems as the most effective way to overcome them. Finally, for many existentialist schools, the main source of the patient's suffering is his closed view of the future, so they direct their efforts toward widening his options.

Therapeutic conceptual schemes also differ in the degree to which they see psychopathology as lying primarily within the individual patient or in the communication network of which he is a part. Existential and psychoanalytically oriented therapies concentrate on the internal life of the individual, on the assumption that as this becomes more harmonious, his social behavior will automatically improve. Behavior therapists also focus on the individual, but try to help him modify his behavior, assuming that this will automatically reduce his internal conflicts, which they regard as outside their purview. In contrast to both these approaches, many group therapies direct primary attention to the interactions in which the patient participates.[19] They see the patient as a node in a pathological communication system, whether it be his family, a neighborhood network,[20] or a therapy group. According to this view, the most effective way of helping an individual is to improve the communications between members of the groups to which he belongs.

As new information emerges under the guidance of the conceptual scheme of any psychotherapy, it results in intellectual and experiential learning. All agree that intellectual insight is not enough. For change to occur, the patient must have a new experience, whether this be related to reliving of his past, discovering symptom-reinforcing contingencies in his environment, or becoming aware of distortions in his interpersonal communications.

Experiential learning implies emotional arousal, the second ingredient of all therapies. Some therapeutic schools see this as the essence of the therapeutic process. At least as old as Mesmer, rediscovered and later largely abandoned by Freud, abreactive, implosive, and emotional flooding methods currently are at the height of fashion. The most prominent are implosion therapy, primal therapy, bioenergetics, Transactional Analysis, and, in the self-help realm, Scientology and Reevaluation Counseling. It is tempting to speculate on why emotional flooding, like hypnosis, undergoes periodic ups and downs of popularity. Part of the reason may be that the techniques are dramatic and produce apparent marked changes, but then disillusionment sets in when most of the gains prove to be transient. In any case, all therapists would agree that some degree of emotional arousal is necessary for the production of change in attitudes and behavior.

Finally, all therapies encourage the patient to try out in his daily life what he has learned in therapy. They do this chiefly by providing him with experiences of success. These maintain his hopes for continuing progress, enhance his sense of mastery over himself and his situation, and reduce his fear of failure. The role of success experiences is most obvious in behavior therapies, which are structured to provide continual evidence of progress and aim to have every session end with a sense of accomplishment. Emotional flooding therapies, by showing the patient that he can survive the full impact of feelings he feared would destroy him, powerfully enhance his feelings of self-mastery. Psychoanalytically and existentially oriented therapies, being less clearly structured, yield more subtle but equally potent successes. Patients who favor these approaches master problems through verbalization and conceptualization, so the achievement of a new insight or ability to formulate a hitherto inchoate state of mind can powerfully enhance their self-confidence.

IMPLICATIONS FOR DIAGNOSIS AND TRAINING

Review of the shared features of psychotherapies suggests a somewhat unconventional approach to diagnosis. Instead of trying to find the right clinical diagnosis, which seldom helps in selecting a suitable therapy, it might be more profitable to classify patients with respect to their relative predilection for or ability to respond to therapies that emphasize one of the shared features above another. We cannot do this as yet, but I can glimpse the directions such an endeavor might take. It would try to explore the expectations patients bring to therapy, their preferred type of success, their arousability, and the like.

Expectations could be determined through inquiry about the psychotherapeutic experiences of the patient's social circle[21] or his own previous therapeutic contacts. Characteristic modes of help-seeking behavior[22] might also yield clues. Persons who seek aid by verbalizing their feelings and have strong motivation for insight[23] would probably respond to a verbally oriented approach; those who convey their need by somatic complaints might do better with a behavioral one; and patients with a strong sense of inadequacy might respond best to techniques providing early and obvious evidences of success.

Degree and nature of arousability might yield clues as to which patients would profit most from emotional flooding procedures. Would they be the most easily aroused, the most phlegmatic, or perhaps those who maintain a placid exterior while seething underneath?

If the analysis offered in this presentation is valid, it raises uncomfortable questions about the goals of training programs in psychotherapy. Until we have a rational basis for choice of specific therapies, one may well ask whether there is any point in mastering any particular one, especially since all have so much in common. Such a conclusion would confuse the content of therapeutic conceptualizations and procedures with their functions. Some therapeutically gifted persons, to be sure, can be effective with very little formal training, but most of us need to master some conceptual framework to enable us to structure our activities, maintain our own confidence, and provide us with adherents of the same school to whom we can turn for support. If any moral can be drawn from this survey, it is that every training program should expose the trainee to several approaches, so he can select and master those most congenial to his own personality.[24] The greater the number of approaches he can handle, the wider the range of patients he will be able to help.

2. The Dynamics of the Psychotherapeutic Relationship

ALL FORMS OF psychotherapy, whatever their underlying theories, and whatever techniques they employ, attempt to promote beneficial changes in a patient's attitudes and symptoms through the influence of a therapist with whom the patient has a close relationship. The purpose of this paper is to review data from diverse sources bearing on the determinants and effects of the patient's emotional dependency on his psychotherapist for relief. The effects may include modifications of the patient's productions in the interview, the duration of treatment itself, and changes in the patient's attitudes and bodily states. Certain mechanisms that may transmit the therapist's expectancies to the patient will be described, and some implications of these data for research and practice will be briefly considered. The major sources of material are reports concerning brainwashing, miracle cures, experimental studies of the psychotherapeutic interview, and the placebo effect.

In general terms, all psychotherapies are concerned with using the influence of the therapist to help patients to unlearn old, maladaptive response patterns and to learn better ones, but they differ considerably in their specific goals and methods. Examples of goals are helping the patient to recover early memories, develop insight, work through transference relationships, release his spontaneity, or modify his self-concept. Methods include, for example, free association, client-centered interviews, and progressive relaxation. These differences in therapeutic approach are reflected in differences in the patient's behavior and in the kinds of change resulting from treatment.

In addition to the differing effects of the psychotherapist's influence, which depend on his particular orientation and method, all forms of psychotherapy seem to produce certain similar effects based on a quality common to the relationships they offer. This common feature is the patient's reliance on the therapist to relieve his distress.

This reliance, which may be forced or voluntary, arises from the interplay of environmental pressures and the patient's subjective state, the relative contribution of each differing from case to case. An example of forced reliance produced primarily by environmental pressure would be the situation of a paranoid patient, placed in a hospital against his will, who believes his incarceration to be unjust, but who is nevertheless forced to depend on the staff to gain his release. An example of forced reliance arising from subjective pressure would be the patient in a panic who flees to the psychiatrist for protection. More commonly, especially in office practice, the patient's dependence on the psychiatrist is voluntary and arises from the interplay of more subtle environmental and subjective factors. These lead the patient to expect relief from the psychiatrist, an expectancy that sometimes may be strong enough to justify the term *faith*.

DETERMINANTS OF THE PATIENT'S RELIANCE ON HIS PSYCHOTHERAPIST

Conditions maintaining or strengthening a patient's reliance on his psychotherapist to relieve his suffering may be conveniently grouped under four headings: the culture, the treatment situation, the therapist, and the patient.

The Culture

The beliefs of members of a culture as to what constitutes illness and its treatment are formed and supported by generally held cultural attitudes.[1] A member of a particular society can regard himself as having an emotional illness—for which the proper treatment is psychotherapy—only if his society recognizes the existence of such illnesses and sanctions psychotherapy as the appropriate treatment for them. The same symptoms that in the Middle Ages were viewed as signs of demoniacal possession to be treated by exorcism, are now regarded as manifestations of mental illness to be treated by a psychiatrist. In World War II Russian soldiers did not have psychoneuroses, which can only mean that the Russian army did not recognize the existence of such conditions. Presumably soldiers with functional complaints were regarded either as malingerers, and thus subject to disciplinary action, or as medically ill, and therefore to be treated by regular physicians. In the American army, by contrast, many commonplace reactions to the stresses of military life were initially regarded as signs of psychoneurosis. Soldiers with these complaints, therefore, often received psychotherapy, which not infrequently culminated in their discharge. Today many of these same soldiers would be promptly returned to active duty.

In midcentury America, mental illness has not fully shaken off its demonological heritage, as evidenced by the stigma attached to it. Both psychotics and neurotics, however, are seen as suffering from bona fide illnesses, and the dominant treatment for most of the conditions subsumed under mental and emotional illness is psychotherapy. Moreover, the psychiatrist is generally regarded as the best-qualified dispenser of this form of treatment, although other professional groups are challenging his right to this preeminence. Therefore an American today, once he has accepted the label of being mentally or emotionally ill, is culturally predisposed to expect relief from psychotherapy and to look to a psychiatrist for this relief.

The Treatment Situation

Certain situations in which psychotherapy is practiced, notably mental hospitals, to a varying degree force the patient to become dependent on the treatment staff. Even when there is no external compulsion, however, many aspects of the psychotherapeutic situation in both hospital and office supply cues that tend to impress the patient with the importance of the procedure and also to identify psychotherapy with other healing methods. In both ways they strengthen his expectation of relief and thus his dependency on the therapist. The cues start to operate before the patient and therapist meet. Most patients reach the presence of the psychotherapist only after some preliminaries. If the patient is hospitalized, the commitment procedure heightens his sense of dependence on the hospital staff for his release. Voluntary admission procedures usually require the patient to sign a witnessed request for admission that contains a "three-day notice" clause. This impresses him with the importance of the step he is taking and underlines the staff's control over him while in the hospital. If properly conducted, the admission procedure can heighten the patient's hope of benefit from his stay and his trust in the treatment staff.

Psychiatrists working with outpatients are rightly concerned that the referral heighten the patient's favorable expectations, rather than making him feel that he is being "brushed off"—a situation that frequently occurs. One of the purposes of the intake procedure of psychiatric outpatient clinics is to predispose the patient favorably to psychotherapy. At the Phipps Clinic of the Johns Hopkins Hospital, for example, for a time each new patient was first briefly interviewed by a trained nurse as a deliberate reminder that he is under medical auspices.

More commonly, patients coming to a psychiatric clinic first have one or more intake interviews with a social worker. The avowed purposes of these are to determine the patient's suitability for psychotherapy and to prepare him for it. The patient may, however, perceive the intake process as a probationary period to determine his worthiness to receive the psychiatrist's ministrations. Thus, subtly impressing him with the importance of psychotherapy heightens his susceptibility to the psychiatrist's influence. In this sense the intake procedure is analogous to the preparatory rites undergone by suppliants at faith healing shrines, with the social worker in the role of acolyte and the psychiatrist as high priest.

Once in the presence of his therapist, the patient's favorable expectancies are reinforced by the setting. Psychotherapy has developed its own trappings, to symbolize healing; like other physicians, psychotherapists display diplomas prominently, but in place of the symbols of the stethoscope, the opthalmoscope, and the reflex hammer, they must rely on the heavily laden bookcases, the couch, the easy chair, and usually a large photograph of the leader of their particular school looking benignly but impressively down on the proceedings. In medical institutions, much of the same effect is created simply by the locale of the psychiatrists' offices, which identifies them with the healing activities of the hospital.[2]

The therapist's activities in the initial interview may also have the function, in part, of heightening the patient's favorable expectancies. Psychiatrists usually take a history, loosely following the model of a medical history, thereby reinforcing their identification with the medical profession in the patient's mind. Psychologists frequently begin by giving the patient a battery of psychological tests, their badge of special competence. Both are apt to conclude the interview by offering the patient some sort of formulation, which impresses him with their ability to understand and help him.

In the early days of psychoanalysis, before the setting and procedures had achieved their symbolic power, the analyst might have found it necessary to impress the patient by other means. This is illustrated by Freud's example of the patient who failed to shut the door to the waiting room. He pointed out that this omission

> throws light upon the relation of this patient to the physician. He is one of the great number of those who seek authority, who want to be dazzled, intimidated. Perhaps he had inquired by telephone as to what time he had best call, he had prepared himself to come on a crowd of suppliants. . . . He now enters an empty waiting room which is, moreover, most modestly furnished, and he is disappointed. He must demand reparation from the physician for the wasted respect that he had tendered him, and so he omits to close the door between the reception room and the office. . . . He would also be quite unmannerly and supercilious during the consultation if his presumption were not at once restrained by a sharp reminder.[3]

In terms of this discussion, Freud interpreted the patient's behavior as expressing a lack of confidence in him as a successful healer, and sought to restore this confidence by a brusque command.

As treatment progresses, the therapist instructs the patient in certain activities which are based on a particular theory. Whatever their specific nature, all implicitly convey that the therapist knows what is wrong with the patient and that the special procedure is the treatment for it. In addition, the underlying theory supplies a frame of reference that helps the patient to make sense of behavior and feelings that had been mysterious and to learn that they are not unique but represent important and widely shared experiences.

Thus from the moment the prospective patient approaches psychotherapy until his treatment terminates, he is confronted with cues and procedures that tend to impress him with both the importance of the procedure and its promise of relief. These heighten the therapist's potential influence over the patient and, as will be discussed below, probably have some therapeutic effects in themselves by mobilizing his favorable expectations.

The Therapist

In addition to as yet ill-defined personal characteristics, two attitudes of the therapist foster the patient's confidence in him. One is his faith in the patient's capacity to benefit from treatment, which is implied in the mere act of accepting him as a patient. The therapist's acceptance of the patient may be influenced by his own feelings. In his first publication on psychotherapy Freud wrote:

> The procedure . . . presupposes . . . in [the physician] . . . a personal concern for the patients. . . . I cannot imagine bringing myself to delve into the psychical mechanism of a hysteria in anyone who struck me as low-minded and repellent, and who, on closer acquaintance, would not be capable of arousing human sympathy.[4]

Similar considerations make some psychotherapists unwilling to accept alcoholics or patients with antisocial character disorders for treatment. Schaffer and Myers[5] have found that middle-class clinic patients, more often than lower-class ones, are assigned to senior staff members, who presumably have first choice. They relate this to the fact that middle-class patients appear to offer better prospects for therapy because their values are closer to those of the psychiatrists. The therapist's faith in the capacities of his patient is a strong incentive to maintain that attitude of active personal participation that helps the patient to develop confidence in him.[6]

The other therapeutically potent attitude of the therapist is his confidence in his theory and method of treatment. How these enhance the therapeutic meaning of the treatment situation in the patient's eyes has been touched on above. Adherence to a definite therapeutic procedure and theory also helps to maintain the psychotherapist's confidence. As one young analyst remarked, "Even if the patient doesn't improve, you know you're doing the right thing."

In fields where there is a common body of validated knowledge and the effectiveness of treatment has been demonstrated—for example, abdominal surgery or infectious disease—the physician's confidence rests on his mastery of the pertinent knowledge and diagnostic and therapeutic techniques. In psychotherapy, which lacks such a body of information, therapists tend to rely for their emotional security on allegiance to a group that represents a particular view. This allegiance is fostered by a long period of indoctrination, as many writers have pointed out.[7] Glover, who deplores the effect of this on the research capacities of young psychoanalysts, writes:

> It is scarcely to be expected that a student who has spent some years under the artificial . . . conditions of a training analysis and whose professional career depends on overcoming "resistance" to the satisfaction of his training analyst, can be in a favorable position to defend his scientific integrity against his analyst's theories and practice. . . . For according to his analyst the candidate's objections to interpretations rate as "resistances." In short

there is a tendency inherent in the training situation to perpetuate error.[8]

The effectiveness of indoctrination in psychotherapy is
suggested by replies of a group of psychotherapists—mainly
Freudian, Adlerian, or Jungian in orientation—to a questionnaire distributed by Werner Wolff.[9] Seventy percent stated that
they believed their particular form of therapy to be the best, a
high figure considering the absence of any objective data that
one form of therapy is superior to another.[10] Only 25 percent,
however, professed themselves satisfied with their theoretical
orientation. It is interesting that these consisted mostly of disciples of Adler and Jung. Wolff comments: "The degree of identification of each member with the leader of the group is greater
in minority groups, which defend their new system against the
system of the majority group."[11] Thus 45 percent, or about half
of those who responded, believed their therapy to be best, not
only in the absence of objective evidence but also without
being sure of the soundness of the theory on which it was
based. This is a striking testimonial to the faith of those
therapists in their procedures.

It seems safe to conclude that training in psychotherapy
tends to develop a strong allegiance in the young therapist to
his therapeutic school. This contributes to his confidence in his
brand of treatment, which, in turn, helps him to inspire confidence in his patients.

At this point it seems appropriate to mention that the factors
so far enumerated that enhance the patient's faith in
psychotherapy in the United States are remarkably similar to
those reported with respect to shamanism in Indian tribes.
Henri Ellenberger, for example, points out that among the
Kwakiutl Indians, "to become a shaman requires a four-year
program in a kind of professional school with strict rules. The
shamans constitute a corporation and possess a considerable
body of knowledge which they are anxious to transmit to qualified pesons."[12] He mentions four factors to which the success
of shamanistic cures is attributed. These are: the faith of the
shamans in their own abilities, the faith of the patient in the
healer's abilities, the acknowledgment of the disease by the so-

cial group, and the acceptance of the healing method by the group. Shamans do not treat all diseases, many of which are treated by natural medications or plants; but there are special diseases for which the intervention of the shaman is the only recourse.

The Patient

The extent to which a patient accepts the cues offered by the culture, the treatment situation, and his therapist as representing potential relief depends, of course, also on his own attributes. Many complex and as yet poorly understood factors influence a patient's ability to develop trust in his therapist. In a recent study of patients in a psychiatric clinic, more of those who remained in individual psychotherapy at least six months than of those who dropped out within the first month were suggestible, as measured by a sway test.[13] This study also confirmed the results of Schaffer and Myers with respect to social and educational status and remaining in treatment.[14] That is, patients whose values were such that the goals and methods of psychotherapy made sense to them were more likely to stay in treatment.

Perhaps the major personal determinant of the patient's faith in treatment is the degree of his distress. The literature is consistent in the finding that with neurotics the degree of reported distress is positively related to remaining in treatment.[15] There are at least two possible, and compatible, explanations of this. One, which is consistent with the little that is known about miracle cures, is that presumably the more wretched a person is, the greater his hunger for relief and the greater his predisposition to put faith in what is offered.[16] The other possibility is that the patient's revelation of distress is in itself a sign that he is favorably disposed to trust the therapist and therapy; that is, it may indicate a willingness on the part of the patient to emphasize aspects of himself that show his vulnerability or weakness.

MODES OF TRANSMISSION OF
THE THERAPIST'S INFLUENCE

That the psychotherapist influences his patients is generally accepted. Early psychotherapeutic techniques such as mesmerism, direct suggestion under hypnosis, and the moral persuasion of Dubois deliberately exploited the therapist's power. Directive forms of psychotherapy still dominate the treatment scene in their modern forms of hypnotherapy, progressive relaxation, directive counseling, and simple advice-giving. Of Wolff's respondents, most of whom, it will be remembered, were trained in the broad psychoanalytical tradition, only 27 percent said they used a strictly nondirective approach.[17]

Nevertheless, beginning with Freud's substitution of so-called free association for hypnosis, the dominant trend in writings on psychotherapy has emphasized the desirability of the therapist's using more indirect methods of influence. The goals of treatment are expressed in more ambitious terms than the relief of the patient's distress and improvement of his functioning. He must be helped toward greater self-actualization, spontaneity, maturity, creativity, and the like. The therapist facilitates the patient's movement by empathizing with him, accepting him, collaborating with him, respecting him, and being permissive. The patient's natural tendency to be dependent on the therapist is to be combated. The therapist is not to persuade or advise, since such activities impede the patient's growth toward emotional maturity.

This trend may spring in part from democratic values, which place a higher worth on apparently self-directed, spontaneous behavior than on that obviously caused by outside influence.[18] The swing from directive techniques also derives in part from the experience that many cures acheived through these means proved to be transitory, although whether a larger percentage of enduring results is achieved by more permissive techniques is still unknown.

I shall now review some ways in which the therapist may transmit his expectancies to the patient and so influence the latter's productions in treatment, often without the awareness of either. Data are adduced from two sources: Chinese thought reform or brainwashing, and content analyses of patients' and therapists' verbalizations in treatment.

Chinese Thought Reform

At first glance, nothing could seem more remote from psychotherapy than methods used by Chinese Communists to obtain confessions from their prisoners. The objects of psychotherapy are patients; those of thought reform, prisoners. Patients and therapists operate within the same broad cultural framework; the cultural values of interrogators and prisoners clash. The goals of psychotherapist and patient are roughly similar; those of interrogator and prisoner are diametrically opposed. In psychotherapy the welfare of the patient is uppermost; in thought reform that of the prisoner is of no account. Thought reform relies on the application of extreme force; psychotherapy typically eschews overt pressure on the patient.

Nevertheless, several psychiatrists have been impressed by certain parallels between psychotherapy and thought reform;[19] in both someone in distress must rely on someone else for relief, and in both the person in distress is required to review and reinterpret his past life in detail. Just as the study of pathological processes increases the understanding of normal ones by throwing certain of their characteristics into relief, a study of thought reform, which may be regarded as a pathological form of psychotherapy, highlights some aspects of the latter that have received inadequate attention.

Thought reform utilizes both group and individual pressures to break down the prisoner's sense of personal identity and influence him to assume a new one incorporating the attitudes and values of his captors. The victim is snatched from his usual activities and abruptly plunged into a completely hostile environment. Present miseries are compounded by threats of worse to come, with the possibility of death always present. Physical tortures are of the humiliating type, such as manacling the prisoner's hands behind his back so that he has to eat like an animal. He receives none of the respect or consideration accorded to his previous status. For example, he is allowed only a few moments to defecate and must do it in public. He is completely immersed in a group which incessantly hammers at his values and demands that he adopt theirs. The group's attitude is implacable and rigidly consistent. For example, the group assumes that the prisoner is guilty and that the enormity of his offenses justifies the harshest punishment. Therefore, any punishment he does receive is a sign of his captor's leniency. The effect of these pressures on the prisoner is strengthened by complete severance of his contact with former associates, and he receives only such distorted and fragmentary news of the outer world as fits the aims of his captors. By these means his sense of personal identity is weakened and his critical faculties are dulled, decreasing his ability to resist.

The prisoner is removed from the group only for the time he spends with an interrogator, whose task it is to obtain the prisoner's "confession" of his "crimes." Certain features of the interrogation situation are relevant to this discussion. It is characterized by rigidity in some respects, by ambiguity in others, by repetition, and by insistence on the prisoner's participation.

The rigidity lies in the interrogator's attitude of infallibility. His position is that the Communist viewpoint on every issue is the only correct one. The prisoner's guilt is axiomatic, and all his productions are judged in the light of this assumption. The interrogator indicates that he knows what the crimes are, but the prisoner must make his own confession. He is encouraged to talk or write freely about himself and his alleged crimes, but he is not told what to write. He may be punished severely, however, if his production does not accord with the desires of his interrogator. Those statements which do meet the interrogator's wishes gain approval, which reinforces them the more effectively because of the prisoner's previous apprehensiveness.[20] No matter what he confesses, it is never enough, but the hope continues to be held out to him that once he makes a proper and complete confession he will be released. The prisoner is thus placed in a perceptually ambiguous situation, which compels him to scrutinize the interrogator for clues as to what is really wanted, while at the same time offering him no target against which to focus his resistance.

The participation of the prisoner in bringing about his own change in attitude is implicit in this procedure. By putting the responsibility for writing an adequate confession on him, his captors force him to commit himself to the process. Schein describes the same procedure in Korean prison camps:

> It was never enough for the prisoner to listen and absorb; some kind of verbal or written response was always demanded. . . . The Chinese apparently believed that if they could once get a man to participate . . . eventually he would accept the attitudes which the participation expressed.[21]

Finally, repetition is an important component of thought reform:

> One of the chief characteristics of the Chinese was their immense patience in whatever they were doing. . . . they were always willing to make their demand or assertion over and over again. Many men pointed out that most of the techniques used gained their effectiveness by being used in this repetitive way until the prisoner could no longer sustain his resistance.[22]

Under these pressures the prisoner's self-searchings produce material increasingly in line with the interrogator's desires, and eventually the victim may be unable to tell fact from fantasy. In extreme cases he accepts his fabricated confession as true. Lifton tells of a man who confessed with conviction and in detail that he had tried to attract the attention of an official representative of his country who passed by the door of his cell, only to discover later that the episode could not possibly have occurred.[23]

The world of the victim of thought reform seems a far cry from that of the mental patient, and yet the analogies are sometimes startling. Some patients are in the same state of terror and bewilderment that the Communists try to produce in their prisoners. To quote Hinkle and Wolff,

> In all [the Communist indoctrination programs] the subject is faced with pressure upon pressure and discomfort upon discomfort, and none of his attempts to deal with his situation lead to

amelioration of his lot. Psychiatrists may refer to a man in such a situation as "emotionally bankrupt." Some of the patients who seek the help of psychiatrists are in a similar state. The pressures and convolutions of their lives have reached a point at which they can no longer deal with them, and they must have help. It is recognized that such a state of "emotional bankruptcy" provides a good opportunity for the therapist.[24]

Furthermore, some interrogators are analogous to psychotherapists in two respects. Their contact with the prisoner is close and prolonged, and they see themselves as trying to promote the prisoner's true welfare by getting him to discard his unhealthy, outmoded values and attitudes and adopt the "healthier" ones of the Communist ideology. Under these conditions it is not surprising that intense transferences and countertransferences can develop between a prisoner and his interrogator.

As Erving Goffman has vividly pointed out, mental hospitals, in the eyes of many patients, may display some of the characteristics of the Communist prisons.[25] Patients are deprived of their usual badges of personal identity and are forced into a humiliating position of complete dependence on the treatment staff for even such small things as cigarettes. They are cut off from their contacts with the outer world and totally immersed in a different culture. They see themselves as completely in the power of the staff, whose decisions often appear to them to be arbitrary or capricious. They know that in order to get out they must satisfy the demands of the staff, but they have no clear idea as to how to do this.

Moreover, the ideology of the mental hospital is consistently and rigidly maintained. Thus all measures applied to the patient, such as transfer from an open to a locked ward, are perceived by the staff as "therapy." If the patient demurs, he is met with what Goffman calls the "institutional smirk," with its implication that "you may think that's what you want, but we know better." Although this somewhat malicious description deliberately highlights the coercive aspects of the mental hospital, the caricature is not so extreme as to be unrecognizable.

The parallels between thought reform and outpatient

psychiatry, whether in clinic or private practice, are much fainter, but they can still be discerned. As with hospitalized patients, the psychiatrist's potential influence on the outpatient depends in part on the latter's expectancy of help. A few office patients turn to the psychiatrist as a last resort after having vainly tried other possible sources. Their favorable expectancy, like that of many hospitalized patients, is based on desperation. A larger group are not sure why they have come to the psychiatrist or how the latter can help them. The psychiatrist then has the task of mobilizing their favorable expectancies by convincing them that they are ill, and that the illness is best treated by psychotherapy. This is usually expressed as arousing the patient's consciousness of illness. As Kubie writes: "Without a full-hearted acknowledgment of the sense of illness a patient can go through only the motions of treatment."[26]

Moreover, he writes, "it is often necessary during an analysis to lead a patient through a sustained period of relative isolation from his usual activities and human associations."[27] It may not be entirely far-fetched to read into such a statement a recognition that a patient, like the prisoner, can more easily be brought to change his ideology if he is removed from the groups which reinforce his current one.

Viewing psychotherapy in the light of thought reform calls attention to another feature which tends to enhance the therapist's influence. This is his interpretation of all of the patient's thoughts, feelings, and acts in terms of a consistent and unshakable theoretical framework. In accordance with his theory, the therapist assumes that the patient's distress is related to repressed infantile memories, parataxic distortions, or an unrealistic self-image, to take three examples. Therapy continues until the patient acknowledges these phenomena in himself and deals with them to the therapist's and his own satisfaction. The possibility that he has not experienced the phenomena in question or that they may be irrelevant to his illness is not entertained. Freud's handling of his discovery that patients confabulated infantile memories may serve as a prototype of this way of thinking. As he was quick to see, "this discovery . . . serves either to discredit the analysis which has led to such a result or to discredit the patients upon whose testimony the analysis, as well as the whole understanding of neurosis, is built up." A bleak predicament indeed, from which Freud extricates himself by a tour de force. He points out that "these phantasies possess *psychological* reality in contrast to *physical* reality," and *"in the realm of neuroses the psychological reality is the determining factor."* [28] Therefore the fact that these infantile experiences were fantasies rather than actualities, far from refuting his theories, actually confirms them. The Freudian theory of neurosis rests on more solid evidence than real or fabricated infantile memories, of course. The purpose of this example is to illustrate a type of thinking which is characteristic of psychotherapists and which contributes to their influence on patients.

The therapist may protect the infallibility of his theoretical orientation in subtle ways. For example, behavior of patients which does not conform to his position is apt to be characterized as "resistance," or "manipulation." Patients' criticism can always be dismissed as based on "transference," implying that they are entirely the result of the patient's distorted perceptions. Faced with such behaviors, the therapist is admonished not to become "defensive"—that is, not to admit, even by implication, that his viewpoint requires defending.

The therapist also has ways of maintaining his faith in his theory and procedures in the face of a patient's failure to respond favorably. He may take refuge in the position that the patient broke off treatment too soon. Or he may conclude that the patient was insufficiently motivated or otherwise not suitable for treatment. Occasionally he may entertain the possibility that he applied his technique incorrectly, but failures rarely lead him to question the technique itself or the premises underlying it. In short, the vicissitudes of treatment are not permitted to shake the therapist's basic ideology.

In calling attention to the means by which psychotherapists maintain their conviction of the correctness of their theories and procedures, I imply no derogation. On the contrary, this conviction probably is partly responsible for the success of all forms of psychotherapy. I stress it here as one of the ingredients which heighten the therapist's influence on the patient.

The methods of psychotherapy, finally, are slightly analogous to those of thought reform with respect to repetition, participation, and ambiguity. In long-term psychotherapy, the patient repeatedly reviews material connected with certain issues, toward which the therapist maintains a consistent attitude. That this may tend to influence the patient in accordance with the therapist's viewpoint is consistent with what is known concerning the role of repetition in all learning.

The desirability of the patient's being an active participant or collaborator in the treatment process is universally recognized. One of the many reasons for encouraging such an attitude is that it forestalls or combats the patient's tendency to become dependent on the therapist. Yet the perspective of thought reform suggests that it may also heighten the therapist's influence in at least two ways. The more the patient's active participation can be obtained, the more he commits himself to the change which the therapist is trying to induce. Moreover, the patient has greater difficulty in mobilizing his resistance against a collaborative than a directive therapist.

It is in the ambiguity of the therapeutic situation, however, that its greatest potentiality for influence probably lies. Like the interrogators in thought reform, some psychotherapists convey to the patient that they know what is wrong with him but that he must find it out for himself in order to be helped. This is one means of enlisting his participation, but it also gives the patient an ambiguous task.[29] This ambiguity is heightened by the fact that the end-point of this process, whether it be unearthing his infantile memories, making his unconscious conscious, correcting his idealized image, or what not, is indeterminate, like that of the confession. The patient is to keep on trying until he is cured, but the criteria which will indicate that cure has been achieved are not clearly specified.

Psychotherapists have always been alert to the possibility of directly imposing their own ideas in the long-term, repetitive relationship of psychotherapy and have advocated certain attitudes to diminish this possibility. One is permissiveness; that is, the therapist leaves the patient free to use the therapeutic situation as he wishes. The perspective of thought reform suggests that, given a patient who expects the therapist to relieve his distress, the latter's permissiveness, by creating an ambiguous situation, may enhance rather than diminish his power to indoctrinate the patient. By failing to take a definite position, the therapist deprives the patient of a target against which to mobilize his opposition. Furthermore, an ambiguous situation tends to create or increase the patient's confusion, which, as Cantril suggests, tends to heighten suggestibility.[30] It also makes him more anxious, therefore presumably heightening his motivation to please the therapist.[31] This motivation is enhanced by the fact that the ambiguity is in a context of threat of unfortunate consequences if the patient does not perform the task properly. In thought reform the threat of punishment for failure is direct; in psychotherapy it is indirectly conveyed by the implication that the patient's distress will not be relieved, and perhaps also by subtle hints of the therapist's disapproval or lack of interest when the patient is not "cooperating." That an ambiguous therapeutic situation may intensify the patient's search for subtle hints as to how well he is doing can be testified to by many analysands, who are acutely aware of changes in the analyst's respiration, when he lights his pipe, shifts in his chair, and so on, even when he is out of their sight.

In summary, factors similar to those in thought reform can, in greatly attenuated form, be discerned in psychotherapy, and may in part determine the strength of the psychotherapist's influence. Changes produced by such means range from mere verbal compliance which vanishes with the disappearance of the influencing agent, to genuine internalization of attitudes and values, depending on personal and situational factors still not understood.[32]

Psychotherapy as Operant Conditioning

A mechanism of transmission of influence which seems analogous to operant conditioning[33] occurs in psychotherapy, according to some experimental evidence, and probably also in thought reform. This technique, which produces extremely rapid learning in animals, consists in reinforcing by a prompt reward some spontaneous act—such as a pigeon's pecking at a target or a rat's hitting a lever with his paw. For example, when the rat hits the lever he receives a pellet of food. Analogously, in psychotherapy the patient's spontaneous behavior is his speech, and the therapist reinforces certain verbalizations by cues of approval which may be as subtle as a fleeting change of expression, or as obvious as an elaborate interpretation.

The reinforcing effect of simple signs of interest lies in the fact that, as Jurgen Ruesch says:

> The driving force inherent in any form of psychotherapy is related to the patient's experience of pleasure when a message has been acknowledged. Successful communication is gratifying; it brings about a feeling of inclusion and security and leads to constructive action. Disturbed communication is frustrating; it brings about a feeling of loneliness and despair and leads to destructive action.[34]

The first experimental support of the hypothesis that verbal behavior might be subject to operant conditioning was offered by Greenspoon.[35] He had graduate students say as many words as they could in 50 minutes. He sat behind the subjects and exerted no ostensible control over them. In accordance with a preconceived plan, however, he sometimes said, "Mm-hm," and sometimes, "Huh-uh," just after the subjects used a plural noun. He also introduced other variations as controls. By statistical analysis he showed that "Mm-hm" significantly increased the number of plural nouns spoken by the subjects and "Huh-uh" significantly decreased them. These effects occurred without the subjects' knowledge that they were being influenced.

Following this lead, experimenters have begun to study the patient's productions in psychotherapy as influenced by the therapist's behavior. Only a few results have been published to date, but they confirm Greenspoon's findings. Salzinger and Pisoni used as subjects 14 female and 6 male schizophrenics newly admitted to the New York State Psychiatric Institute.[36] Each patient was interviewed for 30 minutes, once by a man and once by a woman, on two consecutive days, within one week after arrival. In each interview, for the first ten minutes the interviewer offered no reinforcement. During the next ten minutes he systematically reinforced affect statements by the patient, by simple grunts, looks of interest, and so on. During the third ten minutes, no reinforcement was offered. Affect statements were defined as those beginning with "I" or "we," followed by an expression of feeling. They found that, with both interviewers, even a ten-minute period of reinforcement significantly increased the frequency of affect statements over both the control periods. Apparently patients learn as fast as pigeons. Murray reports a content analysis of two case protocols, one of his own and one of "Herbert Bryan" published by Rogers.[37] In his patient, "defensive statements" as defined by him, and which he disapproved, fell from 140 to 9 per interview, over 17 sessions. Expressions of hostility, which he permitted—and perhaps subtly reinforced—rose from practically none to nearly 80 by the fourth interview. In Herbert Bryan's protocol, statements in categories disapproved by the therapist fell from 45 percent of the total number of statements in the second hour to 5 percent in the eighth. Statements in approved categories rose from 1 percent in the second hour to 45 percent in the seventh.

The case of Herbert Bryan has particular interest because it was offered as an example of nondirective therapy. The therapist presumably believed that he was not influencing the patient's productions, yet different raters were able to classify his interventions as implicitly approving or disapproving with a high degree of reliability. Apparently a therapist can strongly affect his patient's productions without being aware that he is doing so.

Perhaps other conventional psychotherapeutic maneuvers may also function as positive or negative stimuli for operant conditioning, thereby influencing the patient's productions in the direction of the therapist's expectancies. Silence, for example, when used to indicate lack of interest, might be a negative reinforcer, influencing the patient to desist from those verbalizations which elicit it.

An interpretation can be viewed as having both positive and negative reinforcing potential. It acts as a positive reinforcer by implicitly conveying the therapist's interest in the patient's verbalization, and, more specifically, by heightening its significance. This it does by relating the patient's statement to a larger system of thought, often with dramatic overtones, as is implied by such concepts as, for example, Oedipus complex, persona and anima, and self-actualization. On the negative side, an interpretation of a patient's behavior as resistance, for example, as an implicit indication of the therapist's disapproval, would probably act as a negative reinforcer.

Beyond their function as positive and negative reinforcers, interpretations are the means whereby the therapist presents his self-consistent and unshakable value system to the patient and demonstrates his mastery of a body of theory and technique. In these ways they further contribute to the therapist's influence.

The possibility that interpretations might directly influence the patient's productions has long been recognized. Psychoanalysts in particular have sought to deny that interpretations can operate as suggestion in this sense.[38] The material just cited as well as evidence from psychoanalysis itself casts considerable doubt on this contention. Freud's well-known statement that "... we are not in a position to force anything on the patient about the things of which he is ostensibly ignorant or to influence the products of the analysis by arousing an expectation," was made before his discovery that patients fabricated infantile memories in accord with his theories.[39] Glover went to some lengths to draw a distinction between correct and incorrect interpretations, agreeing that the latter might operate by suggestion but offering elaborate reasons why the former did not. That he did not entirely convince himself is suggested by the following quotation, from an article written some twenty years later: "... despite all dogmatic and puristic assertions to the contrary we cannot exclude or have not yet excluded the transference effect of 'suggestion through interpretation.'"[40] Recently Carl Rogers has agreed that even his "client-centered" techniques "institute certain attitudinal conditions, and the client has relatively little voice in the establishment of these conditions. We predict that if these conditions are instituted, certain behavioral consequences will ensue to the client. Up to this point this is largely external control."[41]

Operant conditioning offers a mechanism for explaining the repeated observation that patients tend to express their problems and attitudes in the therapist's language. Stekel said long ago, "Dreams are 'made to order,' are produced in the form that

will best please the analyst."[42] Patients treated by Carl Rogers'
group show a shift of their perceived self toward their ideal
self.[43] Those treated by Murray, who operates in a framework of
learning theory, show a decrease in defensive verbalizations
and an increase in direct expression of feeling.[44] Patients in
psychoanalysis express increasing amounts of hitherto unconscious material as treatment progresses. Heine found that veterans who had undergone psychotherapy expressed the reasons
for their improvement in terms of the theoretical systems of
their therapists.[45] Rosenthal found that improved patients
showed a shift in their value systems to those held by the
therapist.[46]

It may be tentatively concluded that the elimination of
suggestion in the crude sense of directly implanting ideas in the
patient does not exclude reinforcement which may influence
his productions in the directions expected or desired by the
therapist. It would be a mistake, however, to generalize too hast-
ily from these scanty findings. They apply only to what the
patient says, not to how he actually feels. In psychotherapy as in
thought reform, the extent to which changes in verbalization
represent mere compliance or internalization of the attitudes
expressed is unknown.[47] There is a distinct possibility, however, that a person's attitudes may be significantly influenced
by his own words. Most persons cannot indefinitely tolerate a
discrepancy between communicative behavior and underlying
attitudes because such deceit is incompatible with self-respect,
and under some conditions it is the attitudes which yield.[48]

The chief interest of operant conditioning for psychotherapy
at this point is that it can work through cues of which the
therapist is unaware, as in the case of Herbert Bryan. This may
lead the therapist erroneously to assume that the patient's productions reflect actual attitudes or experiences, thereby independently verifying his theories, whereas in fact they are responses to his expectancies.

In operant conditioning no learning occurs unless the reinforcement satisfies a need of the animal's. A hungry pigeon will
quickly learn to peck at a target if his pecks release pellets of
food, but a satiated one will not. By analogy it seems likely that
certain behaviors of a person will be conditioned only if they

are followed by a reinforcement which meets some motivation in him. Greenspoon's graduate students probably were trying to please him by being good experimental subjects. In this connection Verplanck found that students had only "indifferent" success in trying to condition each other. The successful students seemed to have prestige, suggesting that the procedure succeeded if the subject "cared" about the experimenter's behavior.[49] Apparently very slight motivation may suffice if the subject has no objection to learning the new behavior.

When a person does object to the behavior to which others desire to condition him, presumably the strength of his motive to learn the new behavior would have to be sufficient to outweigh the strength of his resistance. Prisoners undergoing thought reform usually had to be made to feel that pleasing the interrogator offered the only hope of escape from an intolerable situation before they responded to his pressures. Psychiatric patients, like political prisoners, are usually committed to a certain view of the world. Sometimes this view may accord with the therapist's, but this could not account for the fact that therapists of all schools obtain confirmatory material from their patients. In some cases, at any rate, the therapist's viewpoint must conflict with the patient's initial one. The apparent ease with which such patients learn to make statements in line with the therapist's expectancies suggests that they are strongly motivated to win his approval. The most likely source of this motivation would appear to be their expectation that he will relieve their distress.

DIRECT EFFECTS OF FAVORABLE EXPECTATION ON THE DURATION AND OUTCOME OF PSYCHOTHERAPY

Any discussion of the effects of psychotherapy involves the thorny issue of how to define and evaluate improvement. Until general agreement is reached on the criteria of improvement and adequate follow-up data are available, many crucial questions cannot be answered. These include, for example, whether the changes brought about by different forms of psychotherapy are the same or different and whether some types of changes are more permanent or basic than others. Under the circumstances I believe that progress can best be made by confining the term "improvement" only to explicitly reported or demonstrable favorable changes in a patient's objective or subjective state. This view regards other commonly used criteria of improvement—for example, greater maturity or personality reorganization—as inferences about the causes of the observed behavioral and subjective changes, or ways of summarizing a group of these changes.[50] In this section, various criteria of improvement are used, depending on the material being reviewed. These are disappearance of a bodily lesion such as a wart or a peptic ulcer, beneficial change in a person's attitudes and life pattern as in religious conversions, and changes in certain experimental measures such as a symptom check list or a self-ideal Q sort.[51] The meager evidence available on the duration of such changes will be presented. No attempt is made to evalute them in terms of "depth" or "extent," and the reader is left free to draw these inferences for himself.

The Temporal Course of Treatment

That the therapist's expectancies, transmitted to the patient, affect the amount of treatment in relation to improvement is suggested by Clara Thompson's observation that frequency of sessions, over a fairly wide range, seems not to affect either the duration or outcome of therapy. She pointed out that American psychoanalysts, possibly because they liked long weekends, soon dropped the frequency of sessions from six to five per week. Later, under increasing pressure from the hordes of patients seeking treatment, they reduced the frequency to three times, or even once a week. She stated that effective psychoanalysis can be done, in rare cases, even at the latter rate. Moreover, "in actual duration of treatment, in terms of months and years, the patient going five times a week takes about as long to be cured as the patient going three times."[52] She concluded that the passage of time required for the patient to consolidate new insights and incorporate them into his daily living is the crucial variable, rather than amount of therapeutic contact. In view of the previous discussion, an alternative conclusion might be that some therapists have changed their expectancies as to the frequency of visits necessary to relieve their patients but not as to the total duration of treatment required. The patients have obliged by taking as long to get well but not needing to be seen as often.

This leads to consideration of some evidence that the speed of the patient's improvement may be influenced by his understanding of how long treatment will last. There has been a tendency for psychotherapy to become increasingly prolonged when there are no external obstacles to its continuance. Psychoanalyses now often last five or six years. At the Counselling Center of the University of Chicago the average number of sessions increased from six in 1949 to thirty-one in 1954.[53]

This development may be a manifestation of the therapist's need to maintain confidence in his form of treatment and thereby the patient's confidence in him. Rather than admit defeat he keeps on trying until he, the patient, or both are exhausted, or until treatment is interrupted by external circumstances, leaving open the possibility that it might have been successful if the patient could have continued longer. In any case, length of treatment probably reflects in part the therapist's and patient's expectancies. Those who practice long-term psychotherapy find that their patients take a long time to respond; those who believe that good results can be produced in a few weeks claim to obtain them in this period of time.[54] There is no evidence that a larger proportion of patients in long-term treatment improve, or that the improvements are more permanent than in patients treated more briefly. On the other hand, there is some experimental evidence that patients respond more promptly when they know in advance that therapy is time-limited.

Particularly interesting in this regard are two papers on the group treatment of peptic ulcer patients. Fortin and Abse treated nine college students with peptic ulcer, demonstrated by X-ray, with an analytic type of group therapy for one and one-half hours twice a week for about a year. The patients simultaneously received medical treatment for relief of discomfort. In these groups "discussion of ulcer symptomatology was ignored and attention became focussed on basic personality problems."[55] Most of the patients had a flare-up of symptoms during the first month, and three required bed rest in the infirmary. However, during the later part of group psychotherapy—presumably after several months—in addition to favorable personality changes the ulcer symptoms lessened in intensity and frequency. Fortin and Abse state that at the end of the year, "Among the four members who were diagnosed initially prior to group therapy, no recurrence was reported; among the remaining six members with chronic peptic ulcers, where the expected rate of recurrence is over 75 percent for a period of three years' observation, only one student reported a hemorrhage."[56]

Chappell, Stefano, Rogerson, and Pike treated thirty-two patients with demonstrated peptic ulcers, which had been refractory to medical treatment, by a six-week course of daily didactic group therapy sessions in addition to medical treatment, and compared the results with a matched control group receiving medical treatment only.[57] The therapy group stressed ways of promoting "visceral rest." They report that all but one of the experimental subjects became symptom-free within three weeks, the period during which Fortin's patients were suffering exacerbations. At the end of three months all but two were symptom-free.[58] In contrast, eighteen of the control group of twenty, after an initial good response to the medical regimen, had had full recurrences of symptoms within this period. At the end of three years, twenty-eight of the experimental group were re-examined, and twenty-four "considered themselves to be healthy." Of these fifteen were symptom-free or nearly so. Only two were as sick as at the start. Thus Chappell's patients began to get better while Fortin's were getting sicker, and the end results seem equally good and at least equally durable.[59]

That patients' expectations concerning the duration of treatment affect the speed of their response is suggested by a finding of a research study on psychotherapy of psychiatric outpatients.[60] Patients were assigned at random to three psychiatric residents for individual therapy at least one hour a week, group therapy one and one-half hours a week, or "minimal individual therapy," not more than one-half hour every two weeks. Each resident conducted all three types of treatment. The residents' obligation extended only to six months of treatment, at which time they were free to drop the patients. The patients were told that at the end of six months a decision as to further treatment would be made by patient and therapist. Two scales were used to measure patients' progress. One was a symptom check list filled out by the patient as a measure of his subjective state. The other was a social ineffectiveness scale, a measure of the adequacy of social functioning, filled out by the research staff on the basis of interviews with both the patient and an informant. At the first reevaluation, at the end of six months, there was a sharp average decline in both symptoms and social ineffectiveness. The decline in symptoms was unrelated to type of therapy or therapist; improvement in social effectiveness was greater, the greater the amount of treatment contact over the six-month period. Although individual variations were marked, discomfort scores and ineffectiveness scores at the end of two years were on the average no higher than they were at the end of six months, regardless of whether or not patients continued in psychotherapy. This raises the possibility that many of these patients achieved their improvement in six months because they understood this to be the designated period of treatment.

Support for this is offered by Schlien. He compared the improvement on certain measures of a group of clients who were told at the start that they would receive only twenty therapeutic sessions over a ten-week period with a group who continued in treatment until voluntary termination. Both groups received client-centered therapy, and the same improvement measures were used for both. The groups were closely matched at the start of therapy by the criteria used. The group receiving time-limited therapy reached the same average level of improvement on these measures at twenty interviews as the others did in fifty-five. Moreover, at the end of the latter period, the group receiving time-limited therapy had maintained their improvement, even though they had been out of treatment several months.[61]

These studies all suggest that speed of improvement may

often be largely determined by the patient's expectancies, conveyed to him by the therapist, as to the duration of treatment, and that a favorable response to brief therapy may be enduring.

Faith as a Healing Agent

For a patient to rely on his therapist for help, he must at least have hope that something useful will transpire. The therapist usually tries to inspire more than this; he seeks to win the patient's trust, confidence, or faith. Many therapists feel that in the absence of such an attitude little can be accomplished; and there is some evidence that this state of mind in itself can have important therapeutic effects.

It is generally agreed that a patient's hope for a successful outcome of treatment can make him feel better, but it is usually assumed that improvement based solely on this is transient and superficial. An example of this type of response is afforded by an obsessional patient who tried several forms of psychotherapy, each lasting many months. He stated that as long as he hoped that the treatment would help him, his symptoms greatly improved. When his hope eventually waned, his symptoms would recur and he would seek another therapist.

Changes following brief therapeutic contact, however, in which little seems to have occurred beyond the arousal of the patient's faith in the therapist, are sometimes deep-seated and persistent. The most plausible explanation for the permanence of these "transference cures" is that the relief the patient experiences from this relationship frees him to function more effectively.[62] He becomes better able to utilize his latent assets and find the courage to re-examine himself and perhaps to modify his habitual maladaptive ways of responding, leading to genuine personality growth.

There is a good possibility, however, that the emotional state of trust or faith in itself can sometimes produce far-reaching and permanent changes in attitude or bodily states, although the occurrence of this phenomenon cannot be predicted or controlled. The major evidence for this lies in the realm of religious conversions and miracle cures.

It is common knowledge that faith in its religious form can

have profound and lasting effects on personality, attitudes, and values. After a conversion experience the convert may have changed so much as to be scarcely recognizable as the person he was before this experience. This is seen not only in persons like St. Augustine and St. Francis but even in an occasional denizen of skid row who becomes "saved" at a Salvation Army meeting.[63] Most such conversions are transient, of course, and backsliding is the rule. In this they resemble the transference cures already discussed. As with such cures, perhaps a conversion sticks when it leads to new forms of behavior which yield more rewards than the old patterns. For purposes of this discussion, the only important points are that religious conversions can lead to profound and permanent changes of attitude in persons who have undergone prolonged hardship or spiritual torment and that they usually involve intimate, emotionally charged contact with a person or group representing the viewpoint to which the convert becomes converted. Conversions which occur in isolation are often, perhaps always, preceded by such contacts.[64] According to William James,

> General Booth, the founder of the Salvation Army, considers that the first vital step in saving outcasts consists in making them feel that some decent human cares enough for them to take an interest in the question whether they are to rise or sink.[65]

The role of divine intervention in producing conversion experiences may be left open. The significant point for this discussion is that they are usually accompanied or preceded by a certain type of relationship with other human beings, which in some ways resembles the psychotherapeutic one. The psychotherapist, too, cares deeply whether his patient rises or sinks.

That faith can also produce extensive and enduring organic changes is amply attested to by so-called miracle cures. There can be little doubt that these cures can activate reparative forces, which, in rare instances, are powerful enough to heal grossly damaged tissue. The best-documented cases are those healed at Lourdes, and evidence for these is as good as for any phenomena that are accepted as facts.[66]

Patients claiming to have been miraculously cured at Lourdes are examined by a bureau of non-Catholic physicians, who certify that a cure has occurred only when there is unquestioned evidence of organic pathology previous to the cure. The cures include healings of chronic draining fecal fistulas, union of compound fractures which had remained unhealed for years, and similar quite convincing manifestations. Although the consciousness of being cured comes instantly and healing is rapid, it occurs by normal reparative processes. A cachectic patient takes months to regain his weight. An extensive gap in tissues is filled by scar tissue as in normal healing, and this repair may take hours or days.

For various reasons the actual number of cures of this type at Lourdes cannot be accurately calculated. The most conservative figure is the number of cures certified by the Church as miraculous, which by 1955 was only fifty-one. This is an infinitesimal percentage of the millions of pilgrims who visited Lourdes up to that time. By the most liberal criteria, only a small fraction of one percent of the pilgrims have been healed. This raises the possibility that similar cures occur with at least equal frequency in ordinary medical practice but are overlooked because no one physician has a large enough sample of patients. Questioning of colleagues, many of whom report having actually treated or at least having heard of one such case, tends to bear out this supposition. In any case, it is clear that faith cures occur, regardless of the object of the patient's faith. All religions report them, and they are also produced by persons who, by the accepted standards of society, are charlatans. That is, the healing force appears to reside in the patient's state of faith or hope, not in its object.[67]

Certain features are common to most miracle cures. The patients are usually chronically ill, debilitated, and despondent. Their critical faculty has been weakened, and they are ready to grasp at straws. The journey to the shrine is long and arduous—persons who live in the vicinity of the shrine having proved poor candidates for cures. After arrival there are many preliminaries before the patient can enter the shrine, and during the preparatory period the patient hears about other miraculous cures and views the votive offerings of those healed.

As Janet says, "all these things happen today at Lourdes just as they used to happen of old at the temple of Aesculapius."[68] In his despair the patient's state of mind is similar to that of the victim of thought reform, and the symbols of cure are present, as in the psychiatrist's office, although in much more potent form. Finally, all three types of experience are similar in that another person or group of persons is involved who represents the promise of relief.

Since it is the state of hope, belief, or faith which produces the beneficial effects rather than its object, one would expect to find the same phenomena in a nonreligious framework, and this is indeed the case. For example, according to Harold Wolff, hope had definite survival value for prisoners in concentration camps: "prolonged circumstances which are perceived as dangerous, as lonely, as hopeless, may drain a man of hope and of his health; but he is capable of enduring incredible burdens and taking cruel punishment when he has self-esteem, hope, purpose, and belief in his fellows."[69]

In the realm of medicine evidence abounds that faith can facilitate bodily healing. In these cases the patient's faith is activated by the doctor's administration of an inert pharmacological substance, which symbolizes his healing function. Such remedies are called placebos, implying that they are means of placating the patient and therefore not genuine treatment. But placebos can have deep and enduring effects.[70] An instructive example of the power of the placebo involves the lowly wart. Warts have been shown by several dermatologists to respond to suggestion as well as to any other form of treatment. One of the most careful studies is that of Bloch.[71] He was able to follow 136 cases of common warts and 43 cases of flat warts over a period of two and one-half years. Of the former group 44 percent, of the latter 88 percent were healed by painting them with an inert dye. About half of the cures occurred after one treatment, while less than 3 percent required more than three sessions. Bloch found that cases which had previously been treated unsuccessfully by the usual means responded just as well as untreated cases, and he adequately ruled out the possibility that his cure rates might represent the percentage that would have healed without any treatment. Since warts are caused by an identifiable virus, their cure by placebo may serve as a prototype of an organic disease cured by faith. In this case the faith seems to operate to change the physiology of the skin so that the virus · can no longer thrive on it.

Placebos can also heal more serious tissue damage, if it is directly related to the patient's emotional state. In a study which compared two groups of patients with bleeding peptic ulcer in a municipal hospital in Budapest,[72] the placebo group received an injection of sterile water from the doctor, who told them it was a new medicine which would produce relief. The control group received the same injection from nurses who told them it was an experimental medicine of undetermined effectiveness. The placebo group had remissions which were "excellent in 70 percent of the cases lasting over a period of one year." The control group showed only a 25 percent remission rate. The cure of warts and peptic ulcers by suggestion is not as spectacular as religious miracle cures, but qualitatively the processes involved seem very similar.

Just as placebos can benefit organic conditions they can help subjective complaints, and the beneficial effects are not necessarily transient. Evidence to support this assertion is still scanty. One scrap is that in a controlled study of the effects of mephenesin and placebo on psychiatric outpatients, it was found that the relief of symptoms by placebo persisted undiminished for at least eight weeks, at which time the experiment was terminated.[73]

Miracle cures and placebo responses suggest the probability that a patient's expectancy of benefit from treatment in itself may have enduring and profound effects on his physical and mental state. It seems plausible, furthermore, that the successful effects of all forms of psychotherapy depend in part on their ability to foster such attitudes in the patient. Since it is the patient's state which counts, rather than what he believes in, it is not surprising that all types of psychotherapy obtain roughly equal improvement rates.[74] This finding also suggests that the generic type of relationship offered by the therapist plays a larger part in his success than the specific technique he uses. The aspects of the therapist's personality that affect his healing power have not yet been adequately defined, but it seems reasonable to assume that they lie in the realm of his ability to inspire confidence in his patients. In this connection the findings of Whitehorn and Betz[75] may be pertinent—that therapists whose relationship with their schizophrenic patients was characterized by active personal participation obtained very much better results than those who failed to show this attitude. The therapeutic forces in such a relationship are complex, but one may well be that the therapist's attitude conveys his belief in the patient's capacity to improve, which in turn would strengthen the patient's faith in the treatment procedure, as mentioned earlier. That psychotherapy produces its effects partly through faith is also suggested by the fact that sometimes these effects occur rapidly, as already discussed, and that the speed of cure need bear no relation to its depth or permanence.

The hypothesis that some of the favorable results of psychotherapy may be primarily produced by the patients' favorable expectancies has led some colleagues and myself to study similarities between the effects of psychotherapy and placebo, with the eventual aim of being able to sort out those effects of psychotherapy which cannot be explained on this basis.[76] Two preliminary findings are of interest in this connection. A subgroup of the psychiatric outpatients who were symptomatically improved after six months of psychotherapy, but whose scores on the symptom check list had gradually climbed back to close to the pretreatment level over a two-year follow-up, were then given placebos. After two weeks, their average score on the symptom check list had again dropped back to the level of the period immediately after psychotherapy.[77] The finding that psychotherapy and placebos have similar effects on this measure has led to questions about the meanings of a patient's report of symptoms, which are now being explored. The other tentative finding which has suggested further lines of research is that a group of patients who improved the most on discomfort and ineffectiveness after six months of psychotherapy had personal characteristics surprisingly similar to those found by other investigators in surgical patients whose pain was alleviated by placebos.[78]

In pulling together the evidence that the patient's attitude of trust or faith may play a significant part in his response to all forms of psychotherapy, I do not contend that all or even most of the processes or effects of psychotherapy can be explained on this basis alone. There are obviously many important determinants of the processes and outcomes of treatment besides the direct influence of the therapist based on patients' trust in him. In this presentation, however, I have attempted to focus on two interrelated themes. One is that because of certain properties of all therapeutic relationships, the therapist inevitably exerts a strong influence on the patient. This influence arises primarily from the patient's hope or faith that treatment will relieve his distress. This favorable expectation is strengthened by cultural factors, aspects of the referral or intake process, cues in the therapy situation which indicate that help will be forthcoming, and the therapist's own confidence in his ability to help, springing from his training and his methods. Analogies between psychotherapy and thought reform have been used to clarify some of the sources and modes of operation of the influencing process in the former. Some examples of the influence of the therapist's expectations on the patient's productions and on the duration of therapy have been given.

The other theme is that the patient's favorable expectation, which is a major determinant of the therapist's influence over him, may have direct therapeutic effects which are not necessarily transient or superficial. Certain implications of these propositions for practice and research may be briefly mentioned.

Since this review points out areas of relative ignorance which need further exploration rather than areas of knowledge, its implication for psychotherapeutic practice must be regarded as extremely tentative. It should be noted first that the likelihood of a common factor in the effectiveness of all forms of psychotherapy does not imply that all methods or theories are interchangeable. It may well turn out that the specific effects of different approaches differ significantly and that different types of patients respond differently to different therapeutic techniques. Until these questions are clarified, it is important that every therapist be well versed in his theoretical orientation and skilled in the methods most congenial to him, in order to maintain his self-confidence and thereby the patient's faith in him. Since the leading conceptual systems of psychotherapy are not logically incompatible, but represent primarily differences in emphasis or alternative formulations of the same ideas,[79] adherents of each school need feel no compunction about holding to their own positions, while tolerant of alternative views, pending the accumulation of facts which may make possible decisions as to the specific merits and drawbacks of different approaches.

If the common effective factor in all forms of psychotherapy is the patient's favorable expectancy, this suggests that psychotherapists should deliberately mobilize and utilize patients' faith in the treatment they offer. The problem here is where to draw the line. The psychotherapist obviously cannot use methods in which he himself does not believe. Moreover, reliance on the healing potentialities of faith to the neglect of proper diagnostic procedures would obviously be irresponsible. Treating tuberculosis or cancer by faith healing alone is none the less reprehensible because it may work occasionally. But a large component of the illnesses which bring patients to psychiatrists—how large is still unclear—consists of harmful emotional states such as anxiety, apprehensiveness, and depression, and for these faith or trust may be a specific antidote. In such conditions, the strengthening of the patient's trust in his therapist, by whatever means, may be as much an etiological remedy as penicillin for pneumonia.

The psychotherapist should be prepared, therefore, to modify his approach, within limits possible for him, to meet the expectancies of different types of patients. Interview types of therapy, for example, tend to fit the expectations of most middle-class patients, but many lower-class patients cannot conceive of a doctor who does not dispense pills or jab them with needles. These patients are very apt to drop out of interview psychotherapy because they cannot perceive it as treatment for their ills.[80] For them the tactics of therapy may involve accommodating to their initial expectations so that they will return for more treatment. The developing therapeutic relationship may then lead to modification of the patients' expectancies in a more psychotherapeutically useful direction. Thus it may be hoped that adequate diagnosis will eventually include an estimate as to the type of therapeutic approach most likely to mobilize the patient's faith.

This review also implies that psychotherapists should be more aware of the extent of their influence on patients. The physician cannot avoid influencing his patients—the only question is whether he should use this influence consciously or unconsciously.[81] As Modell says, "It would be well to remember that in all therapy trouble is apt to follow the ignorant application of important forces,"[82] and this applies particularly when the important force is the therapist himself.

It might be objected that the therapist's direct use of influence tends to intensify the patient's dependency and thereby impede genuine progress. There is no question as to the desirability of helping patients to independence, but the real problem is to determine when this goal is better achieved by freely accepting their initial dependency and using it, and when by resisting this attitude from the start.[83] It is easy for patient and physician to become absorbed in a struggle over this issue, to the detriment of therapeutic movement. For example, sometimes giving a patient a symptomatic remedy he requests may improve the therapeutic relationship and permit discussion to move to more fruitful topics, whereas withholding it impedes all progress.[84] In order to become genuinely self-reliant, a child needs to feel securely dependent on his parents. From this he develops the confidence in the dependability of others which enables him to forge ahead. The same consideration may often apply to patients.

Validation of these tentative implications for practice awaits the accumulation of more knowledge. This review suggests two hopeful directions in which to seek this knowledge. One is the study of conditions contributing to the patient's faith in his therapist, and the effects of this on the processes and effects of treatment. Psychiatry, in its preoccupation with illness, has concerned itself almost exclusively with pathogenic feelings such as fear, anxiety, and anger. It is high time that the "healing" emotions such as faith, hope, eagerness, and joy received more attention.[85] Of these, the physician-patient relationship affords a special opportunity to study the group of emotions related to expectancy of help which may be grouped under the generic term *faith*. A promising experimental approach to elucidating the determinants, psychological and physiological concomitants, and effects of these emotions lies in study of the placebo effect, since the placebo, under proper circumstances, symbolizes the physician's healing powers. Study of the relationships between the placebo response and response to psychotherapy in psychiatric patients may help to isolate and define the role of the faith component in therapy.

The second promising line of research lies in experimental studies of the ways in which the therapist transmits his expectancies, goals, and values to the patient, and the effects of these on the patient's responses in therapy. Until this matter is elucidated, great caution is advisable in drawing conclusions as to the etiology of mental illness from patients' productions in therapy.

It is now clear that psychotherapists of different schools may elicit from their patients verbal productions confirming the theoretical conceptions of that school and that patients sometimes accommodate their memories and dreams to the expectations of the therapist to the point of outright confabulation. The possibility that the patient may be responding to the therapist's cues and telling him what he wants to hear must always be kept in mind, especially since it can occur without either being aware of it. Hypotheses about interpersonal factors in mental illness require validation by observations outside the therapeutic situation.[86]

By the same token, one must be cautious about attributing improvement to other causes until more is known about the limits of the direct effects of the patient's positive expectancies on his state of health, and the expectancies of the psychiatrist as related to them. Until more is known about the factors in the patient, therapist, and treatment situation which determine the degree and form of influence exerted by the therapist, and about the effects of this influence on the patient's behavior and the nature and duration of his improvement, it is impossible adequately to isolate either the factors specific to each form of psychotherapy or those involved in all forms of psychotherapy. In the meantime there is a danger of falling into the trap of attributing the patient's improvement to the particular kinds of productions he gives in a given kind of treatment, overlooking the possibility that both the productions and the improvement may be determined, at least in part, by his faith in the therapist.

3. Treatment of the Focal Symptom

WHEN SIGMUND FREUD invented modern psychotherapy about three-quarters of a century ago, he conceived it as a means of relieving focal symptoms through the abreaction of repressed traumatic early childhood experiences under hypnosis. Dissatisfaction with this direct way of reviving buried memories led him to substitute the method of free association. This, in turn, led to increasingly extensive explorations of patients' life histories, with great enlargement of our knowledge about human nature, to be sure, but with no convincing increase in therapeutic efficacy.

For many reasons, including growing fascination with the complexities of the human psyche, the goals of psychoanalytic therapy diffused from alleviation of the focal symptom to restructuring of the patient's personality, enlarging the area of self-awareness, increasing his autonomy, and the like. Psychoanalysis became longer and longer and its goals vaguer and vaguer.

Following the second World War, psychologists entered the field of psychotherapy, bringing with them their knowledge of conditioning and learning theories. Inevitably, they began to apply these notions to the understanding and treatment of their patients. At the same time many psychiatrists were becoming increasingly dissatisfied with the results of psychoanalytically based treatments and so were accessible to new approaches. These trends have combined to foster the rapidly increasing interest in behavior therapies, the goal of which is elimination of symptoms of mental illness by appropriate conditioning and re-learning techniques. The focal symptom has thereby again become the center of therapeutic interest and we have come full circle.

At this point, it is necessary that I define my terms. For purposes of this discussion, "symptom" will refer to any complaint for which the patient seeks treatment, including states of subjective distress and disturbances of performance or of communicative behavior.[1]

Two categories of focal symptoms must be distinguished, related to two different modalities of treatment. In generalized breakdowns, as in psychoses, the disorganization can be partly combated at the biochemical level through drugs. For this purpose it is the *form* of disturbance rather than its specific content or function that determines the choice of remedies. The psychopharmacologist is interested in whether the patient is hallucinated, apathetic, overactive, or depressed, with little concern for the precipitants or concomitants of these reactions.[2] For psychotherapy, what counts is the specific meaning or *function* of the complaint rather than its form. That is, the psychotherapist is less concerned with whether the target complaint is a depression, conversion reaction, or a phobia, than with its origins in the patient's past and the specific part it plays in his current adjustment difficulties.

Mental illness, like physical illness, can be regarded as a failure of adaptation of the organism to its environment, produced by the interplay of specific vulnerabilities in the former and noxious stimuli in the latter.

In mental illnesses the major noxious agents are stressful interactions with other persons, past or present, rather than bacteria, poisons, and the like, and the chief manifestations are at the psychologic-symbolic level rather than the biologic one.

Psychiatric patients, then, are persons who, as the result of the interplay of congenital or acquired vulnerabilities and stressful life experiences, have developed an image of themselves and the world that makes them particularly vulnerable to certain types of interpersonal events. Typically they suffer from unresolved internal conflicts and feelings of inadequacy and inferiority. Some gradually decompensate but most manage to cope reasonably well with life until they meet a crisis—that is, a sudden heightening of environmental stress that exceeds their adaptive capacities. Like everyone else, they then experience distress and indulge in aberrant patterns of behavior.

These persons become patients—that is, come to the attention of psychiatrists—when their personal distress or the deviant behavior exceeds their own tolerance or that of people close to them and when they view psychiatrists as the proper persons to treat them. Whether or not these conditions are fulfilled in a given case depends on a host of factors besides the severity of the patient's breakdown. These include the level of tolerance of the family, the stigma attached to "mental illness," and the patient's own perception of whether he can recover without help or not. Many persons in the community are suffering more distress and creating more commotion than those who come for treatment.

Furthermore, anyone will decompensate under sufficient stress. In fact, it has been shown that persons caught in a disaster may exhibit the whole range of neurotic and psychotic reactions.[3] What distinguishes psychiatric patients is that they have become caught up in maladaptive patterns and are unable to get out of them unaided. Thus psychotherapeutic efforts must be primarily directed to the factors maintaining the symptoms.

Parenthetically, recovery rates of psychiatric treatments are swelled by those patients whom we happen to be seeing while they are spontaneously recovering. The notoriously high attrition rate of waiting lists for treatment at psychiatric clinics is probably due primarily to patients who made appointments while they were in the throes of a crisis reaction and have recovered by the time the appointment date rolls around.

For purposes of psychotherapy, focal symptoms can be viewed as faulty ways of attempting to cope with both internal conflicts and interpersonal stresses. In general, at least in the neurotic spectrum, they are disguised or oblique attempts to gain a reassuring response of some sort from other persons as a means of allaying subjective distress.

The disguise is necessary because the nature of the relationship is such that the patient cannot admit his real aims to himself or to the others involved—or at least, he believes he cannot do so. Otherwise said, the neurotic attempts to control his environment without taking responsibility for doing so.[4] In this connection, it should be pointed out that controlling a relationship is not necessarily the same as dominating it. A clinging wife, for example, may completely control her husband by forcing him to take the dominant role.

So-called functional or neurotic pain, that is, pain more severe than the underlying tissue damage seems to warrant, may serve to illustrate this formulation, as in the following case:

> A sixteen-year-old high school student had suffered a compound fracture of his left wrist and continued to experience, over the following two years, a "murderous" pain at the site of the injury. When he arrived in the hospital, the family was "at the end of the rope." Against his protests, he soon was transferred to the psychiatric service. There his display of extreme suffering was completely ignored, and all analgesics were cut off. In therapy, he realized that he had many aggressive feelings.
>
> This boy had been spoiled greatly by his parents, but had never been allowed to express any resentment. He wanted to be liked and would hold back the anger he felt toward his parents who were constantly arguing and who expected a lot from him. Following the injury he found out that whenever he had pain, the parents would stop fighting, comfort him, and desist from any demands made upon him. His "murderous" pain also served him as a safe means to get revenge on his parents. . . . After he began to verbalize his annoyance, the pain in the wrist diminished and soon disappeared. He was discharged after six weeks on the psychiatric service. He received weekly outpatient psychiatric care for several months, from a therapist closer to home, and has remained symptom-free.[5]

This adolescent's choice of complaint was determined by a specific body vulnerability, in this case an acquired one. It indirectly expressed his anger toward his parents and at the same time elicited behavior from them that allayed his anxieties. Thus the pain effectively controlled the nature of his relationship with his parents, but at the cost of considerable suffering and disability. When he could accomplish the same ends more effectively at less cost by verbal means, the symptoms diminished and disappeared.

Turning now to psychotherapy, all forms share features that strengthen the patient's morale, and in all, arousal of the patient's hope of relief is a powerful nonspecific therapeutic ingredient.[6] The patient's hopes are raised, first of all, by his conviction that the therapist is really trying to understand and help him. Truax and his co-workers have accumulated substantial evidence that, with many different patients and forms of treatment, therapists who offer high degrees of "accurate empathy," "nonpossessive warmth," and "genuineness" obtain better results than those who offer less of these qualities. If these qualities are sufficiently lacking, many patients get worse.[7]

Gaining the patient's trust is an art in itself and often requires great skill and patience. Existential and Rogerian schools seem to maintain that this is the be-all and end-all of therapy—that, supported by the therapist's "unconditional positive regard," the patient finds the courage to let previously unacceptable parts of his psychic life into awareness, and can then modify his behavior accordingly. The weight of evidence, however, is that even the most nondirective therapist molds his patient's responses by very subtle positive and negative reinforcers, so subtle that the therapist may not be aware that he is emitting them. The nondirective therapist, like those of all schools, also shapes the patient's behavior by serving as a model with whom he identifies.

Schools of therapy differ primarily in their preferred ways of attempting to influence the patient's attitudes and behavior. Therapies based on psychoanalytic models stress uncovering the early origins of the patient's current attitudes, on the hypothesis that if the patient becomes fully aware of their inappropriateness to his present life, he will be able to modify them. They attribute major importance to exposing the unconscious conflicts underlying the symptoms. Both client-centered and analytic approaches deemphasize the focal symptom because their aim is to heighten the patient's general sense of security and self-confidence through increasing his self-awareness. This, in turn, enables him to become more spontaneous and direct in his interpersonal dealings, at which point it should be relatively easy for him to overcome his target complaints.

At the other extreme are those forms of behavior therapy that use highly specific techniques to counteract particular focal symptoms.

A third approach, which, to give it a label, may be called adaptational,[8] and which seems useful with many patients, resembles the other two in some respects and differs from them in others. Unlike many forms of behavior therapies, but like analytic ones, it views most symptoms not primarily as habits that can be deconditioned—though this is undoubtedly possible with certain types of symptoms—but as meaningful communications that are miscarrying. Hence reliance is placed not on deconditioning techniques, but on therapeutic conversation aimed at increasing the patient's awareness of the meaning of his symptomatic behavior.[9] Like behavior therapies, but unlike analytically oriented ones, it is less concerned with historic intrapsychic causes of the symptom than with what currently perpetuates it, and searches for these perpetuators in the interactions between the patient and his present social environment. This general orientation is represented by the therapies of Ellis and Berne, for example.[10]

It implies that the therapist must attend not only to the patient himself but to the role requirements of his life situation and to the other persons involved in his illness. The focus of therapy is not on the patient exclusively, but on the social atom[11] of which he is the center—that is, on his communication network. Efforts are made to help other members of the network understand what they contribute to the patient's difficulties, and to gain their aid in helping him to master them. This implies the use of group, marital, and family therapy approaches as well as cooperation with community agencies when appropriate.

In this connection, we might take a leaf from the experience of military psychiatry as to defining goals of treatment. Today the evacuation rate of psychiatric casualties has dropped to below 1 percent, and 65 percent are returned to combat duty. This has been achieved by a sharp change in the military psychiatrist's perception of disability. Instead of viewing it as an expression of intrapsychic conflicts, he treats it strictly as a response to battle stress. He knows the standard of performance to which the patient must return, and focuses treatment on getting him back up to that level as rapidly as possible.

Analogously, the adaptational point of view implies attention to the role demands of the situations to which patients must return, and termination of treatment when they are able to meet these demands. Many patients with paranoid delusions, for example, never really get over them but learn to keep quiet about them and to go about their jobs. Occasionally symptoms may flare up to the point where they are unable to function, but a brief period of hospitalization is enough to restore them to their previous state. This is regarded as an entirely legitimate goal for psychotherapy of such patients.

This view implies that, ordinarily, therapy should end when the focal symptom is relieved. Some maintain that presenting symptoms are superficial manifestations and that real therapeutic improvement depends on correction of underlying psychopathology. The view of mental illness outlined here does not permit such a distinction. The symptom is a form of communication which both expresses and attempts to cope with the person's personal problems. To the extent that it is alleviated, his communications with others must improve, and thereby his personal problems diminish. It is true that very occasionally disappearance of one symptom will be followed by appearance of another, but this has been shown to be much rarer than initially supposed. It is probably an indication that the patient has not yet found a more appropriate way of coping with the stress that led him to treatment.

Occasionally a patient will recover and later on relapse. This does not necessarily mean that the earlier treatment has failed, but rather that environmental stresses have again exceeded the patient's adaptive capacity, as in the example cited below. The analogy of the common cold may be appropriate here. This is an expression of a change in the balance between immunity and infection. Cold viruses are always present in the respiratory passages. Occasionally they become more virulent or the person's immunity drops and he has a cold. It does not follow that treatment of any particular cold is pointless because this does not protect against relapses. Analogously, electroshock therapy has no effect on the frequency with which depressions recur, but shortening a given episode from months to weeks is certainly worthwhile.

In keeping with its modest and circumscribed goals, therapy based on an adaptational approach ordinarily will be relatively brief. Many patients, of course, do not show much response to short-term therapy, but one wonders how many of these would improve much more with long-term treatment. Many have severely limited adaptive capacities due to weaknesses of constitutional endowment, or to early life experiences so pervasive and destructive that the damage cannot be undone. Prolonged contact with a psychotherapist may help keep such patients afloat, but often little beyond this occurs.

Another limitation to therapeutic response is posed by essentially unmodifiable real life stresses. When this is the case, therapy comes to focus on what can be done to make the environment more bearable, keeping in mind, of course, that it is probably not as bad as the patient pictures it and that, as Viktor Frankl has so movingly portrayed in his account of life in a Nazi death camp,[12] no matter how catastrophic one's situation, one is always free to determine the position one will take toward it.

When there are no insuperable environmental or personal obstacles, the duration of treatment is probably determined by two factors. The first is the time required to win the patient's confidence. As described above, the therapist does this primarily through his ability to sense and respond appropriately to the patient's attitudes. With schizophrenics, who are by definition distrustful, the achievement of this may represent the essential therapeutic task. Once the patient begins to trust the therapist, he can begin to trust other people a little more and so function more comfortably and effectively.

The second reason for prolongation of therapy is that a patient needs time to apply what he has learned and to reinforce the new patterns of behavior. Many patients who are seen weekly or more frequently for months really establish the basis for their improvement in the first few weeks. The remaining sessions are essentially devoted to reporting how they are doing and dredging up more bits of past history to comply with the therapist's therapeutic philosophy. With such patients, probably as much can be accomplished by spacing appointments out at monthly or longer intervals after the initial gains had been achieved as by going on seeing patients at the same frequency through force of habit.

Even if therapy proves to take longer than initially anticipated, little is to be lost by trying to instill in the patient an expectation of prompt improvement.[13] If the patient has stayed in treatment long enough to be disappointed at its duration, by the same token his relationship with the therapist will usually be strong enough to survive the disappointment.

Four causes of the perpetuation of focal symptoms are accessible to psychotherapy. The first—the so-called secondary gain—requires only brief mention. As in the boy with the painful wrist, the focal symptom serves to elicit anxiety-allaying attitudes from others or to relieve the patient of certain responsibilities.

The main point to be made about secondary gain is that its role in maintaining symptoms is easily exaggerated. The gain is usually achieved at such great cost in distress and disability that the patient is glad to relinquish it as soon as he develops sufficient self-confidence to find better ways of handling his problems. This scarcely needs elaboration.

A second source of symptom perpetuation modifiable by psychotherapy is the vicious circle—the patient's aberrant behavior elicits responses which reinforce it, partly because the person at whom the behavior is directed cannot decipher the real message the symptom attempts to convey.

For example, a young engineer who was chronically angry at his mother because she gave him so little emotional support in childhood married a girl who was undemonstrative and shy. While strongly attached to her, he also felt compelled at times to seek sexual gratification elsewhere, which made him feel very guilty. These episodes seemed to be precipitated by periods when his wife seemed cold and withdrawn. It soon appeared that these states were reactions to his own behavior. When he felt especially in need of her affection, he would show it by flying into a rage over a triviality—for example, he would dress her down because supper was not ready promptly or because she made him wait a few minutes before he picked her up in the car. These outbursts frightened and angered her, causing her to become still more withdrawn. When they were seen together, it became clear that she had more control over her responses than he did over his. She learned to recognize his bursts of irritability as a perverse way of expressing a need for her affection and, at least on some occasions, was able to respond by becoming more supportive rather than less. This rapidly led to considerable improvement in the marital relationship.

A third well-known source of symptom perpetuation is that it has come to serve a stabilizing or homeostatic function in the patient's social system. Either it helps to resolve problems of other family members as well as the patient's or the family has made adjustments to it which would have to be changed if the patient changed. As a result, while ostensibly collaborating in treatment, everyone may conspire to maintain the status quo. It is easy to multiply examples of the homeostatic functions of symptoms. One involved the husband of a patient to be described presently.

> The patient's crippling obsessions made her very difficult to live with, but the husband managed to be outwardly loving and tolerant until about six months after she had recovered. Then he came to see me secretly in great distress because he had lost all interest in his wife. He developed ulcer pains, lost about ten pounds, felt very restless and could not concentrate. He himself recognized that when his wife was obviously sick, he could maintain a protective attitude toward her. This fulfilled his need to be the dominant member of the marriage and helped to counteract his anger at her behavior. Her recovery deprived him of these defenses.
>
> The wife had been aggravating his condition by reproaching him for his coolness, and trying to "help" by analyzing his feelings. Since he had to be the dominant spouse, her attempt to cast him in the role of patient was intolerable to him. Fortunately, his mood lifted rapidly after a joint discussion in which I recommended that his wife leave him alone for a while to give his spontaneous recuperative powers a chance to operate.

A fourth reason why symptoms persist is that an important

component of them is unconscious. The term is used here as synonymous with "out of awareness." There are many aspects of psychiatric symptoms that may be unconscious and many reasons why this may be so. One, often overlooked, is that the symptom has become so habitual that the patient no longer attends to it.

> One patient in group therapy, for example, complained that others ignored her. They then told her that they were afraid to talk to her because she wore a perpetual scowl. She was no more aware of this than we are of blinking our eyes, yet it greatly disturbed her communications with others. Merely bringing it to her attention enabled her to explain that she did not mean to appear unfriendly, whereupon her relations with the other group members sharply improved.

Most focal symptoms, in contrast to this example, are conscious. The patient knows that he is in pain, afraid, depressed or troubled by thoughts he cannot banish. What he is unware of is what he is trying to accomplish through his symptoms. The boy with the painful wrist was presumably unaware that the pain was a way of keeping his parents from fighting, gaining their sympathy, and expressing his anger at them. To take a more complex example, the patient already mentioned, whose husband became depressed when she got better, suffered from severe obsessional fears, increasing since her first meeting with her future mother-in-law, who, she felt, disapproved of her. She had undergone a very traumatic childhood, was filled with impotent resentments toward her own family, and had a strong feeling of self-hatred coupled with a fear of rejection by others. Her husband, himself a rather obsessional lawyer, was angered by his wife's efforts to change him and had demanded that she leave her first therapist because he felt that the therapist was trying to change him through his wife. He told her he could not see why a wife should ever be angry at her husband. The patient was consciously angry at her husband for his "indifference" and not showing her enough tenderness, but was unable to tell him so directly because of fear of her own destructiveness and of rejection by him.

Among her obsessions was a fear that she had run over old

people who were standing by the side of the road when she was driving.

Her husband one day urged her to stop eating sweets because she was overweight. She kept eating them and he expressed his anger. She said nothing but instantly had a flare-up of obsessive fears that she had run over an old lady while driving home from work the day before.

The next day, while out for a drive with her husband, she meant to ask him to stop at the place to make sure nothing had happened, but forgot to mention it. After he drove past, she demanded that he turn around and go back. Quite naturally he refused. Then she flew into a violent rage at him for refusing. Her symptoms enabled her to express her anger at her husband, which had a legitimate basis, but only on grounds that were obviously absurd, so that neither he nor she took it seriously. At the same time he could not respond appropriately because he did not know what she was really angry about.

After some months of treatment she announced that she had discovered she really could "trust" her husband—that is, that his feelings for her were genuine and that his apparent indifference was often simply preoccupation with other matters. This enabled her to talk more openly with him about her feeling of neglect, and he was able to respond with some show of affection. Thereupon her obsessions sharply diminished. Her greatly improved condition persisted without further therapy for three years

There were, of course, many components of her symptoms that were not conscious, including some early childhood attitudes that contributed to their choice, and more to her treatment than is implied by the one feature that has been singled out for comment.

An important aim of therapy, however, was to bring into her awareness the connection between flare-ups of her irrational fears and occasions for legitimate anger at her husband. That is, their "unconscious" purpose was to elicit more consideration from her husband for her as a person. They did, to be sure, gain his consideration for her as a patient, but this was ineffective because it was given on the basis that she was sick, not that her demands were legitimate.

A final example may serve to pull this rather discursive presentation together because it graphically illustrates the meaning of the focal symptom as an ineffective response to environmental pressures, its disappearance when the patient became able to cope with these pressures more effectively, and its brief reappearance when the patient was intimidated by a new interpersonal relationship.

A soft-spoken, somewhat depressive appearing, twenty-eight-year-old school teacher had had bouts of fear of cancer of the tongue for at least three years, sometimes reaching such a pitch that he was tempted to commit suicide. Reassurance from various physicians had assuaged the fear only briefly. His family of origin was full of illness and hypochondriasis, and he had felt intimidated by his father and unable to speak up to him. He also had doubts about his masculine identification and was very shy with girls.

By the third interview I was able to document the interpretation that his symptoms seemed related to fear of speaking up for himself lest he make others angry. This permitted others to take advantage of him, increasing his anger and frustration. (Though the probable symbolic connection between his symptom and his repression of anger seemed obvious, this was not mentioned.)

After the fourth interview, he confirmed this relationship for himself. At the last moment his principal told him he would have to work two extra days before vacation. He could not express the anger he felt but had a severe bout of anxiety over cancer. He then went home on vacation and asserted himself in various ways for the first time. He had sex relations with a girl. He took a drink in his mother's presence, which he had always previously been afraid to do, and told her he was old enough to do as he liked. He refused to yield to his father's insistence that he let him make out the patient's income tax, as he had done in previous years. Concomitantly his symptoms virtually disappeared and his self-confidence with respect to his work and his social life greatly increased. As he became more assertive with his parents, his feelings toward them became less hostile. A follow-up six months later revealed that his improvement had been maintained.

A year and a half later he returned for one visit because of a recent recurrence of his obsessional fears. They began when his wife, whom he had married in the interim, took a job of her own.

It appeared that she was a dominating person with whom he had many covert conflicts. She was used to a higher standard of living than his and often humiliated him by indirectly reminding him of it. Whereas his parents would sympathize with his symptoms, she would not. These and other sources of his anger and guilt were discussed and he determined to be more assertive with his wife. His symptoms again subsided almost completely.

SUMMARY

A psychotherapeutic viewpoint has been presented that focuses on the adaptive functions of focal symptoms. They are viewed as more or less disguised efforts to express certain feelings toward other persons and gain certain responses from them. They are perpetuated primarily by the fact that neither the patient nor the others involved can read their meanings correctly. The goal of therapy is to help the patient to clarify his feelings and find more effective ways of expressing them. This requires that therapy be focused on the patient's current transactions with others rather than on the origins of his difficulties.

Although this therapeutic approach is not applicable to all patients and has modest goals, it often obtains results that compare favorably with those of more prolonged and ambitious forms of treatment.

4. On Illness and Healing in Nonindustrialized Societies

ACCOUNTS OF ILLNESS and healing in nonindustrialized societies may, at first glance, appear to have little in common with psychiatric illness and healing in the industrialized West. Those who read such accounts may feel like visitors at a zoo or passengers on a luxury cruise to exotic regions of the earth. They may be entertained, even fascinated, by the outlandish healing rites of various societies and impressed by the wealth of creative imagination they reveal, but they do not immediately recognize that these phenomena have anything to do with modern medical practice. And indeed conceptualizations of illness and healing in nonindustrialized societies are superficially very different from those in industrialized ones. Nor, at first glance, do the dramatic and emotional activities of the shaman appear to have anything in common with the detached, quietly competent ministrations of the modern physician.

In nonindustrialized cultures, illness is believed to have a variety of causes, both natural and supernatural. These causes include noxious environmental agents, the enmity of other persons, and the disfavor of the gods, incurred perhaps by unwitting offenses against them. All illness, therefore, arouses fear and self-doubt in the victim and disturbs his relations with his compatriots. Since illness may be evidence of the displeasure of supernatural forces and reduces the patient's contribution to his society, it may also adversely affect the attitudes of others toward him. Their concern may be tempered with fear and even

71

rejection, which feed back into the patient's own emotions, aggravating his condition.

The shaman, like the physician, tries to cure the patient by correcting the causes of his illness. In line with his culture's concept of disease, this cure may involve not only the administration of therapeutic agents but also provision of means for confession, atonement, restoration into the good graces of family and tribe, and intercession with the spirit world. The shaman's role may thus involve aspects of the roles of physician, magician, priest, moral arbiter, representative of the group's world view, and agent of social control. His success may often depend more on his ability to mobilize the patient's hopes, restore his morale, and gain his reacceptance by his group than on his pharmacopoeia.

Industrialized societies hold quite a different concept of illness and healing. We fondly expect someday fully to comprehend the human being as a complex machine controlled by a computer in the skull. Disease will then be merely a derangement of the machine's functioning produced by noxious environmental agents in interaction with inborn or acquired vulnerabilities or errors of metabolism. Psychiatric illnesses are distinguished primarily by the fact that they manifest themselves in disturbances of thinking and behavior, leading to complications in the patient's interpersonal relationships. Ultimately, however, their etiology too will be found in derangement of brain function. Support for this position is afforded by the finding that the incidence of psychosis seems to be about the same in every culture. This finding suggests that cultural factors may not be causative but may merely determine the behavioral expressions of psychotic processes caused by physicochemical abnormalities. It seems reasonable to expect, furthermore, that gains in knowledge of the biological bases of mental illness will lead to increasing effectiveness of pharmacological and neurophysiological remedies.

In this view, the physician is an expert scientist-technician whose job is to get the body into good running order again, and many psychiatrists dream of the day when they too can obtain triumphant cures with pills and injections.

The phenomenal triumphs of modern scientific medicine

have been made possible by this emphasis on the physico-chemical aspects of health and disease, and greater triumphs are undoubtedly in store. Yet in one vital respect it will always remain insufficient. It does not take into account the powerful influence of meanings derived from the interplay of the individual with his family and his culture on his bodily states. Illness always implies certain meanings. It is never merely bodily pathology, but has implications for the patient's view of himself and for society's view of him. In industrial as well as in primitive societies, illness may create noxious emotions, raise moral issues, disturb the patient's image of himself, and estrange him from his compatriots. Barred from the front door, these intangibles sneak in at the back, and, unless the physician takes them into account, he will often fail. The widespread popularity of nonmedical and religious healers in twentieth-century America attests to the fact that the physician must be more than a skilled technician if he is to help many of his patients.

The importance of cultural and spiritual factors in disease and healing is seen clearly in the chronically ill. The patient's loss of earning power, the constant reminder of the fragility of life and the inevitability of death conveyed by his disease, and the pity, scorn, or distaste of those about him are assaults on his self-esteem that often contribute more to his suffering and disability than the disease process itself. To rehabilitate him, the physician must not only treat his body but inspire his hopes, mobilize his environment on his behalf, and actively help him to resume a useful place in society. Sometimes this task includes helping the patient to achieve a philosophy of life compatible with his reduced expectations.

The complex interplay of illness, the physician, and society is also exemplified in suits for damages or workman's compensation following alleged injuries. The physician's estimate of the claimant's disability is supposed to be based solely on the latter's bodily condition, yet every physician knows that such motivational factors as discouragement or hope of financial gain may be much more significant. Furthermore, the ease with which physicians can be found to testify on both sides of such suits suggests that professional judgments involve implicit attitudes toward personal responsibility and self-reliance; the relation of the employee to the employer, of the private citizen to the state; and the like.

If the nonpsychiatric physician often cannot remain the impartial, objective scientist, the psychiatrist is even less able to do so. Not only is little known about the biological bases of mental disorders, but most such disorders also involve disturbances of the patient's self-image and social behavior. The diagnosis of mental illness is usually first made, not by a physician, but by persons in contact with the patient and is based on behavior that deviates from the accepted norms of the culture.

The social aspects of mental illness often require the psychiatrist, like the shaman, to function as a representative of the values of his society. Mention of damage suits is a reminder that the most difficult ones usually involve the testimony of psychiatrists, and they too can always be found to testify on both sides. Another example is afforded by the vexing question of criminal responsibility. One social function of psychiatrists is to make a judgment of the sanity of an accused person to determine whether he is able to stand trial for his acts. Unfortunately, the concept of insanity continues to elude precise definition. In actual practice the psychiatrist's judgment may be influenced by all kinds of considerations, implicit and explicit, that are remote from medicine. Judgment of the sanity or insanity of a defendant may be affected by cultural standards and by the psychiatrist's personal views on the nature of crime, guilt, expiation, and the interests of society.

Outside the courtroom but next door to it, as it were, society expects psychiatrists to "treat" certain socially unacceptable or morally reprehensible forms of behavior as if they were illnesses. Sexual deviations, for example, in some cultures may have a high social value or religious significance, while in others they are regarded merely as unfortunate or ludicrous quirks. Some Western societies, however, view sexual deviation as a cross between vice and illness. When he is asked to treat persons with these behavior patterns, the psychiatrist is really being asked to reform them.

Addicts and alcoholics dwell in the same no-man's land between medicine and morals. At what point does heavy drinking cease to be a vice and become a symptom of the disease called "alcoholism"? Morphine and heroin, though addictive, are physiologically less harmful than alcohol in excess and, in societies that do not interdict their use, produce no antisocial behavior at all. Yet in the United States narcotics addiction is viewed as a more heinous vice than alcoholism, and in most communities an addict cannot get treatment unless he is branded as a criminal by being convicted as an addict. Furthermore, since opiates are obtainable only through illegal channels, they are forbiddingly expensive, so that most addicts are forced to steal. Behavior that is not even recognized as a problem in some cultures can thus become a severe medical and social problem in others.

These examples illustrate that, in industrial as in preindustrial societies, the definition of psychiatric illness is at least in part social, and successful treatment of psychiatric patients must take this point into account.

In industrialized cultures, the efficacy of medications and even of some surgical procedures may depend on their capacity to arouse the patient's hopes for cure, as do the shaman's charms and incantations. For example, patients with coronary artery disease have experienced spectacular relief of anginal pain and showed greatly improved ability to function following the tying of a blood vessel in the chest wall, which supposedly shunts more blood to the heart. Yet, a mock operation, mimicking the real one in all respects except the tying of the blood vessel, has proved equally effective. The ability of placebos—pharmacologically inert pills that serve as symbols of the physician's healing power—to relieve pain even in patients with organic disease is further evidence of the healing properties of emotions and attitudes aroused by the physician. In fact, since until recent years most medical remedies were either inert or harmful, the reputation of the medical profession actually rested largely on the power of the placebo. Since the effectiveness of placebos lies in their ability to counteract psychonoxious emotional states, it is not surprising that some of the beneficial results of psychotherapy can be duplicated simply by giving the patient a placebo. The psychiatrist, therefore, must recognize, however reluctantly, that his treatment methods may rely on an important component of faith.

Furthermore, although his own thinking may be firmly anchored in the naturalistic world, not infrequently he must deal
with supernatural or magical aspects of the world-views of his
patients. Three patients recently treated in the psychiatric outpatient department of one teaching hospital, a veritable citadel
of modern scientific medicine, come to mind. None was in any
sense psychotic. One, born in Sicily, complained of intense
nervousness and restlessness. He had flirted with someone
else's girl and sheepishly confessed that he believed his
symptoms had been produced by the evil eye. He had gone to
several fortune tellers whose reassurances had left him unconvinced. He is the spiritual brother of an Australian aborigine at
whom the bone has been pointed. Another patient raised in the
hills of West Virginia attributed her severe anxiety to a fortune
teller's prophecy that her father was about to die. She stoutly
affirmed the existence of vampires and was convinced that her
grandmother was a witch. A third, a devout Catholic who had
divorced her husband and married a Protestant, was more than
half convinced that a miscarriage was God's punishment for
having broken a religious taboo. For these patients, a priest or
sorcerer might well have been a more suitable therapist than a
scientifically trained psychiatrist.

These patients came from foreign or lower-class cultures
and did not trouble to disguise their concern about possible
supernatural causes of their distress. The better educated are
more circumspect, but, as the current vogue among intellectu-
als for drugs that alter consciousness attests, some of them also
try to solve their problems by seeking experiences that border
on the supernatural. The introduction of these drugs into Western societies closes the circle between science and mysticism.
Mind-altering agents are powerful tools for scientific investigation of brain processes in relation to conscious states, but some
scientists and scholars take them in the hope of achieving experiences they do not hesitate to describe as "sacred." The
parallel between an LSD party held in a setting designed to
evoke religious emotions and a peyote ritual, for example, is
uncomfortably close.

Most psychiatric patients seek to couch the moral or
spiritual problems for which they seek psychiatric help in

pseudoscientific terms, principally derived from psychoanalysis. Under the influence of the scientific world view, the psychiatrist too views himself as morally neutral and believes that his therapeutic maneuvers are based on scientific principles. Yet much of his effectiveness depends not only on his capacity to inspire the patient's hopes but also on his value system. The current popularity of existential forms of psychotherapy is in a sense no more than belated public recognition of what psychotherapists knew all along, although many were unwilling to admit it even to themselves. Although the psychotherapist may state his interpretations in neutral terms, many are nevertheless covert exhortations or criticisms based on implicit value judgments.

In all cultures, phenomena called "mental illnesses" disturb all levels of the person's functioning: bodily, psychological, and spiritual. They involve the sufferer's world view, ethical values, self-image, and his relationships with his compatriots. These disorders result from or express the interaction of sociocultural stresses with vulnerabilities resulting from combinations of genetic, physicochemical, and life-experience factors. The healer, whether psychiatrist or shaman, derives his healing powers from his status and role in the sufferer's society and functions, among other ways, as an evoker of healing forces, a mentor, a role model, and a mediator between the sufferer and his group. His task is to help the patient, whether he be a stockbroker, a research scientist, or an African tribesman, to mobilize his psychological and spiritual as well as his bodily resources.

5.   The Two Faces of Psychotherapy

PSYCHOTHERAPY, like all healing arts, has always presented two faces: one, as old as mankind, the religio-magical; the other, of much more recent vintage, which may be termed the scientific. The scientific approach emerged with the rapid rise in the prestige of science in the seventeenth century. It is based on a Newtonian world view in which entities in space and time relate to each other by cause and effect. By and large, it is conducted with the patient in an unaltered state of consciousness. This statement, of course, has to be qualified to make room for hypnosis, fantasies, dreams, and the state of reverie which may accompany free association in psychoanalysis. The most scientifically sounding therapies, however, notably those of behavior modification, depend on full ultilization of the patient's waking intellect.

Healers in the scientific tradition invoke science as a sanction for their methods. At a conference in New York several years ago at which leaders of various schools presented their methods, each one started by establishing his scientific credentials. One showed anatomical charts; another cited some conditioning experiments with rats; and a third showed some kymographic tracings of visceral responses.

Religio-magical psychotherapy is grounded in what has been termed the perennial philosophy. This underlies all major religions and avers that we are all manifestations of "the divine ground" which links us into a kind of seamless web. Each individual, as it were, contains the universe. The conventional or sensory reality in which we live is only one form of reality.

Health is a harmonious integration of forces within the person coupled with a corresponding harmony in his relations with other persons and the spirit world. Illness is a sign that he has transgressed the rules of nature or society, thereby disrupting his internal harmony and creating vulnerability to harmful influences from other persons and spirits.

Such a conceptualization takes for granted that mental states can powerfully affect bodily functions and that the state of bodily health, conversely, can affect mental functions. The therapist's goal is to restore the patient's harmony within himself, with his group, and with the spirit world through special rituals requiring the participation of the patient and, usually, those important to him, the purpose of which is to intercede with the spirit world on the patient's behalf.

Although the religio-magical healer is as well trained in special techniques as his scientific colleague, he attributes his healing powers to supernatural sources which are linked to a religious system that he and the patient share. Healing involves a special state of consciousness of both healer and patient, in which both temporarily enter another reality characterized by such phenomena as clairvoyance, communication with the spirit world, and out-of-body experiences.

Interest in religio-magical healing has received a powerful impetus through the discovery that some of its features are amenable to study by the methods of science. A compelling example is a study demonstrating that a scale including such items as trust in the surgeon, optimism about the outcome of treatment, and confidence in one's own ability to cope, regardless of the outcome, was highly correlated with speed of healing from retinal surgery.[1]

Expectant faith is responsible for the so-called miracle cures which occur at healing shrines such as Lourdes. It need hardly be said that since these cures have been reported at the shrines of every religion, their existence is irrelevant to the validity of the beliefs to which they are attributed. Moreover, they are not miraculous in the sense that they cannot be explained by natural laws. To be sure, the sense of having been healed is instantaneous, but the actual healing is by normal reparative processes, albeit greatly accelerated. No one has ever grown a new eye or limb as the result of a miracle cure. It is as if the mental and emotional states of the pilgrim to a healing shrine accelerate or release dormant healing forces.

The same process in an attenuated form may account for the placebo effect—the response of patients to an inert medication—which depends on the patient's perception of the medication as a tangible symbol of the physician's healing power. The power of the placebo is considerable. Many double blind comparisons of placebo with active analgesics concur that the placebo is 30 to 60 percent as effective as the medication, regardless of the strength of the latter;[2] that is, the more powerful the medication, the more powerful the effect of the placebo with which it is being compared. It seems as if the physician somehow transmits his belief in the power of the active drug to the patient.

The placebo effect is not incompatible with the Western world view, but other phenomena introduced from the East are harder to reconcile with it. Fortunately, some also prove to be amenable to scientific investigation. One currently receiving much study is meditation. It has gained acceptance through the demonstration that Westerners can learn through biofeedback to control their viscera, a feat long thought to be the exclusive prerogative of Yogi. Although the technology is fairly simple, the successful application of biofeedback training proves to require the same kind of clinical acumen as other treatment procedures. From a therapeutic standpoint, its main usefulness may be as a method of learning meditation.[3]

Meditation has been shown to have bodily consequences, all related to increased tranquility, such as increase in the galvanic skin reflex, drop in heart rate, and change in blood chemistry indicating reduction in metabolic rate. Above all, it seems to facilitate a synchronization of electrical phenomena throughout the cortex. With both biofeedback and meditation, success depends on a strong relationship with the teacher. In this, both strongly resemble psychotherapy.[4]

An exciting finding is that meditation combined with conventional psychotherapy may be helpful in arresting, or even reversing, the growth of cancer, as is being suggested by the results of one program to change the mood of the patient and his family from fear and depression to hope, and in this context to train the patient to meditate and imagine his white cells devouring the cancer.[5]

The most unsettling aspect of religio-magical psychotherapy is its utilization of phenomena that depend on the existence of a reality which does not obey the laws of conventional time and space. The evidence for some of these, particularly telepathy and the healing power of the laying on of hands, is so overwhelming that it can no longer be disregarded.

The laying on of hands is an ancient healing method which has never disappeared. The healers explain their power in various ways. Some believe that they are condensers or focusers of healing energy from God, others that they transmit the healing power generated by the other persons in the group, and still others believe that the power emanates directly from themselves. Those undergoing healing by this means often report that they experience intense heat, but this does not register on a thermometer. Laying on of hands appears to accelerate wound healing and seedling growth;[6] evidence that this procedure's apparent effectiveness in humans involves more than suggestion.[7]

As to telepathy, recent studies suggest that this capacity is much more prevalent than is generally realized. A possible reason for failure to be aware of it is that telepathic communications, being weak signals, are drowned out by sensory inputs. If these are reduced, telepathic reception is greatly increased. The most convincing recent demonstrations of telepathy are the carefully controlled studies of the Maimonides Dream Research Laboratory, first utilizing dreaming subjects and, more recently, subjects placed in a situation of nonpatterned sensory input.[8]

What is the relevance of telepathy to psychotherapy? Almost all schools stress the importance of the therapist's empathy with the patient, and existentialist schools speak of the essence of therapy's being the therapist's ability to merge with the patient. Are these euphemisms for telepathy? The psychologist Lawrence LeShan has gone a step further. He claims that by proper exercises he can place himself in clairvoyant reality while in the presence of his patient and that when he does this sometimes something useful occurs.[9] He has been sufficiently impressed to train many other therapists in this technique.

It would appear that clairvoyance, a phenomenon closely related to telepathy, can be used diagnostically. A neurosurgeon who has placed a clairvoyant on his staff reports that he was able to make a correct diagnosis of the site and source of the patient's pain in almost three-quarters of the cases simply by looking at the patient's photograph, which contained only name and date.[10]

This raises a disquieting question. Rorschach and Thematic Apperception Test (TAT) interpreters and handwriting analysts, no less than palmists and astrologers, range enormously in skill. Some show an uncanny ability to describe persons' inner lives, while others give only superficial or ambiguous readings. Most practitioners of all of these arts of divination make a great show of deriving their findings from mathematical systems which are highly complex with many interacting variables. This permits considerable flexibility in their use. Could it be that the gifted interpreters reach their insights intuitively and then select the calculations which yield quantitative support for them? In other words, are gifted Rorschach interpreters and palmists really using telepathy and clairvoyance without knowing it?

If, in the light of this discussion, we peer more closely into the scientific face of psychotherapy, we may begin to suspect that in reality it may turn out to be a mask, thinly covering the religio-magical one. For one thing, much of the therapeutic effectiveness of Western therapies may depend on the same healing factors as religio-magical ones. Therapists of the existential-humanist persuasion, who have never donned the mask of science, would probably accept this statement without question. But what about therapies which claim to be scientific? Their scientific base may not be as solid as it seems. The scientific objectivity of the psychoanalytic method, for example, is severely contaminated by overt and covert effects of the therapist's expectations on the patient's productions. As to behavior therapies, although many of their procedures are apparently grounded on laboratory findings, how much of their effectiveness depends on these and how much on features of the relationship is still an open question.

Despite striking differences in their underlying world views, religio-magical and scientific therapies have much in common. Both approaches depend on a belief system shared by the patient and the therapist which both believe to have been empirically validated. This is as true for the religio-magical systems of prescientific cultures as for the scientific systems in our own. The therapeutic procedures express the belief system in tangible form, thereby reinforcing it. In both, a trained healer derives his power from the belief system—whether it be as a scientifically grounded Western practitioner or a supernaturally inspired shaman—and in both he serves as an intermediary between the patient and his group.

Finally, healers of both persuasions expend considerable effort to mobilize the patient's expectant faith. To be sure, this is de-emphasized in therapies which pride themselves on their scientific rationales, such as behavior therapy, but observers of two leading practitioners of this method, Wolpe and Lazarus, report: "The explicit positive and authoritarian manner in which the therapist approaches the patient seems destined, if not designed, to establish the therapist as a powerful figure and turn the patient's hopes for success into concrete expectations."[11]

The line of thought presented here raises an awkward question, namely criteria for the selection of candidates for training. Suppose, as seems very possible, persons differ innately in such qualities as healing power, ability to mobilize expectant faith, and the like. Healing ability may well be analogous to musical ability; that is, it may be distributed unequally in the population but in most it can be trained. We cannot all be Rubinsteins, but most of us can learn to play the piano. Unfortunately, some people are really tone deaf. Are there analogous people who should be excluded from the practice of psychotherapy?

Current methods for evaluating the therapeutic potential of candidates for graduate training programs in psychotherapy are at best indirect. Interviews, personality tests, the candidate's previous experience, and the like yield only inferential conclusions as to his therapeutic efficacy. The studies here reviewed suggest that it might eventually be possible to devise direct tests of healing ability—for example, the ability to receive telepathic messages or to stimulate the growth of seedlings—which could be included among screening procedures. Whether this will happen and whether, if it does, any admissions committee would have the courage to use such tests are interesting questions.

From the standpoint of training, we must recognize that all forms of suffering involve the total person. This implies that on the one hand, pharmacological adjuncts to the psychotherapy of all forms of psychological distress may eventually be discovered, and on the other, that psychotherapy may be an important component of the treatment of many bodily diseases. In fact, according to one careful review of data on outcome of psychotherapy, the only conditions in which it seems of unquestioned benefit are asthma, peptic ulcer, and ulcerative colitis.[12] It follows that training programs in psychotherapy should place more emphasis on familiarity with psychotropic drugs and their use and on human physiology, especially of the autonomic nervous system.

Finally, perhaps training programs should consider ways of acquainting students with methods for mobilizing healing forces that involve altered states of consciousness. These range from the easily acceptable, such as progressive relaxation, autogenic training, and biofeedback, to the far out, such as forms of meditation and trance states that foster telepathic, clairvoyant, and mystical experiences. Here, too, drugs like LSD may serve as useful adjuncts. Fortunately, states of altered consciousness are proving to be amenable to scientific investigation, at least up to a point, which legitimizes their study.

In short, the religio-magical and scientific faces of psychotherapy are coming increasingly to resemble each other. Perhaps the ideal psychotherapist of the future should be able to use methods of either or both when appropriate, thereby enhancing his psychotherapeutic effectiveness.

ON GROUP THERAPY

6.   *Conflict in Therapeutic Groups*

THIS GENERATION FACES two conditions of life which have never before existed. The first is that the major threat to human survival comes from man instead of nature. The second is the incredible speed of technological advance, especially in means of communication and the control of energy. As a result chronic problems of human relationships—in particular, hostility—suddenly demand solution as a price of survival, at the same time that the past experience of mankind in dealing with such problems offers little guidance. Some fifty years ago the philosopher Alfred North Whitehead remarked that this was the first generation in human history that could not use the precepts of its grandfathers as reliable guides. Today, at least in some respects, we cannot even rely on ideals that were valid six months ago. As Richard Rovere wrote: "Under the impact of our dizzying technological advance, the validity not only of military and political strategies but of basic ideas is often almost as short-lived as the design of a fighter plane. Concepts that once seemed as if they might endure at least through our epoch are ready for mothballs a few years or months after they have been grasped and disseminated."[1] The combination of the imminent threat of destruction and the unreliability of time-tested guides for conduct tends to produce an attitude of fatalism in the individual and pressure to conformity in the group. Chronic anxiety paralyzes initiative—we become preoccupied with what may happen to us rather than with what we can do. It also causes us to cling more tightly to each other and to regard every sign of independence of spirit in an individual as a threat to the survival of the group.

What are the qualities needed to function successfully in such a world? Two may be singled out which are especially relevant to psychotherapy. These are self-confidence and communication skill. From self-confidence springs the initiative and independence of thought which are required if we are to create and apply the new ideas needed to solve mankind's dilemma. Self-confidence includes three related aspects: self-esteem, mastery over one's impulses, and a feeling of mastery over one's environment. Self-esteem or self-respect probably arises initially from perceiving oneself as inspiring respect in others. Later it becomes autonomous, and is perhaps best defined by the refrain of a popular song of some years back: "No matter what you say, I still suits me." In more technical terms, signs of self-esteem might be an approximation of one's perceived real self to one's ideal self,[2] or the attribution of more favorable than unfavorable qualities to one's self.

The feeling of self-mastery is partly related to absence of strong feelings of, for example, guilt, anxiety, and hate. More importantly, it involves the ability to withstand the onslaught of such feelings, which may at times assail everyone, that is, to let one's self consciously experience these feelings so that they can be resolved without resorting to either neurotic defenses or ill-advised acting out. To the extent that a person has mastered himself in this sense, he has also achieved some feeling of mastery over his social environment. That is, he can withstand attack from others and so maintain an inner freedom from the pressures of the group.

With self-confidence must go ability to communicate, that is, to convey one's own ideas and feelings to others, and understand theirs. This includes capacity to communicate freely with one's self, that is, to have clear awareness of one's own feelings and motives, ability to express what one means so that others receive the message correctly, and ability to perceive without distortion the communications of others.

Self-confidence and communication skill are closely interrelated, and a person must possess both for successful social functioning. The ability to communicate depends on self-confidence in the sense of being able to stand one's ground until one's own feelings and thoughts are clear. Conversely, one's feelings of mastery over the environment and over himself depend directly on his success in getting his ideas across and understanding the position of others.

Among other goals psychotherapy tries to help patients develop self-confidence and communication skills. Psychotherapists have tended to stress the importance of warmth, acceptance, kindly understanding, and similar attitudes in promoting this development. In rightly emphasizing the therapeutic value of these attitudes, however, we sometimes forget that conflict and antagonism, under proper conditions, are important stimuli to personality growth. Conflict can increase self-respect in various ways—through defeating one's opponent, through the discovery of hidden reserves and unsuspected strengths, or that one's convictions may be worth fighting for. Through it we can learn to withstand the pressures of other personalities, and to keep our heads in the face of such emotions as the anger of the battle, the fear or depression engendered by defeat, and the elation of victory. Defeat, if not too drastic, may strengthen the capacity for self-discipline. Sometimes, if the opponent is right, defeat may lead to a beneficial change in attitude. Conflict situations, under favorable circumstances, also increase communication skills. In them one learns to size up the strengths and weaknesses of others and to assert one's own position in the most effective way. Conflict teaches the skills of compromise, for if there were no disagreements, there would be nothing to compromise about. The ideal outcome of conflict, finally, is a new interpersonal integration between the opponents based on reaching a solution which meets the needs of both better than either of the original solutions whose incompatibility led to the conflict.

Related to these considerations some recent writers have called attention to certain therapeutic values of the therapist's assuming a severe, even angry, attitude under certain conditions.[3] In individual therapy, however, the power relationship between therapist and patient severely limits the freedom of motion of both when they are in conflict. Group therapy, in contrast, abounds in conflict situations which can develop freely because the antagonists enjoy roughly equal status. Through observing struggles in therapy groups we have learned that the neurotic, despite his special vulnerabilities, can profit from strife, provided that its intensity does not exceed his tolerance and that the setting has special properties.

In this paper I should like to consider some of the ways in which the antagonism of patients, under the special conditions of the therapeutic group, can contribute to their self-confidence and communication skills. I shall not discuss antagonism to the therapist, which also comes to light more readily in group than in individual therapy, as is well known.

Initially antagonisms between patients are largely based on the contempt that neurotic patients have for each other, arising from their self-contempt. This finds expression in the "peer court"[4] . . . that early period of group development in which members offer advice and admonitions and pass more or less open judgments on each other in terms of conventional norms of behavior and attitude. Patients may come into conflict as they vie for a role which only one can play, such as therapist's favorite, most respected member, sickest member, or group leader. Antagonisms also develop on the basis of real differences in outlook based on differing life experience, as for example, between a black schoolteacher and a southern white housewife over racial integration of schools in a southern city. Or antagonism may arise between patients who attempt to handle a common problem in opposite ways. Allied to this is the antagonism which may arise from mirror reactions.[5] Thus in one group a prolonged feud developed between two Jews, one of whom flaunted his Jewishness while the other tried to conceal it. Each finally realized that he was combating in the other an attitude he repressed in himself. The militant Jew finally admitted that he was disturbed by certain disadvantages of being Jewish and the man who hid his background confessed that he secretly nurtured a certain pride in it. Finally, transference reactions in their multitudinous forms are prolific sources of antagonism.

How does it come about that a group of persons, contemptuous of themselves and each other, often filled with resentments and hostile feelings, and with many opportunities for reinforcing these attitudes in the group, can generate self-respect and develop communication skills? This is brought about, I believe, through the development of a group climate and code which encourage certain attitudes and activities that tend to make conflict useful rather than destructive. In essence these are that everyone is taken seriously, that the group is cohesive, and that communication among members is maintained, no matter how angry they become at each other, in an effort to discover and resolve the sources of antagonism. Forces toward these ends are initially set in motion by the therapist, who strives from the start to develop an atmosphere of free discussion in which the contributions of all are heard respectfully and honest expressions of feeling are encouraged provided the patient uses them as occasions for self-examination. Much depends on the therapist's ability to manifest these attitudes with sufficient strength and clarity so that the group members can learn them from him. Until they have done so, he may try to forestall or mitigate conflicts. Later, when the group code is fully accepted by the members, he neither encourages nor discourages expressions of hostility, but tries to help each antagonist use such occasions to gain a better understanding of himself and his opponent. In a sense he supports both parties, while expecting each to assume responsibility for his own behavior.

Reflecting the therapist's attitudes, members begin to take each other seriously. This differs from acceptance in the usual sense in that a positive feeling is not necessarily implied. In the therapeutic group each member has status simply by being there, not by virtue of any particular accomplishment or strength, or because he is likable. On the contrary, the ticket of admission is that one openly admit a weakness, or the existence of personal problems he has been unable to resolve. Furthermore, a member gains status to the extent that he can freely reveal his deficiencies and unacceptable feelings, rather than through his ability to put up a front. These qualities make therapy groups unique forms of group activity in our society, and may, in part, account for their popularity.[6]

Being taken seriously by other group members is often a more powerful support to a member's self-respect than being so regarded by the therapist, because he perceives them as more like himself. As one patient put it: "A 'doctor of psychiatry' might be smarter than the average but he lives in his own little world. It is good to have things come from a bunch of guys."

As members listen seriously to each other, the group begins to develop cohesiveness which further enhances the self-confidence of its members. Cohesiveness begins to emerge as each patient discovers that his problems or symptoms are shared by others, with relief of demoralizing feelings of isolation. It progresses to the development of what can best be termed group spirit. Members come to feel that they are an in-group, that they are participating in something special from which others are excluded. Although there is, strictly speaking, no common group goal, in that each patient is present solely to help himself, as group spirit develops most members derive an access of self-confidence from seeing other members improve or hearing reports of how other members have successfully tackled a problem in living similar to one which they had failed to master.

Group cohesiveness may be fostered by patients meeting informally without the therapist. They usually begin by stopping for coffee after the group session and occasionally progress to meeting in each other's homes. Though such meetings, which seldom involve all the members, may foster clique formation, they allow patients to establish bonds and test their modes of relating away from the inhibiting eye of the therapist. At the same time, since they occur only under the shadow of the group, in that members are expected to report back to it what transpires in these informal meetings, their divisive aspects are minimized.

It should be emphasized that feelings of being taken seriously and group cohesiveness, though helped by mutual liking, can develop and even increase in the face of considerable antagonism. In this, members of a successful therapy group are like members of a closely knit family who may battle each other, yet derive much support from their family allegiance.

In addition to its seriousness and cohesiveness, the therapeutic group makes for the useful outcome of conflict situations through its pressure on members to continue communicating despite mutual hostility, with the aim of clarifying their behavior and feelings. As has been pointed out by New-comb,[7] one of the unfortunate effects of hostility is that, by rup-turing communication, it prevents the correction of possible misunderstandings on which it may be based. Conversely, if antagonists continue to communicate, not only do they increase their communication skills, but the antagonism itself may be a road to increased mutual understanding and respect.

Communication skills in therapeutic groups are fostered by the expectation that members will continually examine them-selves and each other in an effort to bring to clear awareness certain aspects of their functioning. Of these, three may be mentioned. The first is the patient's habitual interpersonal be-havior, of which he is often unaware, and its effects on others. Secondly, the group tries to uncover the more or less uncon-scious or secret wishes and fears that might be motivating a pa-tient's behavior. Finally, it tries to bring to light past experi-ences which cast light on current behavior and motivations.

In a cohesive group in which members take each other seri-ously and strive to increase their understanding of themselves and each other, conflicts may enhance the self-esteem of the antagonists in several ways. When patients become angry at each other, this itself may be experienced as a sign that they take each other seriously. In the group setting, furthermore, it is often clear that an attack on a member is directed at some neurotic manifestation, and carries the implication that his at-tackers are angry with him because they know he can do better. This enhances rather than damages his self-respect. An-tagonisms also increase communication skills in that patients learn to remain in mutually useful contact despite their anger.

I should like to give examples of three of the ways in which a conflict in a group can be therapeutically useful. First, the result of a struggle may be to make each antagonist more certain that his position is right for himself and more willing to agree that his opponent's position may be right for him. In the process of agreeing to disagree each has become better acquainted with the reasons for his position and may even discover new and better ones. Each also has discovered that he can successfully withstand pressure from others. The feud between the two

Jewish patients already mentioned may serve to illustrate a conflict leading to this type of conclusion.

Secondly, a conflict may lead each antagonist to reveal more and more of himself in an effort to make his position clear to his opponent. This may result in the uncovering and dissolution of the distorted perceptions on which the mutual hostility is based and the emergence of more positive reciprocal feelings.

For example, in one group were two patients who took an instant dislike to each other. One, Hare, was a chronic "drifter," always rebelling against convention and authority. The other, Trojan, said he would have made a good Nazi storm trooper. He was all for obedience, discipline, law and order. When Hare spoke critically of red tape in government, Trojan asked him whether he thought people should just go their own sweet way. When Hare complained about how unpleasant it was to work in the mess hall in the army, Trojan wondered whether Hare thought other people should do his work for him. When the doctor asked what was going on, Trojan, who seemed quite uncomfortable, said he was just trying to convince Hare of the values of self-discipline. They sniped at each other a little longer, both obviously ill at ease, and then Hare began to talk about his past—how his parents were separated, how he had no goal in school or in the army, and how he was just drifting. Trojan listened intently. He seemed especially impressed with Hare's account of his unhappy home life. Then Trojan began to talk about himself. He said that he ran away from home at 16, after he had planned a bank robbery. From then on he had made his own rules for living. Hare laughed and seemed quite pleased that Trojan, instead of being a pillar of society, had rebelled against his family.

This encouraged Trojan to go on. He told how his sisters never got spanked, but he got a thrashing every day, what an inferiority complex he had had at school, and so on. Hare and Trojan had no further fights.

These two patients became uncomfortable quarreling with each other, leading each to tell something about himself in an effort to make the other man understand his attitude better. Trojan discovered that Hare had had a hard time at home too, and wasn't just a chronic malcontent. Hare learned that Trojan had once been a rebel. As a result Hare switched from sniping at Trojan to approving him, and this encouraged Trojan to tell still more about himself.[8]

Since the chief sources of antagonism in our groups are neurotic distortions, usually based on mirror or transference reactions, maintaining communication in the face of antagonism is perhaps the chief means for their correction, as in the example just given.

Thirdly, conflict can lead a patient to experience a beneficial change in attitude through admitting defeat, and modifying himself as his attackers demand. For example, an aloof, intellectualizing group member was subjected to prolonged attack because of his attitude. He typically responded by counterattacking, until the group, in a particularly forceful attack, finally succeeded in conveying to him that their anger was based on his refusal to let them like him. Although apparently unmoved at the time, he went home, listed all the girls he had known, and realized that every time a girl had shown interest in him he had driven her away. He reported this to the group with a burst of tears at the next meeting, the first time he had wept in years. After this dramatic admission of defeat he continued, better able to express his feelings. His next relationship with a girl culminated in a happy marriage. Several years later he still remembered this as the most significant episode in his treatment.[9] In such a situation the winners also gain. Their self-confidence is strengthened by the discovery that their views are helpful to someone else. At the same time, they find that their anger is not as destructive as they may have feared.

The potential therapeutic value of conflicts in therapeutic groups differs, of course, for different types of patients. For some, group therapy may be contraindicated because of its potential for engendering antagonisms. These include excessively timid patients, and, at the other extreme, those who are so aggressive that they cannot be successfully controlled in free discussion. Patients who are moderately timid or overaggressive, however, can both benefit from antagonisms, though in somewhat different ways. The timid patient may profit by others' accounts of battles conducted successfully outside the group, but more from observing struggles between group members.

Through this he comes to learn that expressions of antagonism are frequently followed by greater understanding and emotional closeness as the misunderstandings or distortions underlying the hostility are exposed. He discovers, further, that the group offers many avenues of graceful retreat without having to undergo the humiliation of openly admitting defeat, such as shifting the conversation to another member, or introducing a diversionary topic. Other patients offer various models of behavior under attack which may help him to decide how he would behave. Through vicarious emotional participation he may increase his tolerance for hostility. By these means he may eventually reach the point of being able to venture into the field of battle himself.

The moderately overaggressive patient, accustomed to blind self-assertion, may discover more acceptable ways of making his points by observing that better-controlled behavior in other members leads to a more satisfactory outcome. More commonly, he is held in check initially by finding himself having to take on several members at once. Later he may be especially helped by the therapist and group holding him responsible for exploring the motives for his belligerency.

It must be emphasized, finally, that the successful outcome of hostility in a therapeutic group depends on the creation and maintenance of certain group properties. To the extent that members do not take each other seriously, the group lacks cohesiveness, and there is little pressure toward self-examination, hostility will have damaging results. This is especially true in the formative stages of the group, when it behooves the therapist to forestall or divert expressions of hostile feelings lest members be unduly upset, forced back more solidly into their neurotic defenses, or driven from the group. Scapegoating of a deviant or outspoken member is especially to be watched for and, if possible, prevented. In a cohesive group with a strong therapeutic climate, however, members seem able to turn even very strong antagonisms to constructive use.

In summary, two especially valuable personality attitudes in today's changing world are self-confidence and communication skill. Psychiatric patients are characteristically deficient in these qualities, and both individual and group psychotherapy try to foster their development. This paper considers only one of the many types of interaction in therapy groups whose therapeutic potential is insufficiently stressed, namely conflict between members. Conflicts in therapeutic groups have many sources, among them patients' contempt for each other, their rivalry for the therapist, real differences in outlook, and neurotically based distorted perceptions of each other. For conflicts to eventuate usefully the members must take each other seriously, the group must be cohesive, and the group code must require that members keep communicating despite hostility. Examples are given of three ways in which conflict under these conditions can be therapeutically helpful: it can strengthen each antagonist's confidence in the correctness of his own position for himself while increasing his appreciation of the rightness of the opponent's view for him, can stimulate antagonists to more successful communication, and can produce a helpful change of attitude in one or more of the contending parties.

7. *Cohesiveness in Therapeutic Groups*

GROUP THERAPY, like all therapy, attempts to foster change in individual patients. Group therapists, therefore, tend to conceptualize phenomena in therapeutic groups exclusively in terms of the influence of personal characteristics and behavior of the members and therapist on each other, the group itself being merely the arena in which these events occur.

It is clear, however, that a person's responses are determined not only by the other persons with whom he comes in contact but by the properties of the groups to which he belongs. Group standards and codes which a member has internalized may be relatively independent of the particular members of the group. In this sense the group is not so much an arena as a social field. The properties of this field are determined by many factors, in addition to personal attributes of the members composing it at any one time, and each member is influenced by these properties. The attitudes of a professional soldier, for example, are determined to a larger degree by the codes and standards of the army than by the personal characteristics of his fellows. And these standards are only very slightly modified by any individual soldier.

Recent experimental studies of small face-to-face groups suggest that, as with larger, more permanent organizations, certain of their properties which are relatively independent of the personal attributes of the members, may strongly influence aspects of the behavior of each participant. Since these studies are based on "a face-to-face social organization involving a lasting, personally meaningful communication relationship,"[1] it would seem that they might be relevant to group psychotherapy. One such property is cohesiveness. This is defined experimentally as the degree of the members' sense of belonging to a group or, more simply, as the attractiveness of a group for its members. This concept seems to have special relevance for psychotherapy, because it has been found that the greater the cohesiveness of a group the more influence its standards exert on its members.

While recognizing the indispensability of conceptualization of group therapy in terms of the interplay of the particular personalities of the group members, this paper attempts to explore some implications for therapy of group cohesiveness, viewed as a property of the group in itself. Some well-known phenomena will be looked at as determinants, manifestations, and effects of the cohesiveness of the therapeutic group.[2]

GREGARIOUSNESS AND ITS MANIFESTATIONS

A major source of cohesiveness in therapeutic groups may lie in the fact that man is gregarious and can gain complete self-fulfillment only through harmonious interactions with his fellows. The tendency of groups to maintain themselves is seen in all gregarious creatures.[3] An example of its operation in humans is the way committees and institutions strive to continue their existence after they have fulfilled the purpose for which they were created.

Certain phenomena occur so regularly in therapeutic groups as to suggest that, although they may be convincingly explained on the basis of the psychodynamics of the individuals involved, they may also represent the tendency of all human beings to make those groups of which they are members cohesive. Our patients, like the rest of mankind, seem to strive to make the groups they are in the kind of groups they want to belong to. Thus, in early meetings of a group members try hard to find bases for mutual attraction. They hasten to identify themselves and others in ways which they believe will be acceptable. They search for superficial similarities, but fail to pursue these to the point where important points of difference might emerge. Expressions of hostility are directed toward the environment of the group rather than toward the group itself. In a hospital mutual griping about the conditions of hospitalization occurs universally. In outpatient groups complaints are usually directed toward influential members of the social environment of the patients. This type of activity serves not only to find common grounds on which the group may coalesce, but to displace expressions of hostility from the group to the environment. Attacks on those outside the group may also serve to increase the attractiveness of the group to its members as a source of prestige, as when an attack is based on the failure of the outsider to understand the value of this type of experience or to appreciate his own need for it.

The universal tendency of members to continue interacting outside of the regular group meetings may be viewed as a manifestation of their efforts to become cohesive. Patients chat animatedly before the therapist enters the room or after he leaves, only to freeze up in his presence. Social contacts soon progress to stopping for coffee after the group therapy sessions or sharing rides to and from them. There may develop, even without the therapist's encouragement, meetings of segments of the group or even the total group in members' homes, although this seldom eventuates well unless it occurs with his sanction and guidance. In these subgroups patients have a chance to dissipate disjunctive feelings generated at the group sessions and to strengthen mutually attractive forces. In this connection, it has been shown experimentally that the more the members of a group communicate in a friendly way with each other, the more they like the group.

It has also been found that splinter groups tend to disrupt a parent group when their goals are incompatible with it, but strengthen it when their goals are the same as or supportive of the larger body's goals. Many disadvantages of informal subgroup formation outside the therapeutic group have been noted. Hostile patients may utilize such meetings to disrupt the functioning of the larger group. Social meetings may dispel the social incognito which some therapists feel must be maintained if there is to be a free interchange of feeling in the group.[4] Occasionally they intensify the scapegoating of a member who does not participate in any of them. It is, however, my impression that the activities of most informal subgroups are primarily concerned with "fence mending"—that is, seeking increased intimacy and dispelling hostilities and anxieties which the larger group may have conjured up. As these goals are compatible, though not identical, with those of the parent group, participation in subgroups probably tends to increase its attractiveness. The conflictful attitudes of therapy groups to new members may express one of the problems inherent in a group's efforts to maintain cohesiveness. A group wishes to exclude strangers as threats to its cohesiveness, but if it kept them out forever it would eventually perish by attrition. The initiation rites of organized groups may be viewed as resolutions of this problem. Members are accepted only after they have demonstrated their adherence to the group's code by undergoing suffering for its sake.

Applying this thought to therapy groups, we may note, first, two circumstances under which new members are usually accepted without difficulty. One is in early sessions before much feeling of cohesiveness has developed; the other is when the group is so small that its survival is doubtful. Patients of such a group often request that members be added.

A well-established therapy group, however, resents newcomers, and the behavior of the regular members vacillates between attempts to integrate and to exclude them. At one extreme are activities that can be interpreted as efforts to freeze the newcomer out, such as discussion of incidents in earlier sessions or of members who are absent. The flurry of questions about absentees, which the entrance of a newcomer often provokes, may also represent efforts of old members to reassure themselves as to the stability of the group. An intermediate activity is close personal questioning of the newcomer, often maliciously tinged, which may simultaneously express urges to identify and assimilate the stranger as rapidly as possible, to test the strength of his willingness to accept the group, to demonstrate how the group functions, and to drive him out. It often seems somewhat analogous to hazing. Finally, old members may try to facilitate the integration of the newcomer by demonstrating through their own interactions how the group functions, or by offering information about its goals and procedures.

Aspects of patients' management of hostility may also be viewed as related to the need of the group to remain cohesive. Although the group facilitates expression of hostility to the therapist, if the group is at all cohesive, the latter can always count on some members of the group coming to his rescue, and on the tone of the group as a whole not remaining hostile for long. This seems related to the fact that the attractiveness of the group depends partly on the members' preserving their perception of the therapist as a potential source of help and a figure of prestige, through identification with whom they gain status.

With respect to hostility toward fellow members, the kind of patient who most often receives the group's ire is more easily defined in terms of his effect on the group than his underlying psychodynamics. Common to all patients who are strongly attacked by the group is that their behavior tends to disrupt the group's cohesiveness or prevent its increase. It has been noted in research groups that members tend to leave when others are felt to be too dominating. In therapy groups, similarly, the compulsive monopolist, who grossly impedes the development of a cohesive interaction network, regularly arouses hostility in other group members. Those members who cannot vent their hostility often leave; and if the compulsive monopolist cannot be brought to modify his behavior, he may disrupt the group. The frequent scapegoating of patients who have a derogatory attitude to the group, even if they are outwardly pleasant, may be related to their being a threat to the attractiveness of the group for the other members.

One of the puzzling phenomena of group psychotherapy is that attacks under certain conditions are therapeutically helpful to their object rather than the reverse. The attacked member may emerge with increased self-confidence and with a beneficial change of attitude. Some of the conditions making for this fortunate result are considered in another paper.[5] Reviewing this subject in the light of its possible relationship to group cohesiveness, I have been struck by how frequently helpful attacks have been made, as it were, in the name of the group.

Criticism of a member because he is behaving in such a way that the group cannot negotiate him into their activities seems especially likely to eventuate usefully. When a patient yields to such an attack and modifies his behavior accordingly, he is promptly rewarded by experiencing a greater sense of acceptance by the group. This may shield his self-respect from the damage that it would otherwise have suffered and also reinforce the new pattern of behavior.

OTHER SOURCES OF COHESIVENESS

The gregarious drive as a source of group cohesiveness is probably impossible to manipulate experimentally. Experimenters with small groups have distinguished four general sources of group cohesiveness which can be manipulated, and therefore have implications for the management of therapeutic groups. They have found that a member tends to find a group attractive to the extent that (1) he perceives it as potentially meeting a personal need; (2) he likes the other members; (3) he likes the group activities; and (4) he sees the group as conferring prestige or status because of its relation to its social environment. Let us consider some implications of these points for the handling of therapeutic groups.

Satisfaction of Personal Needs

The attractiveness of a group can be increased either by heightening the satisfaction the members get from participating in it, or by increasing their awareness that they can fulfill their needs through it. The therapist can increase members' satisfaction from participation, through his definition of the therapeutic task, as discussed below. With respect to the second point, many patients do not see how a group can do them any good. Cultural traditions in our society portray the therapeutic relationship exclusively as a private one between patient and therapist. Furthermore, many patients do not initially perceive the kind of activity that goes on in a therapy group as even re-

motely useful to them. Thus, to foster the development of cohesiveness the therapist should keep before the members the
ways in which the group can help them.

Attractiveness of Members

With respect to the mutual attraction of members, it should
be mentioned first that members of a group need not like each
other in order for it to be cohesive. Individuals may have a
strong sense of belonging to groups in the face of considerable
mutual antagonism. Family loyalty, for example, is entirely
compatible with dislike of certain members of the clan, and
even the healthiest primary groups inevitably contain components of competition, rivalry, jealousy, and other disjunctive
feelings.[6] Nevertheless, mutual liking is undoubtedly a strong
source of group cohesiveness, and in this respect the therapeutic group is initially at a great disadvantage. Mentally ill patients characteristically are contemptuous of themselves and
therefore of each other. In line with their rather immature level
of functioning they are apt to be self-centered and to lack a
genuine interest in others. Because of damaging past experiences with people, many of them have little expectancy of gaining anything from close relationships. The normal fear of the
stranger is heightened in psychiatric patients and tends to
create mutual hostility.[7] Moreover, mutual attractions of patients are often based on transference reactions, "set-up operations," and so on, and are therefore apt to evaporate or change to
antagonisms as patients' self-understanding increases.

The group therapist, however, has certain opportunities to
facilitate the development of mutual attractions. He can exploit
patients' initial attraction to himself as the major source of help
by clearly assuming his role as leader, a role which is definite
even in the most permissive of groups. Through identifying
with him, patients are helped to identify with each other.
Moreover, many patients who cannot relate comfortably as
peers can do so as help-seekers. Links formed on this basis may
afford a starting point for developing more mutually satisfying
relationships. The leader can tacitly or openly encourage the
"fence-mending" activities described earlier, not only in the

group but outside it, so long as the material brought up in these situations is regarded as grist for the mill of the group itself. He can help members to see similarities in their problems or experiences which might make them potentially useful to each other. In short, the therapist can foster transient and superficial sources of mutual liking as a temporary scaffolding until sounder relationships develop. A major source of these is patients' eventual discovery that they can be helpful to each other. This does not always increase mutual liking, but it invariably leads to increased self-respect, which makes the group more attractive.

Attractiveness of Group's Activities

Therapy groups as ordinarily conducted pay little attention to this. Often it is not clear just what the activity or the goals of the group are. This contributes to the confusion many patients feel in early sessions. Nor does the group have a goal outside itself which would serve to guide its activities and to minimize personal clashes, as patients work toward a common end.

Whatever the activities of a therapy group, the therapist can help make them attractive to the members by selecting those which are within the patients' competence but sufficiently difficult to be challenging, and by making clear what they are and how success in carrying them out is to be judged. He should do this more by example than precept so as not to intensify the patients' conflicts about submission to authority. In the process of defining the group's activities, he is at the same time implying how they can be expected to meet the patients' needs.

These considerations apply as much to free discussion groups as to therapeutic social clubs or psychodrama, for free discussion is a specific task with definite standards of success. These include the extent to which participants express their feelings honestly and accept responsibility for the consequences, and their skill at analyzing their own and others' motives.

The activities of a therapy group yield two kinds of rewards which help to make them attractive. The first is the approbation of the therapist and other group members for performing successfully in the group. A patient may gain a real sense of achievement by, for example, being the first to recognize a distortion of perception in another patient or himself. The second source of satisfaction lies in the patient's increased success in dealing with persons outside the group as a carry-over from his successful performance in it.

Attractive and Restraining Forces in the Group's Environment

A group in relation to its social environment may exert attractive forces on its members, or the environment may exert restraining forces impeding members from leaving it. The most common source of attraction is the prestige and status that accrues from belonging to it. Initially, therapy groups are at a gross disadvantage in this respect. Most members feel stigmatized at having to come to them. In successful groups, however, patients gradually develop some pride in membership. They come to look down on persons they know who have similar emotional problems but who lack the sense to seek treatment. They come to perceive the values and standards of the group as better than those of the world at large, in that, for example, they are more tolerant and stress the value of self-knowledge.

Restraining forces play a significant part in securing members' attendance at many therapy groups. Quite a few patients, especially in the lower cultural and economic class, come to therapy under pressure from family, employer, or social agencies. Obviously a group maintained by outside pressures, although it may obtain overt conformity of behavior, is unlikely to produce genuine changes of attitude and motivation. Not too infrequently, however, patients who come to a group under compulsion undergo a change of heart and find it genuinely attractive. We have seen this phenomenon particularly in alcoholics. An example from daily life is that of a draftee who struggles against being inducted but once in the army wholeheartedly accepts its activities and values.

GROUP COHESIVENESS AND THE AIMS OF PSYCHOTHERAPY

Having considered some of the sources of cohesiveness in therapeutic groups and certain behavior patterns of members in the light of this concept, I should like to mention some effects on members of attraction to a group as related to the aims of psychotherapy.

All forms of psychotherapy try to help patients achieve beneficial and permanent changes of attitude through resolution of conflicts. Essential to this aim is the maintenance and strengthening of the patient's self-esteem so that he gains courage to face his problems and to try new means of resolving them, and the mobilization of his emotions, which supply the motive power for change. A cohesive group with proper standards protects and enhances the self-esteem of its members, fortifies their ability to consolidate and maintain beneficial changes in behavior or attitudes, helps them to resolve conflicts, and facilitates constructive release of feeling.

Maintaining Therapeutic Change

A cohesive group not only exerts pressure on members to change but also strengthens their ability to maintain the changes it has helped bring about. Allegiance to a group helps members to hold to their decisions. If these decisions arise out of group discussion and have its sanction, the member feels that he cannot let the group down by recanting. It has been shown that group discussion leads to more permanent change of behavior than individual persuasion.[8] It seems likely that the more cohesive a group is—that is, the more each member feels himself a part of it—the stronger this force will be. Thus, the group helps its members to maintain changes which in the eyes of the group are beneficial to him until they can gain sufficient reinforcement from experiences outside the group. A paradoxical example is that of the submissive member who, in compliance with the group's standards, forces himself to act aggressively; that is, he acts aggressively because he is basically submissive. This pseudo-aggressiveness, bolstered by his allegiance to the group, may lead to beneficial changes in his relationships with important persons in his life.

Cohesiveness and Resistance

The cohesiveness of a group might conceivably impede therapy if its standards were such as to strengthen members' resistance. Emotionally ill persons cling to their symptoms and have distorted perceptions of themselves and others; hence groups composed of them might well be expected to develop antitherapeutic norms. Although this misgiving seems plausible, its validity is dubious. Foulkes has suggested that "The deepest reason why ... patients ... can reinforce each other's normal reactions and correct each others' neurotic reactions is that *collectively they constitute the very Norm from which, individually, they deviate.*"[9] An important safeguard against a therapy group's becoming cohesively resistant is that it can develop cohesiveness only by incorporating the standards of the therapist. It cannot remain in a stable league against him because the patients come to it in order to get his help. If certain members find his terms unacceptable, they will leave. Thus the therapist, provided he makes his expectancies for the group clear, can be confident that, despite forces toward resistance, the group as it develops cohesiveness will incorporate the standards which he considers desirable. In this connection it is worth pointing out that cohesiveness does not necessarily imply pressure toward conformity, which is undesirable in therapeutic groups, because the standards of even a cohesive group may encourage diversity. According to Cartwright and Zander, "Groups may sometimes agree that they will not allow pressures for conformity to develop in certain areas in order for example ... that freedom of thought may be respected."[10]

Cohesiveness and Members' Self-Esteem

The feeling of belonging to a group is a powerful supporter of self-respect. The self-esteem of a member of a cohesive group rests partly, of course, on the group's prestige in his eyes. One thinks of the family pride of a scion of the upper class as compared to the self-derogatory feelings of some members of slum families. Membership in any group, however, seems to convey more self-esteem than membership in no group at all. It heightens the member's sense of personal importance because each knows that he has an influence on the others, even when absent; that is, they will act differently in his absence than when he is present. In therapy groups, furthermore, each patient gains confidence and encouragement from watching others improve; he then identifies with them, which in turn would seem to be a function of the cohesiveness of the group.

Members of a cohesive group come to occupy definite roles and to have clear role expectations for each other. In this way, each is helped to clarify his self-image, at least in respect to those aspects of himself that are relevant to the group's functioning.

Cohesiveness and Resolution of Conflicts

Most mental patients are in deadlocked conflicts with certain aspects of their social environment, reflecting their inner conflicts. Individual therapy attempts to resolve the latter and so facilitate resolution of the former. But the converse also holds; in the process of resolving a neurotically based conflict with another person, internal integration may be increased. In a cohesive group patients can work out such conflicts, if the group standard is that antagonists must continue communicating no matter how angry they become with each other. Mutual hostilities disrupt communications, permitting mutual distortions to develop, which increase the hostility, leading to a vicious circle.[11] A cohesive therapy group increases the ability of patients to tolerate a conflict by protecting their self-esteem. By putting pressure on them to continue communicating, it can often carry them to a successful resolution based on deeper and more accurate mutual understanding.

Cohesiveness and Expression of Feelings

Finally, a cohesive therapy group with the proper code mobilizes and guides the release of emotion in its members in such a way as to be most helpful to them. The code must encourage each member to express his feelings freely and honestly, but only on condition that he take full responsibility for them. This implies trying to understand his own motivations and being willing to accept the consequences of his actions in the reactions of other patients. Under these conditions the free expression of emotion can be a powerful aid, if not a necessary prerequisite, to therapeutic changes of attitude.

This leads to another presumed drawback of group cohesiveness, namely, that the more members are attracted to a group, the more they may be inclined to guard expressions of feeling which might be disruptive. This may result in the group's being "too comfortable." Though it is true that in early group meetings members, out of their urge to develop cohesion, may struggle to establish a code of superficial conformity and social politeness, the therapist's attitude and the desire of members to express themselves more freely are usually sufficient to counteract this. In my experience groups seldom become too comfortable. They may become apathetic, but this is rarely an expression of comfort; it is rather an indication that patients are concealing hostile feelings which they do not yet dare express. It should be added, however, that for certain groups of psychotics, alcoholics, and aggressive psychopaths the norm should be one of greater control of feelings rather than freer expression of them.

CONCLUSION

The thesis of this paper is that interactions of members of a therapy group may be understood in part as manifestations of properties of the group per se rather than as exclusively determined by personal characteristics of the members. As an illustration, some therapeutic implications of the concept of group cohesiveness, as used by researchers in group dynamics, are explored. The therapeutic relevance of group cohesiveness lies chiefly in the fact that the more a group's members are attracted to it, the more they are influenced by its standards. If these approve diversity of outlook, nondefensive expressions of feelings and honest attempts at self-examinations; if they reward maintenance of communication no matter how angry patients get at each other; and if they put a premium not on mutual liking but on mutual respect—then the more cohesive the group is, the more likely it is to induce therapeutic changes in its members.

ON PSYCHOSOMATICS

8. Emotional Reactions to an Unfamiliar Disease

In WORLD WAR II American soldiers were repeatedly exposed to unfamiliar diseases about which medical knowledge was incomplete at the time they were first contracted by our troops. In the Pacific theater the first of these was malaria—which was a major problem before atabrine therapy was standardized—and was followed by filariasis,[1] scrub typhus, and schistosomiasis. Each of these diseases when first encountered by our troops was surrounded by an inevitable atmosphere of uncertainty. This tended to encourage emotional reactions in patients, which themselves might produce symptoms or modify symptoms due to strictly organic causes. As a result, the duration and amount of invalidism caused by these illnesses was greater than might have been expected from their organic manifestations alone. As knowledge of each disease increased there was a decline in the amount of disability it produced, even without change in the methods of treatment. This improvement must be attributed to better attitudes on the part of both patients and physicians resulting from increased certainty as to the nature and treatment of the condition.

The problem of emotional reactions to an unfamiliar disease became acute at a general hospital in the Pacific area, where a group of patients were being treated for schistosomiasis. Many patients showed a degree and persistence of invalidism so out of proportion to the objective findings that medical officers in charge of them requested a psychiatric evaluation of the situa-

tion. This study was an attempt to meet this request. It was undertaken at a time when uncertainties as to pathogenesis, organic manifestations, effectiveness of treatment, prognosis, and
disposition were at their height. Furthermore, the outbreak was
of epidemic proportions, taxing hospital facilities to the utmost.
The necessity for treating large groups of patients made it impossible to give each patient the individualized attention he
would have received in more favorable circumstances. These
conditions heightened certain emotional reactions which are
probably present to some degree in all illnesses in which the
patient is uncertain about his condition. Similarly, they brought
into focus certain problems of therapy and aspects of the
physician-patient relationship which under normal circumstances might tend to pass unobserved. It is believed that
the findings of this study apply in some degree to patients' attitudes in all illness. In particular, it is hoped that they will
supply clues as to how to cut down emotionally aggravated invalidism, not only in patients with schistosomiasis, but in other
unfamiliar diseases.

Schistosomiasis is caused by a fluke transmitted by a snail
found in fresh-water streams. The cercariae enter the unbroken
skin and develop into adult worms which lodge chiefly in certain internal veins. These worms lay eggs, some of which ulcer-
ate through the wall of the intestinal tract and appear in the
stools. It is believed that most of the early symptoms of schistosomiasis are caused by allergic reactions to the ova. Common
initial symptoms are malaise, fever, urticaria, puffiness, upper
abdominal pain, constipation, stiffness of the neck, and cough.
Occasionally more or less severe neurological manifestations
are seen. There is usually an accompanying change in the blood
count. A positive diagnosis is established by finding mature ova
in the stools.

Little is known of the remote effects of the disease in white
men who have had only a brief exposure. In native populations,
liver cirrhosis with ascites may eventually occur. However,
they differ from our troops both in having repeated reinfesta-
tions and in the presence of acquired immunity.

At the time of this study it was difficult to evaluate the course
of schistosomiasis after the acute stage had passed. Most pa-

tients had no physical findings after the initial reaction was over. Enlarged lymph nodes and palpable liver and spleen were occasionally found, but they might be absent in the presence of definite persisting infestation, and of course might be present due to other causes in the absence of this disease. Laboratory findings might be equally inconclusive. Although mature ova in the stools indicated the continued presence of infection, their disappearance did not necessarily mean that a cure had been effected. The ova frequently disappeared following treatment, only to reappear at a later date. Blood count findings were influenced by too many extraneous factors to be reliable guides of the course of the illness. Other tests gave promise of aiding in evaluating the progress of the infestation but were still in the investigative stage. Finally, patients' complaints, as will be seen, were useless as indicators because practically none were specific to the disease, and most were characteristic of emotional rather than organic disturbance.

The situation was further complicated by uncertainty as to the action of the trivalent antimony compounds used as therapeutic agents. It seemed that though they might cause the ova to disappear temporarily from the stool, they often failed to kill the parasite. At the same time they not infrequently caused toxic reactions, usually mild, but occasionally accompanied by manifestations such as nausea, vomiting, and muscular pains, which complicated the symptom picture.

In short, at the time of this study acute schistosomiasis was a poorly understood clinical entity with protean symptomatology and no certain objective means of evaluating severity or progress, for which the only remedy was not completely efficacious and was often somewhat toxic. One did not know how to be sure a patient was cured, or what part of the symptoms of a given patient at a given time were due to the parasite, what part to the treatment, and what part to his emotional reactions. Disposition policies were in a state of flux necessitated by changing understanding of the disease. The result was an atmosphere in which rumors flourished and disability-producing attitudes throve.

OBSERVATIONS

General Survey

The study group consisted of a random sample of 50 patients who had had schistosomiasis proven by the finding of ova in their stools, who had had one or more courses of treatment with antimony compounds, and who had been hospitalized continuously for a long period of time. They had all passed the acute stage. When it was bruited about that there was an opportunity for a psychiatric interview, a few patients asked to be seen by the psychiatrist, and a few were referred specifically as psychiatric problems. Although the information obtained from these patients influenced the considerations to be reported, they are not included in the statistical summary of the results. Each patient was seen for a single interview lasting one-half to one hour. The results obtained from this interview were supplemented with information from the clinical record.

The average hospital stay of these patients at the time they were seen was 105 days, with a range from 68 to 148 days; that is, the shortest period of hospitalization was something over 2 months, the longest almost 5 months. These abnormally long periods in hospital resulted from the need to observe the patients for a sufficient period to determine the effectiveness of treatment.

Schistosomiasis was the main reason for hospitalization for all the patients studied. However 15 had other pre-existing or concomitant organic disease such as hookworm, amebiasis, and hepatitis, and 6 showed evidence of pre-existing psychoneurosis or simple adult maladjustment. It is believed that these more or less incidental findings did not appreciably influence the results.

With respect to the treatments given, 40 of the patients had received fuadin, 10 of them after a course of tartar emetic. The remaining 10 had received tartar emetic alone. Toxic reactions occurred during or immediately following 18 of the 20 tartar emetic treatments. Although less frequent after fuadin, they were not unusual, being reported in 27 of the 40 patients receiving this drug. Almost all these patients were seen several weeks after the last course of treatment so that acute toxic reactions played no significant part in the findings.

Of the 50 patients, 35 were hospitalized because they had clinical symptoms of schistosomiasis sufficiently severe to cause them to report to sick call. The remaining 15 were hospitalized on the basis of ova found in their stools on routine surveys. No relation between the severity of the original attack and the degree of disability at the time the patients were seen could be determined.

Clinical Status

An overall evaluation of the degree of disability of each patient based on history and impression at the time of the examination was attempted. Although this estimate may have been highly inaccurate for some individuals, it indicated a clear trend which is felt to be reliable. This was that the vast majority of the patients were neither in robust health nor strikingly incapacitated. Only 2 were considered to be so sick as to require further hospitalization. One of these was a severe hypochondriac the major part of whose symptoms long antedated his schistosomiasis. In the other a large functional element was suspected but could not be proven. At the other extreme only 2 patients seemed essentially symptom free and ready for full combat duty. All the remaining 46 were judged able to perform at least light noncombat duty, but still not entirely restored to health.

Objective findings attributable to schistosomiasis were infrequent. Only 7 of the 35 patients who were checked in this respect had physical findings which might possibly have been due to the disease. Of these, 5 had palpable cervical glands, one a palpable liver, and one a palpable spleen. As regards the laboratory findings, only one stool showed mature ova and 3 immature ova, the remaining 46 being negative. Only 2 patients had a total leucocyte count over 15,000. Eosinophilia was not uncommon, being over 5 percent in 38 patients and over 15 percent in 10. Subjective symptoms, usually of a mild sort, were

as common as objective findings were rare. Although in many
cases they were elicited only in direct questions, only one patient produced no symptoms at all.

By far the most common complaints were weakness or
fatigue, present in 40 patients, and shakiness, reported by 35.
These two usually occurred together, the patient complaining
that they came over him in waves, or that he became shaky on
mild exertion. Next most frequent were headaches, which occurred in 23, upper abdominal cramps present in 19, blurring of
vision found in 12, aching or stiffness present in 11, insomnia in
11, irritability in 9, and restlessness in 9. Of the less frequent
complaints, 6 patients complained of loss of appetite, 5 of
epigastric swelling, 4 of chest pains, 4 of loss of interest in
things, and 3 of concentration difficulty.

The most striking characteristic of the more frequent
symptoms was the inability to allocate the relative roles of
parasitical infestation, antimony, and psychogenic factors in
their production. Some of the rarer ones, such as insomnia, restlessness, loss of interest, irritability, and concentration difficulty, would appear to be essentially expressions of emotional
tension. Blurring of vision and stiffness or aching of muscles
and joints occur as acute toxic effects of antimony. Whether
their continued presence long after the drug has presumably
been totally excreted may still be attributed to this, is doubtful.
The most prevalent symptoms however—weakness, shakiness,
headaches, and epigastric cramps—could be caused by any
combination of several factors. All are frequently seen on a
purely psychogenic basis. On the other hand, epigastric cramps
and headaches are bona fide symptoms of schistosomiasis, and
some patients reported that shakiness and weakness occurred
only during treatment, stopping soon after antimony was discontinued.

A further factor which must be considered in the evaluation
of these symptoms is the effect of long hospitalization per se.
Questioning of a small group of ambulatory surgical patients
without schistosomiasis who had been hospitalized several
weeks showed that a large proportion complained of weakness
and shakiness, the most common complaints of the patients
with schistosomiasis. A study of soldiers hospitalized for many

months following hepatitis stresses the prevalence of the same symptoms, presumably on a psychogenic basis.[2]

In summary, it seems likely that a considerable part of the incapacity of these patients was not directly related to schistosomiasis, but should be attributed to such factors as emotional strain and the effects of prolonged hospitalization.

Attitudes

In an attempt to gain an understanding of the emotional stresses under which many patients seemed to labor, questions were asked about such topics as the disease itself, the treatment, the ward officers, the problems of immediate disposition and the more remote future and, finally, about the sources of the information that the patients had accumulated and its effect on them. In evaluating the answers to these questions it must be kept in mind that the situation was not conducive to frankness. Most patients knew that the interviewer was a psychiatrist, which at once tended to put them on the defensive. An effort was made to circumvent this difficulty by explaining to the patients at the start of the interview that they had been picked at random, not because it was felt that the ministrations of a psychiatrist were needed, that the purpose of the interview was to get information on attitudes which would be helpful to all concerned in planning future treatment, and that nothing they said would be entered in their clinical record. Although most patients seemed to accept these statements and replied in good faith, it may be assumed that some patients suppressed unfavorable attitudes and opinions. On the other hand those who seemed most distrustful of or hostile toward the interviewer were usually the ones who expressed themselves most freely. So all in all the findings probably bear a reasonable approximation to the actual state of affairs.

These men displayed the attitudes which might be expected to develop under the circumstances in which they were placed. Their illness had begun usually with an unpleasant array of symptoms, which had been compounded by the discomforts of treatment. This had been followed by a necessarily lengthy period of hospitalization with ample time to brood and daydream. Due to the large number of patients under treatment, there was little opportunity for the individualized reassurance which might have counteracted unhealthy preoccupation. Material for worry was supplied at every turn. Treatment was prolonged and uncomfortable, then might be repeated after it was supposed to be finished. Disposition appeared to the patients to be arbitrary and capricious—some men were said to have gone home, others went back to their units, still others were discharged and then showed up in the hospital detachment. The air was full of information and misinformation, and there was no way of separating the wheat from the chaff. The information supplied by doctors seemed to be contradicted by radio broadcasts which took an alarmist view of the illness in order to discourage bathing in infected streams. Some men wrote to friends at home to look the disease up and write them about it, others found an article in an encyclopedia or read the circular that came in the packages of fuadin. Every man tossed his scrap into the witches' cauldron of rumor.

The dominant attitudes which appeared in this setting were resentment, anxiety, and confusion. In only 7 patients could none of these three clearly be detected, and in several of them it was felt that these attitudes were present but concealed. Thirty-three patients or just two-thirds expressed some resentment, and 24 each indicated some degree of anxiety or confusion.

With respect to their feelings about their present condition, only 2 patients were willing to say categorically that they thought they were cured. On the other hand, 26 were convinced that they still had the disease. The remaining 22 were undecided, but most leaned toward the belief that they were still sick. As might have been expected the chief reason given for disbelief in a cure was that they still didn't feel well. These doubts were fortified by the noncommital attitude of the ward officers, and by the retreatment of some patients after an interval.

Uncertainties about cure were frequently accompanied by concern about the future, a worry admitted by 31 patients. However, the attitudes taken toward this varied widely. Some patients were frightened and depressed. Others seemed mainly concerned that the army care for them until they were well. A few took a highly realistic and sensible attitude. For example, one, who had made a good recovery from cerebral schistosomiasis, stated that he was making plans to open a toy store in connection with his uncle's lumber yard, if his strength did not return sufficiently for him to go back to his old job as carpenter.

Lack of faith in cure was paralleled by lack of faith in the treatment. Only 23 patients, or slightly less than half, seemed convinced that the treatment had helped them. Twenty-two were uncertain. The remaining 5 believed that the treatment had left them worse off than they were before. As has already been pointed out, treatment was of necessity experimental to the extent that the most effective dosage and compound of antimony in fresh schistosomiasis infections had not yet been worked out. Most of the patients were aware of this, 28 being willing to express the belief that they had been used as "guinea pigs." It is believed that this opinion was more nearly universal than this figure suggests. It is difficult to tell a medical officer that one believes other medical officers are experimenting on him. The significant point is that 17 of the 28 who thought they were being experimented on recognized the necessity of this and seemed to harbor no resentment. Typical remarks expressing this attitude were: "We have been guinea pigs of necessity. Experiments have been made with our welfare in mind." "Someone had to be in on it to keep someone else from getting it. Someone had to give it a trial." "If they ain't got no cure for it they might as well practice on me as anyone." "If it's necessary for them to experiment on me to clear it up, it's the best they can do."

The patients' doubts and uncertainties were also reflected in their attitudes towards the harassed ward officers caring for them. Only 12 seemed to have full confidence in their physicians. On the other hand, 15 made unfavorable comments and the remaining 23 wouldn't commit themselves. Of this group some may have been afraid to express their views. The criticisms were directed chiefly at four points. The first of these, a clear manifestation of anxiety and uncertainty, was that they were not being kept sufficiently informed about the treatment:

"I'm disgusted. Nothing ever seems to be done. We just keep around and they keep doing something to us and we don't know what's going on." "I know I'm being used as a guinea pig. I felt kinda peeved at first but I can't do much about it." "Everyone would have felt a lot better if they explained it first."

The second criticism was directed at what was felt to be a lack of consistency: "They say it isn't serious, yet they keep us around here and won't let us work." "They tell you one thing one day and kind of contradict themselves. Like they say the sickness is all in your head, and then they want to give you more shots." "If they told me I was completely cured, I don't see any necessity for being kept under observation. If they're going to keep me under observation they deny themselves."

The third complaint was that ward officers appeared insufficiently interested: "When a man tells you a pain you can't stand is in your mind, you know the feeling you get." "I tell them something and they just pass it off as though it didn't exist." "You go to a doctor with a little complaint and he says its schisto. I feel I might as well be talking to myself." These comments were, probably, more a reflection of the insecurity and irritability of the patients than of the actual attitudes of the ward officers, most of whom gave as much individual attention as possible under the hectic conditions which prevailed.

Resentment in a very few patients, finally, reached such a pitch as to result in the absurd suspicion that the physicians were trying to make a name for themselves at the patients' expense: "The talk is going around that someone is trying to make a name for themselves. It's logical. We're in no position to act on it."

With respect to attitudes towards disposition, perhaps the most significant finding was that in spite of the prevailing atmosphere of invalidism, only 30 patients expressed a wish to be sent home. Many felt that all that mattered was to regain their health, and that they preferred to stay in this theater if this result could be achieved here. One motivation which played a part in this attitude was unwillingness to distress their families by returning home as invalids. Another was a feeling of responsibility to comrades still fighting. For some patients, being invalided home was equivalent to deserting their friends. Such men pleaded to be returned to their organizations, or failing this, to be allowed to support their comrades by working in rear areas.

From the standpoint of rehabilitation the most important fact about the attitudes toward disposition was that many of these patients were receptive to the thought of remaining at some form of duty in this theater. The unconfirmed possibility of being sent home was probably more disturbing than definite knowledge that they were to remain here would have been.

Information

The patients' understanding of schistosomiasis varied widely, but on the whole it was poor. Of the 50 patients, only 12 were considered to be well informed about the disease. Their knowledge was accurate, with an adequate evaluation of those aspects of schistosomiasis about which no certain knowledge existed. Ten patients had only very meagre and usually inaccurate information. They seemed to have remembered primarily the alarmist rumors. The remaining 23, or about half, had a certain amount of accurate knowledge heavily spiced with rumor and conjecture.

One item used as a check on how well these patients were informed, was whether or not they knew that the worms could not reproduce in the body. This fact is particularly significant because it can be used therapeutically as evidence for the self-limited nature of the disease. Of the 50 patients, 17 were sure that the worms did not reproduce, but 6 were sure they did, and 27 didn't know. It was disconcerting to discover that quite a few of these admitted having been told by the doctors that the worms did not reproduce, but stated that they didn't know whether to believe it or not. In other words, they had reached the point of doubting anything from any source.

Although a certain amount of confusion was inevitable in as poorly understood a disease as schistosomiasis, part of it was attributable to inability to control the dissemination of information. There were many sources which sometimes contradicted each other, and the implications of the material presented were not always adequately clarified. The chief sources of information were rumors, the statements of the doctors, the radio broadcasts cautioning men to stay out of streams, and an exhibit of the disease, either a travelling one or one presented at a lecture by a member of the staff of the hospital. A few patients had managed to read about the disease in an encyclopedia or a text on tropical medicine, and some had seen the circular accompanying their fuadin ampoules. Of the major sources, all but the physicians apparently increased apprehensiveness or resentment rather than allaying it. Even the doctors were felt to be reassuring by only 19 of the patients. All other sources were universally reported as either neutral or upsetting in their effects. These may be considered briefly in turn.

The rumors which seemed to make the most impression were either connected with immediate disposition or concerned with future disability. Fifteen men thought they knew that some patients had been sent home, and 13 had picked up the notion, to support this, that the disease shows a more rapid recovery in a cold climate. A chance sentence in *Time* magazine about dogs with schistosomiasis being rushed to the United States by plane was the source of this. Twelve men reported the rumor that one would soon die of the disease, 8 that it made one a permanent invalid, and 12 that it produced prolonged invalidism.

The radio broadcasts were highly colored statements of the supposedly disastrous effects of schistosomiasis. While the broadcasts were fully justified by their striking success in stopping the further spread of the disease, their effect on those few who had already contracted schistosomiasis was often unfortunate. This was not only because of their alarmist nature, but because they contradicted other more reassuring sources. Since the voice of radio always carries a certain authority, the result was to produce confusion in the patients' minds: "Either the radio or the doctors are screwed up about something. I suppose the doctors are right, but then I suppose the doctors write the radio program." "They tell you in the hospital schistosomiasis isn't serious. On the radio they say it kills. That breaks down the morale of the fellows who got it." Because of this aspect, these broadcasts were discontinued at about the time this survey was undertaken.

The schistosomiasis exhibit occasionally alarmed patients who had not realized that it required massive or repeated infections to produce ascites or destroy livers. This point, if clarified, could perhaps have been turned to good advantage, by pointing out how much better off the patients, with their single brief exposures, were by contrast.

The only important criticism made of the information supplied by doctors was that it was so extensive as to be confusing. As one man put it: "The doctors gave us so much information it got all balled up in my head."

The question arises as to the desirability of trying to inform patients about their illness. A few of these patients apparently tried to combat their anxiety by attempting to shut their minds to knowledge of their own condition or of the disease itself. One man said: "I think I shouldn't be told (about my stools) for my own peace of mind. If you told some their stools were normal and didn't tell others, the others would worry." Another put it more simply: "What you don't know won't hurt you." As might be expected, this "head in the sand" attitude was seldom successful. Most patients maintaining this pose were mines of alarmist rumors. The majority showed a desire for information, based on a realistic and healthy attitude, expressed in such terms as: "I'm old enough to know the truth. If I'm going to die tomorrow I've faced it before." Since all patients, regardless of their expressed attitudes, were certain to pick up information in one way or another, and since accurate knowledge, even if not entirely roseate, is one of the best antidotes for anxiety, efforts to give patients accurate and clear information about their illness would seem to be fully justified.

Individual Reactions

The reactions of the individual patient to schistosomiasis were of course determined not only by the circumstances already discussed, but by his own personality and attitudes. He tended to seize on those aspects of the situation which fitted in best with his own preoccupations. The following two cases, one of whom reacted primarily with anxiety and the other with hostility, may serve to illustrate this point.

CASE 1.—This 20-year-old infantry man was apparently infected by marching through rice paddies. He had a moderately severe onset with pain in his eyes and back of his neck, stiffness, chills, and fever. He received nine Fuadin treatments. At the time he was seen he had been 128 days in the hospital.

In the interview he made the impression of a youth who has been accustomed to the society of older people and was at ease with them. His dominant mood was one of apprehensiveness, and he appeared somewhat depressed. His opening words were, "I hope you don't think I'm crazy." He complained of constant headaches, extending down the back of his neck, anorexia and shakiness, and difficulty concentrating. He spoke of his "overall weakness" and easy fatigue. Finally he complained of anxiety dreams, of which an example was trying to fire his pistol at charging enemies but being unable to pull the trigger.

A brief survey of his background revealed him always to have been a serious-minded, insecure type of person. He described himself as "not frivolous." As a child he walked in his sleep, feared spiders, and for years had a light burning all night in his bedroom. Although he had had no serious illnesses, his health had never been robust. He was taking a premedical course at the time he was inducted, which may have been related to his exaggerated concern over his condition. It is interesting to note the patient's statement that in combat on Leyte and Samar: "I was surprised to find that I wasn't frightened at all." In other words, the enemy seemed to have been less of a threat to him than a bodily illness.

With this background of anxiety and hypochondriacal tendencies, it is not surprising that, despite a good intelligence and the fact that he had a clear picture of the pathogenesis of the disease, he tended uncritically to accept all alarmist rumors. An example was: "One doctor was supposed to have told one of the fellows that untreated you have 5 years to live, treated you have at least 20 years." He found the radio "kind of difficult to reject, since it comes from the same official source as the other things come." He was chiefly worried by his persistent weakness and wondered if he would ever feel better. He was open to the thought that the doctors didn't know what they were doing, but "if it's necessary for them to experiment on me I suppose it's the best they can do." He didn't care whether he was sent home or not, as long as he was cured.

CASE 2.—This 25-year old combat engineer apparently contracted the disease by swimming in an infected stream. He had a moderately severe onset with cramps, backache, aching in his bones and moderate diarrhea. He had received both tartar emetic and fuadin. When seen he had been 111 days in the hospital.

His attitude in the interview was one of brash cheerfulness, with an undercurrent of suspiciousness and hostility. He showed no anxiety in his manner. He tended to use a vocabulary above his educational level and made a great show of superficial but poorly digested information, in general giving the impression of striving for effect. He was essentially symptom free, but stated that he felt a little shaky at times, occasionally slept poorly, and was somewhat sluggish for lack of exercise.

He was a Mexican whose life had been dominated by an urge to "independence," and defiance of authority. He described himself as an "individualist." He left school early in order to achieve financial independence, and made a great point of saving his money, as a means of being self-sufficient. He changed jobs frequently, usually because the new job offered more money. Apparently he had a knack for picking up skills. His aggressiveness found an additional outlet in prize fighting.

In his four-year army career he had repeatedly received recognition for his abilities, then lost it because of difficulties with those in authority. He reached the rank of 1st sergeant once, staff sergeant twice, and sergeant three times, according to his story. When seen he was a private and had been for a year. He stated that all his reductions in rank were due to refusals to obey orders he thought were unreasonable.

With this background, he met the threat to his future independence implied by schistosomiasis by attacking the doctors, the implication being that if he could discredit them he might be able to convince himself that he didn't have the disease after all. His opening remark made clear that his main concern was that he be able to make his own way when the army discharged him: "As long as I have schisto and they don't cure me I won't accept a discharge." The implication was that the army planned to discharge him as an invalid. He tended to exaggerate rumors concerning the severity of the disease, in such a way as to hide his own anxiety by making it seem ridiculous. The following typical statement was made in a tone not of alarm but of scorn: "They said I was cured but from what I read and heard on the radio I don't believe it. It's liable to wreck your brain or to paralyze you. The encyclopedia says it can give you cancer." He seemed bitter because he wasn't allowed to examine his own stools before treatment was started, and said flatly: "They treated me without showing me I had it, just on their own word. I still believe I didn't have it. The doctor himself told me I was a guinea pig. He may have been joking but that wasn't the time to joke. I would like to tell a few of the doctors what I think."

DISCUSSION

It seems clear from this survey that worry, resentment, lack of confidence, and similar unhealthy attitudes were at least partly responsible for the prolonged disability of patients who had schistosomiasis. The reduction of invalidism in this disease as in all others depends not only on the administration of the proper drugs, but on the maintenance of the proper therapeutic atmosphere. The most important healing attitudes seem to be faith in the physician and expectancy of recovery, which in the army implies expectancy of return to duty. Certain directions in which efforts to encourage these attitudes may profitably be expended are suggested by this study.

With respect to expectation of recovery, it should be pointed out that in the army hospitalization often represents a rather desirable state, in contrast to hospitalization in civilian life. The hospitalized civilian has powerful incentives drawing him toward recovery. Leaving a civilian hospital means terminating the expense of hospitalization, returning to the emotional support of one's family, and resuming gainful work. In the army, hospitalization not only involves no financial sacrifice but is sometimes a refuge from arduous or unpleasant military duties. In addition, there is always the hope that if one remains sick long enough, one may be sent back to the United States, a hope encouraged in schistosomiasis patients by rumors that some had already been sent home. These factors are counteracted to some extent by the strong desire to regain one's health, present in almost everyone. In addition, it is often possible to appeal to the individual soldier's self-respect in at least two ways. One is through his feeling of responsibility to his comrades, whom he may feel he is letting down by remaining an invalid. Another is reluctance to be discharged from the army with a certificate of disability. This implies worrying his family, perhaps a handicap in obtaining work, and the problem of explaining to civilians why he is not in uniform when his friends are still fighting.

Maintaining the patient's faith in the physician, which is an automatic matter in illnesses which are well understood, becomes a real problem in relatively unknown conditions like schistosomiasis. Since each patient reacts to the situation in accordance with his own particular needs, the obvious first requisite is to regard each patient as an individual. A few minutes at the end of the initial examination devoted to discovering and attempting to meet the patient's personal worries are usually well worthwhile from the standpoint of creating a good therapeutic relationship.

Confidence is best maintained by creating a situation in which the patient relies on his physician as the main source of information.

The purpose in presenting information is not primarily to instruct the patient, but to create in his mind the feeling that his physician has fully grasped his condition and has the entire situation thoroughly in hand. Therefore the material should be selected with a view to stressing those points which are most likely to have this effect. An attempt to give the complete picture of the disease, as one might to a group of medical students, often only creates confusion by swamping the patient with more facts than he can digest.

Those aspects of the disease which lend themselves to an optimistic interpretation should be emphasized. One such in schistosomiasis is that the flukes cannot multiply in the body. It will be remembered that only a third of the patients seen had fully grasped this fact. It was found that clarifying this for patients who had not appreciated its significance had a powerfully reassuring effect in many instances.

While the presentation should be as optimistic as is consistent with accuracy, false optimism should be avoided, since it often tends to decrease the patient's confidence. For example, one patient stated he lost all confidence in his physician when he said that schistosomiasis was no worse than a bad cold.

When potentially alarming information is presented, as it must be at times, in order to counteract even more alarming rumors, the mitigating aspects should be stressed. Thus, of the schistosomiasis patients who saw pictures of Filipinos with ascites or a liver destroyed by parasites, very few realized that this was the end result of repeated or massive infestation, in contrast to their own brief and limited contacts with the parasite. Similarly, while it is futile to deny the existence of severe reactions since patients quickly learn of them, it can be pointed out that, with rare exceptions, they seem to occur only at the time of the original infection. Patients who have had the disease for several weeks without a severe reaction need not fear one.

When uncertainty exists, it is better to admit it than to offer reassurances which time is apt to disprove. However, it is important to specify carefully the area of uncertainty and to indicate the means by which it is to be minimized. In schistosomiasis this problem is most acute with respect to the question of cure. If the patient is led to believe that a course of antimony will cure him and then the treatment must be repeated, his confidence in the doctor is certain to suffer. On the other hand, an admission that a single course of treatment, while helpful, might not be curative and might therefore require repetition would have allayed rather than increased anxiety in many patients. At least it would have helped to counteract the demoralizing and completely groundless belief of some that they were being irresponsibly experimented on.

In general, in an unfamiliar disease the question of prognosis should be formulated in terms of ability to perform one's duties rather than in terms of cure. The patient with schistosomiasis should be told that the presence of a few parasites is perfectly consistent with full efficiency, that he will be checked at regular intervals, and more treatment given if indicated. The situation is closely analogous to that of tuberculosis. Many patients with this disease are able to face life with confidence in the presence of obviously persistent infection. In this connection a rehabilitation program, such as that found in many army hospitals, is of the greatest value. Such a program effectively combats the physical and moral deterioration resulting from prolonged inactivity. It not only helps to restore muscle tone but reduces the time available for fretting. By its very existence it creates a stronger expectation of recovery in the mind of the patient than merely verbal reassurance.

In poorly understood diseases one must be alert to the appearance of new rumors. These are constantly emerging as patients seize and elaborate upon any scraps of information which present themselves. Meeting rumors promptly not only stops the spread of false information, but tends to consolidate the physician's control of the situation.

The importance of consistency need hardly be stressed. Contradictions between authorities are obviously highly destructive to confidence. In an army setting care must be taken that ward officers do not contradict each other or other supposedly authoritative sources such as the radio. Self-contradictions are at times difficult to avoid when knowledge is constantly changing. The danger can be minimized by presenting only what is definitely known at a given time, and avoiding speculation.

CONCLUSION

This survey indicates that patients suffering from unfamiliar diseases, of which schistosomiasis is an example, tend to develop emotional reactions which impede recovery, such as anxiety, resentment, and confusion. To keep disability at a minimum, therapeutic efforts must be directed not only to overcoming the pathogenic agent but to maintaining the patient's confidence in the physician, and encouraging his expectation of return to useful activity.

9. Psychosomatic Aspects of Illness and Healing

THE ROLE OF PSYCHOTHERAPY in the treatment of bodily diseases obviously depends on how big a part psychological factors play in their etiology and course. This presentation reviews a few studies demonstrating the intimate relations of mental states to bodily illnesses, and then considers some possible implications for the role of psychotherapy in their treatment.

First, however, since the term "psychotherapy" covers a lot of ground, it requires a definition. For the purpose of this paper, psychotherapy includes all systematic interactions between a sufferer and a socially designated healer, both operating in terms of the same belief system, in which the healer undertakes to relieve the sufferer's distress by symbolic communications. These are primarily and characteristically words, but can also include administration of placebos—inert substances that serve as tangible manifestations of the therapist's healing power—as well as bodily rituals and exercises believed to have healing effects. Active pharmacological agents may be used to facilitate psychotherapy but are not integral to the process itself.

Western healing arts, both psychological and medical, have been dominated by the Cartesian split between mind and matter, with the body being a form of matter. For various reasons, its hold has been so strong as to prevent full acceptance of the implications of the obvious fact that psychological responses and bodily diseases are intimately intertwined. The great eighteenth-century English surgeon John Hunter, who suffered from syphilitic heart disease (allegedly contracted experimentally), said, "My life is in the hands of any rascal who chooses to annoy and tease me," and indeed dropped dead after an argument.

According to a recent bestseller in the United States, *Type A Behavior and Your Heart*,[1] persons with a type A behavior pattern, described as aggressive involvement in "a chronic incessant struggle to achieve more and more in less and less time . . . against the opposing effects of other things or persons," are three times as likely to develop coronary disease within 10 years as persons without this pattern. And, of course, the psychosomatic literature burgeons with studies exploring mind-body interactions.

Yet, while paying lip service to the importance of treating the total person rather than his disease, physicians in actual practice seldom do so. Nor does the recognition that psychic and bodily states interact sit comfortably with psychotherapists. Many vigorously maintain that their healing procedures have nothing to do with the "medical model," which they caricature as the treatment of bodily disease by drugs and operations, and some still resist accepting the etiological and therapeutic importance of genetic and metabolic components of psychoses.

In recent years Westerners have started to pay more attention to the so-called holistic concept of illness and healing held by most of the rest of the world, which views the human as a psychobiological unity integrated within himself and with his environment. Illness is a perturbation of this harmony, and treatment the effort to reinstate it through integrated bodily, psychological, and social interventions.

One reason for this new receptivity to the holistic view may be that, after a century in which the West gained ascendancy over the East, we are now seeing the piston reverse itself as the philosophy, art, and power of the East begin to penetrate our lives and consciousness.[2] Simultaneously, ways are emerging of testing Eastern concepts with Western scientific instruments, thereby making them more palatable to us.

In short, the time is ripe for what has been termed a "paradigm shift".[3] It is time we freed ourselves from the thrall of Cartesian dualism and learned to adopt the holistic view that illnesses can be arranged in a continuum with respect to the relative importance of bodily and psychological components. The psychological component is greatest in neuroses and personality and behavior disorders, the bread and butter of psychotherapists. The bodily components of most of these are still obscure, but they will eventually be found. Next are addictions, including alcoholism, and psychoses, which are now recognized to involve genetic vulnerabilities. Next come psychosomatic illnesses, in which there is no question as to the existence of organic pathology but the etiology and course of the disease are clearly affected by psychological states. The finding that these are the only conditions for which psychotherapy is demonstrably more effective than no psychotherapy[4] is especially intriguing. Finally, there are the bona fide organic illnesses, which can presumably be explained without reference to the mind, such as injuries, infections, and metabolic or degenerative diseases. This presentation focuses on psychological features of these conditions, which represent the hardest cases for the holistic view.

With respect to stress, a retrospective statistical study of the relation of environmental stress to illness in 100 expatriated Chinese reached the following major conclusions:

1. Illnesses appear in clusters, involving more than one organ system.

2. These occur during periods when the patient is trying to cope with a difficult situation—he is stressed.

3. The stress comes mainly from his *interpretation* of the events—it is *psychological*. Often life experiences that appeared to be benign to an "objective" observer were seen as stressful by the patients and associated with illness. Conversely, when stresses that appeared horrendous to the observer—such as poverty, bereavement, alcoholic spouses— were not associated with illnesses, the patient also did not report them as stressful.[5]

By use of a proportional rating scale, it has been found possible reliably to rate both recent life experiences and illnesses in terms of degree of severity on a scale of 1–1000.[6] This has made possible quantification of relations between life stress and illness. For example, a large-scale study of naval crews revealed a statistically significant positive relationship between their scores on the scale of life experiences during the six months prior to going to sea and the total number of illnesses they reported during the cruise period.[7]

In another study, hospitalized patients were asked to score the life experience scale retrospectively with respect to the preceding two years. The correlation of severity of these 'stresses and seriousness of illness was 0.73 (p=.001). This held for chronic illness only and, confirming earlier findings, the severity of the life experiences did not predict specific illness, but only the greater likelihood of becoming ill.[8]

What about circumscribed trauma? Surely the consequences of a blow or a wound would be thought to be fully explained by the bodily damage they cause. All biological organisms respond to noxious agents by bodily changes involving the pituitary and adrenal glands, which Hans Selye has termed the general adaptation syndrome.[9] Recent studies suggest that this syndrome is set off only by injuries to a conscious animal or human, not to an unconscious one, raising the possibility that the psychological significance of the injury rather than the bodily damage is the crucial factor.[10]

A specific example of the contribution of environmentally caused psychic stress to bodily changes is the syndrome known as psychological dwarfism. This consists of retardation of growth, motor development, IQ, and sexual maturation which are promptly reversed if the child is removed from his home.[11] The home environments are usually stormy and frightening to the child. Apparently this is a source of retardation.[12] Once out of the home, growth and development immediately resume.

Hospitalized patients provide an especially good opportunity to observe the effects of psychonoxious and psychotherapeutic forces because patients are exposed to them around the clock and because they can be directly observed and modified.[13] A chronic-disease hospital, where patients are immersed in an atmosphere of monotony and hopelessness and are more or less abandoned by their families, would be expected to be especially damaging. Fortunately, as a project conducted in a veterans hospital for chronic neurological diseases has shown, this damage is reversible. A rehabilitation team developed a program to change the emotional atmosphere of the hospital from a warehouse in which patients were expected to remain indefinitely to a rehabilitation center with the goal of discharging patients back into the community. The program fostered this change in several ways. Within the hospital patients were reindividualized, in that each was reexamined and his medications were changed if indicated. Group activities aimed at raising morale and overcoming isolation were instituted. With respect to the relation between the hospital and the community, social workers reestablished links between the patients, their families, and prospective employers.

This program was applied to 289 patients who had been hospitalized 3 to 10 years, some of whom were bedridden, some incontinent, with striking results. In the first series of 80 patients, in 3 months 70 percent left the hospital. This discharge rate continued over the next 2.5 years. Since this result could conceivably be explained by lowering of the hospital's criteria for discharge and the community's standards for acceptance, the crucial finding is that 40 percent of the discharged patients became self-supporting. The program thus impressively demonstrated the effectiveness of a holistic approach integrating pharmacological, psychological, and social interventions in rehabilitating patients regarded as hopeless.[14] This example illustrates that physicians in a position to counteract *unfavorable states of mind* engendered by aspects of hospitalization can considerably benefit their patients.

Another example is that of children undergoing a tonsillectomy. Both the child and the mother typically experience considerable apprehension before the operation. To determine whether this might affect postoperative course, a simple controlled study was done comparing 22 children who received only routine preoperative care with 22 who, with their mothers, received a brief interview with a special nurse who explained the operation and how the child might expect to feel after it. The interview was aimed at allaying apprehension of both child and parent. At the end of a week, while half of those who received the preparatory interview had been discharged, all of the children who did not receive this interview were still in the hospital.[15]

Shifting the focus now from the patient's milieu to the person himself, the widespread clinical impression that a patient's emotional state may affect the course of illness and healing has received strong support from studies concerning speed of convalescence from infectious disease and speed of healing following an operation. One such study of patients with undulant fever (brucellosis) concerned 24 patients (all male but one), 8 who had recovered in 2 to 3 months and 16 who still complained of headache, nervousness, and vague aches and pains. There were no differences between the two groups in medical findings at onset or at time of reexamination, but 11 of the 16 who were still ill, as compared to none of the 8 who had recovered, had experienced a seriously disturbed life situation within 1 year before or after the acute infection. This finding confirms the results obtained with the life experience scale reported above. All patients were given a morale loss index, consisting of items selected from the Minnesota Multiphasic Personality Inventory (MMPI). Scores on this index were significantly higher in the chronic than in the recovered group.[16]

An explanation of this finding which cannot be completely excluded is that the low morale of the chronic patients was the result of their delayed convalescence, not the cause of it, although the authors adduce additional evidence that this was unlikely. To be conclusive, the morale loss score would have to be obtained before the patients became ill. Fortunately, the ability to predict influenza epidemics made such a study possible. All personnel at a military installation were given the morale loss index before such an epidemic was due to strike, yielding a sample of 26 who contracted the disease. Of these, 14 recovered after an average duration of 8 days, while 12 continued to complain for more than 3 weeks. The initial severity of the illness was the same for both groups, but the slow recoverers had significantly lower morale before they became ill.[17]

Since symptoms of influenza and undulant fever resemble those of depression (lassitude, weakness, vague somatic complaints) and the physicians had to rely on patients' reports, these studies still do not rule out the possibility that patients and doctors were mistaking depression for delayed convalescence. To be conclusive, a measure of improvement that did not depend on patients' reports would be needed. One study used such a criterion, speed of healing following operation for detached retina. Patients about to undergo this operation were administered a scale of "acceptance," which included such items as trust in the surgeon, optimism about outcome, and confidence in one's own ability to cope regardless of outcome. The speed of healing was rated independently by the surgeon, who did not know the patients' scores on the acceptance scale. A correlation of 0.61 was found between acceptance and speed of healing ($p < 0.001$). The authors conclude:

> Despite the psychological make-up of the person or the intensity of the threat . . . high acceptance and rapid healing occur . . . when the patient has faith in the healer, his methods of healing, and feels that these methods are relevant to the cause of his illness . . . the person seeking to help the slow healer . . . should focus primarily on what variables enhance or destroy the patient's attitude of expectant faith.[18]

It must be emphasized that the findings of these three studies are correlational, which leaves open the question of causality. For example, it may be that both the attitude of acceptance and speed of healing are two aspects of a generally high level of vitality. That expectant faith may be causal, however, is suggested by results obtained by procedures which evoke this attitude, of which the most dramatic are those of shrines of religious healing such as Lourdes.

Leaving open the question of the role, if any, of supernatural forces in so-called miracle cures, two points should be stressed. First, since miracle cures are reported by adherents of all religious faiths, their occurrence must depend on the pilgrim's state of mind, not on the validity of the object of his faith. Second, these cures are not miraculous. The consciousness of cure comes instantaneously, but thereafter healing occurs through normal reparative processes, which, to be sure, are greatly accelerated.[19] No one has grown a new limb or an eye at Lourdes. Furthermore, mysterious cures of organic disease occur in doctor's offices, but since such cases are very rare, no one physician sees enough of them, so they are easily overlooked. If they had occurred at Lourdes, they would have been called miracles.

There is no question that religious shrines release powerful healing emotions of hope and exaltation in most pilgrims.

Certain features of shrines of religious healing which mobilize the expectant faith of pilgrims are easily identified. These features activate expectant faith by embodying and reinforcing the belief system about illness and healing shared by all concerned. The shrine is an impressive structure containing a variety of chambers, some open to the public, some secret, staffed by a priesthood, usually hierarchically organized, who have dedicated their lives to its service. The priests are believed to have been initiated into sacred mysteries and perform ceremonies, conducted in a special language unintelligible to the laity, which invoke the healing deities for the benefit of the pilgrims.

Actually, despite their emphasis on the technology of healing, most great teaching hospitals like Johns Hopkins have by no means dissipated the image of the healing shrine in the eyes of many patients. William Osler in a paper entitled "The Faith That Heals" wrote: "Faith in St. Johns Hopkins as we used to call him ... worked just the same sort of cures as did Aesculapius at Epidaurus."[20] One need only substitute Science for the supernatural healing powers invoked at faith-healing shrines to discover striking similarities.

Let us imagine, if you will, how Johns Hopkins might look to an anthropologist from Mars studying healing shrines in Baltimore. He would learn that it has an immense reputation as a site of amazing cures, and he would promptly note the statue of Jesus in the rotunda and eventually would ferret out the chaplain's office and the chapel, tangible vestiges of a belief system still widely held but clearly secondary to the faith in Science. He would note that the organization of St. Johns Hopkins is highly structured, each echelon having its own insignia of rank and function. All levels of the priesthood use a special language, unintelligible to the layman, and prominently display on their persons healing amulets and charms, such as reflex hammers, stethoscopes, and opthalmoscopes. At the lowest level are the postulants in their short white jackets. The junior members of the priesthood wear white suits; their seniors are impressively garbed in long, white, starched coats. All are expected to dedicate themselves to the service of the shrine, regardless of personal hardship or interference with connubial felicity and other satisfactions of life.

Our anthropologist would probably be especially impressed with the massive labyrinthine buildings, situated on a hilltop, through whose many orifices pilgrims seeking health are continually streaming. Inside he would find a complex structure with certain areas open to the public, such as the wards, and others where members of the staff perform arcane healing rituals and to which they alone have access, such as laboratories, operating rooms, radiotherapy rooms, and intensive care units. These rooms contain spectacular machines that beep and gurgle and flash lights or emit immensely powerful but invisible rays, thereby impressively invoking the healing powers of Science. The operating rooms are the holy of holies where the most dramatic and difficult healing rituals are conducted and which even the priests can enter only after donning special costumes and undergoing purification rites known as "scrubbing." So jealously guarded are the mysteries of the operating rooms that patients are rendered unconscious before entering them.

While the physician can seldom mobilize expectant faith as powerfully as healing shrines, he can foster this state in many patients directly by his words, or indirectly by medications and operations.

The physician's power comes from two sources. He occupies a social role of respect, power and trustworthiness analogous to that of a parent, so he mobilizes the attitudes of trust and dependency that an infant feels toward a good parent; and his treatment is based on and validates a theory which expresses the world-view of the society in which both he and the patient function. Since a shared world-view both makes sense out of life and reinforces the sense of group belongingness, medical (like psychological) treatment helps to combat the demoralizing sense of isolation that typically accompanies illness.

Let us consider a striking example of the healing power of patients' expectation of help elicited simply by the doctor's words. The patients involved were: (1) Mrs. Anna Ha., 61, with chronic gall bladder inflammation and gallstone colic; (2) Mrs. Margarete Di., 66, who failed to convalesce after operation for pancreatitis seven months before and was reduced to a skeleton, suffered from obstipation, and was in complete despair; (3) Mrs. Olga Schm., 61, with inoperable cancer of the uterus, who had massive ascites, edema of the legs, anemia, and was too weak to get out of bed.

Learning that an eminent faith healer, who healed by absent healing, was in town, the patients' physician persuaded him to try to heal these patients for 12 sessions, without the patients' knowledge. This had no effect on their condition. He then talked up the healer for eight days to the patients until each expected "most longingly" to be cured and told them the healer would practice absent healing on the three following days between 8 and 8:15, when he *did not* work.

The results were striking. The patient with gall bladder disease immediately became free of pain, and her slight fever fell to normal. She got out of bed, left the hospital, and was symptom-free for a year. The patient with pancreatitis got out of bed after the first treatment, her bowel function returned to normal; she rapidly gained 30 pounds, and remained well. In these two, the improvement was fairly easy to understand, since their disabilities probably had an important emotional component. Gall bladder function is affected by the state of the autonomic nervous system, while the lady with pancreatitis had no active disease process. More interesting is the course of the patient with metastatic cancer. She lost her edema and ascites in a few days; her appetite returned to normal; and her hemoglobin rose in ten days from 52 percent to 73 percent. She returned home in five days and remained feeling well and able to resume her normal household duties until her death three and one-half months later.[21]

These results demonstrate, as do religious healing shrines, that *expectant faith can be healing*, regardless of whether or not it is objectively justified.

A tangible symbol of the physician's role which mobilizes patients' expectant faith is medication. The psychological effects of medication have been studied by giving patients placebos. Since the effectiveness of placebos depends entirely on their symbolization of the physician's healing role, their administration is a form of psychotherapy as defined in this paper.

The patient's response is termed "the placebo effect," an unfortunate term on several counts. Placebo is Latin for "I will please," which implies both deceit by the physician and absence of therapeutic power in the pill. "Expectant faith effect" would be more appropriate to the placebo's power. In this connection, until this century most medical remedies were either ineffective or harmful, so the physician's reputation depended primarily on the placebo effect.

The determinants of strength of the placebo effect are very complex, and seem to depend on the interaction between the patient's state and aspects of his situation at the time the pill is administered. However, in general a placebo is between 30 and 60 percent as effective as the active medication with which it is compared, regardless of the power of the medication. For example, as a pain reliever, placebo is 55 percent as effective as aspirin, a weak analgesic, and 55 percent as effective as morphine, a powerful analgesic. Apparently the therapist transmits his belief in the active drug's potency to the patient.[22]

A physician demonstrated that expectations can reverse the pharmacological action of ipecac, an emetic, by giving it to two vomiting patients through a stomach tube with the statement that it would cure their vomiting. The normal stomach contractions resumed and nausea vanished at the same time interval after administration that stomach contractions cease and nausea starts when ipecac is given as an emetic.[23]

If medication can have powerful psychological effects, one would expect surgical operations to have even stronger ones. As compared to a person seeking medical treatment, someone about to undergo surgery is more apprehensive and is totally dependent on the surgeon—he literally places his life in the surgeon's hands. Furthermore, the operation is a single dramatic act which is expected to produce a prompt cure. Surgery on the heart, the organ of life itself, is an especially impressive demonstration of the surgeon's power, so it should not come as a surprise that the expectant faith effect of heart surgery for anginal pain accounts for a large part of its effectiveness. This was first demonstrated by study of an operation for relief of angina which consisted of tying off an artery in the chest. The results were encouraging in that 40 percent of the patients experienced marked symptomatic relief. But then someone decided to do a mock operation, that is, to give the anesthesia and open the skin, but not touch the artery—and it proved to be fully as effective as the real one in reducing patients' pain, causing them to cut down their use of nitroglycerin tablets and increasing their exercise tolerance.[24]

Recently a new operation has become popular, in which diseased portions of coronary arteries are bypassed by segments of veins, in an effort to improve the heart's blood supply. The rationale for this operation is completely convincing—angina is caused by poor circulation to part of the heart muscle, because a coronary artery is partly occluded; therefore it can be treated by restoring the circulation by bypassing the diseased portion of the artery with a segment of vein.

The results have been spectacular. About 90 percent of patients report reduction of symptoms and improved quality of life. Of these, 82 percent (76 percent of total) also improve on stress test—they can tolerate more exercise without pain. Clearly coronary bypass is a very successful procedure. It would appear absurd to question that improvement following it is caused by better blood flow to the heart as the result of the bypass. But when compared with a matched group of patients *treated medically*, operated patients showed no difference in two-year survival rate. Furthermore, on several objective tests of cardiac function, about 60 percent showed no change, 20 percent were actually worse, and only 20 percent showed some improvement. In short, symptomatic improvement occurred in 90 percent, improvement in heart function in 20 percent, so 70 percent improved with heart function the same or worse.[25]

Breaking down improvement rate differently, it was found that 90 percent of patients with all grafts open improved, but so did 60 percent with *no* grafts open.[26] So improvement could have occurred in two-thirds of those with all grafts open even without the bypass.

How does it happen that so many patients are better symptomatically in the face of no improvement or worsening in heart function? The investigators suggest three possibilities:

1. Full occlusion of an artery may stop pain because the part of the muscle supplied by that artery dies.

2. Perhaps the operation cuts the nerves from the painful area.

3. The improvement is attributable to nonspecific effects of the operation, not further defined.

It should be noted that the first two suggestions could not account for the success of the earlier operation in which the heart was not touched. In terms of our discussion, the nonspecific effects could result from the patient's *expectant faith*, reinforced by a convincing *rationale* according beautifully with the scientific world-view of American culture, and a *procedure* which is spectacular and expensive. It involves stopping the patient's heart and then reviving him—in a sense the surgeon kills the patient and brings him to life again. Few shamans can demonstrate equal healing power.

Turning at last to psychotherapy, its rituals are unlikely to be able to inspire expectant faith as powerfully as those of the physician or surgeon, but the psychotherapist is able to induce other states of mind which contribute to healing, notably hypnosis and meditation. Through hypnosis the therapist can influence a wide range of the subject's bodily processes including such unlikely ones as changes in chemical constituents of blood and bile,[27] but hypnosis has the disadvantage of leaving control in the hands of the hypnotist. Meditation, on the other hand, enables a person to gain conscious control of his own bodily functions, so that he does not have to depend on someone else. The burgeoning interest in meditation is in part attributable to the growing influence of Eastern thought, already mentioned, but also to the emergence of biofeedback, a means of self-regulation of cortical states and thereby bodily ones that depends on equipment and is therefore appealing to Westerners.

Biofeedback studies have demonstrated that thought and behavior continually affect brain activity; for example, whistling or simply imagining the tune of a song produces changes in the right cortex, reciting or imagining its words activates the left. Since we are always controlling our brains, the obvious next step with the sick would be to teach them to exert this control to promote health instead of illness.

It has been shown that normal persons can learn through biofeedback to control many bodily functions.[28] Its effectiveness in treating illnesses, however, seems to be less striking. This is to be expected, since conquering a chronic illness requires changes in life-style, not simply learning a technique. So far, the effectiveness of biofeedback training with patients has been clearly demonstrated only in enabling them to gain voluntary control of skeletal muscles that have escaped this control (as in tension headaches, nocturnal bruxism, and torticollis); to control cardiac arrythmias and other aspects of the circulatory system, for example, skin temperature; and to control fecal incontinence.[29] However, with increasing sophistication in its use, there is reason to think that biofeedback training will aid in the treatment of a wider range of conditions.

The gadgetry of biofeedback must not be allowed to disguise the fact that it is essentially a form of psychotherapy in that the therapeutic interaction is transmitted by symbolic communication. It is readily (although perhaps incorrectly) conceptualized as a method of operant conditioning, and experts agree that its successful use depends on a good therapeutic relationship, a high level of motivation and self-discipline in the patient, and considerable clinical sophistication in the therapist.[30]

The ultimate aim of biofeedback, furthermore, is to transfer control of his bodily states to the patient. It is essentially an informational aid to him in his effort to achieve self-regulation of his bodily processes. In this it resembles meditation, a state in which virtually unlimited conscious control of bodily organs can be achieved, as the Yogi have shown. Meditation has been receiving increasing attention as an adjunct to psychotherapy[31] and seems a promising aid in the treatment of schizophrenia,[32] which, if one chooses to regard it as primarily a bodily disease, comes within our purview.

Since cancer has long been regarded as a bodily disease relatively uninfluenced by mental states, a particularly interesting recent development has been the accumulation of evidence that psychological states may contribute to its causation. This raises the possibility that psychotherapy may have a place in its treatment. Western medicine has conceptualized cancer as an invasion of the body from inside by cells that have gone wild, and treatment consists of an effort to remove or destroy them by surgery, radiation, or drugs. The outcome of this struggle is determined by whether the cancer cells or the destructive agents are stronger. The patient is a helpless bystander or, better, the arena in which the battle is fought. This theory cannot explain spontaneous remissions of definitely diagnosed cancer, which sometimes occur. Two surgeons have accumulated 176 examples of such remissions from the literature, but offer no explanation for them.[33]

Recently a holistic concept of cancer has emerged, the so-called surveillance theory, which offers a possible explanation for at least some of these spontaneous remissions, and suggests additional therapeutic approaches. According to this theory, cancer cells are formed throughout life but are promptly detected and destroyed by the person's immunity system. Clinical cancer appears when this fails; hence factors which influence its strength, including psychic ones, are relevant to both cancer's emergence and treatment.

What is the evidence in support of the surveillance theory? First, an increasing number of studies have found that persons with a certain personality style are especially prone to cancer. As compared to matched healthy controls or those suffering from other illnesses, they repress or deny unpleasant affects such as depression, anxiety, and hostility.[34] Under a facade of cheerfulness and self-confidence, they feel isolated and that life is a hard struggle. This attitude is consistent with the findings that cancer patients, more than controls, reported experiences before the age of 7 which led the child to feel that close emotional relationships brought pain and destruction.[35]

This finding has recently found unexpected confirmation from a prospective study of medical students.[36] A total of 914 male medical students graduating from 1948 to 1964 filled out a questionnaire including a closeness-to-parents scale. By June, 1973, 26 had developed malignant tumors. The 20 on whom complete data were available had scored significantly lower on the closeness-to-parents scale (p = 0.01) than a group matched by age, sex, and class who were in good health. This background would not be inconsistent with the finding that cancer-prone persons are especially shaken when someone they have come to trust dies or otherwise withdraws support. In any case, cancer patients were found to have suffered such a loss 6 months to 8 years before the clinical onset of the disease significantly more often than controls.[37]

The surveillance hypothesis is also consistent with the relation of emotions like hope to remission of cancer, as in the example of the absent healer cited earlier. In the following example, which is even more impressive, the patient's hope was powerfully stimulated by a medication which proved to be a placebo.[38]

The patient was dying of generalized lymphoma. He had large tumors all over his body, his chest was full of fluid, and he was anemic. He had become resistant to treatment and had been given a prognosis of less than a month. As part of a clinical trial of Krebiozen, a widely touted cancer cure, the drug was given to him because he begged for it and had great hopes from it, although he was not eligible because he was so ill. Two days after the first injection, the tumors had shrunk to one-half their original size and the chest fluid was gone. He continued to get injections thrice weekly and was discharged in ten days.

After two months of practically perfect health, on reading conflicting press reports about the efficacy of Krebiozen, he relapsed to his original state. His physician told him to ignore the reports, that the reason for the relapse was that the Krebiozen had deteriorated on standing, and offered him a new "double-strength, super-refined" batch. The patient again developed a very strong anticipation of cure. This time the injections consisted of distilled water, but the patient's remission again was dramatic. The tumors melted and the chest fluid vanished, and he was again symptom-free for two months. Then he read the final AMA report that Krebiozen was worthless. After this, his health precipitously declined and he was dead in two days. To be sure, it isn't certain that life was actually prolonged as his total course seems to have been only about six months. Nevertheless, as with the patient described earlier, the remissions were spectacular.

The possibility of training cancer patients to cultivate healing mental states is currently being explored by a radiotherapist and his wife, a psychiatric social worker.[39] Based on the surveillance theory, they reason that if depression and similar emotions can facilitate the growth of cancer, contrary emotions could retard it. On the basis of this somewhat shaky rationale, they use group and individual psychotherapy to try to change the belief of the patient and his family that the cancer is incurable to faith that it can be cured. Concurrently they train the patient to enter a state of meditation three times a day in which he visualizes that his white cells are devouring the cancerous ones.

They make no extravagant claims for this approach. The radiotherapist continues to use radiotherapy with patients who can still tolerate it and states that less than a quarter of his patients can muster the necessary self-discipline to participate in the psychotherapeutic program. Nor will he publish results until he can report 5-year follow-ups. He has, however, observed spectacular remissions in some patients with far-advanced disease. At the very least, these therapists have raised the strong possibility that psychotherapy can sometimes beneficially affect the course of cancer.

This survey of selected studies could well lead the reader to exaggerate the effectiveness of psychotherapy for bodily disease. It therefore should be made explicit that, despite striking exceptions, by and large psychotherapy will probably prove to be an adjunct to conventional medical and surgical treatments for such illnesses, rather than a major treatment method. This review does suggest, however, that if psychotherapists can persuade physicians of their usefulness, they can make diagnostic, preventive, and therapeutic contributions.

Diagnostically, psychotherapists can bring into the open emotional stresses that may be aggravating the disease process, including those resulting from the treatment itself. For example, a legitimate problem for psychotherapy would be the exploration, and perhaps mitigation of the severe psychonoxious effects of dialysis for kidney failure, resulting in a suicide rate of patients undergoing this treatment some 400 times that of the general population.[40]

As to prevention, in view of the demonstrated close relationship between life stresses and subsequent illness, programs of crisis intervention may already be functioning in this way. With respect to treatment, both group and individual psychotherapy could be used much more than they are at present to overcome the demoralization of patients with chronic disease, which aggravates their distress and disability, and to foster more health-promoting attitudes. Furthermore, since procedures such as autogenic training, biofeedback, and meditation are forms of psychotherapy, psychotherapists are better qualified by training than nonpsychiatric physicians to teach patients how to gain conscious control of involuntary bodily functions as a means of combating illness and promoting health. We are entering a period in which the holistic conception of illness and healing is gaining ever wider acceptance. As a result, psychotherapists will be collaborating increasingly with nonpsychiatric physicians in diagnosing, preventing, and treating organic disease.

10. Self-Centeredness Versus Social Action in Contemporary American Society

A PERMANENT FEATURE OF the human condition is the potential conflict between an individual's drive to self-enhancement and his or her need for the approbation of the groups to which he belongs. One's group membership is in a real sense an integral part of oneself. The group's welfare is perceived as necessary to one's own to such an extent that under some circumstances the need to maintain the solidarity of the group affects members' behavior more strongly than the need for food, sex, or even self-preservation. Soldiers in closely knit combat units, for example, have frequently sacrificed their own lives to protect their fellows.

Humans are aware of the brevity of life, and identification with the group is an expression of the need to identify with something larger and more enduring than one's individual self. This need is met in stable societies by institutionalized religions and by allegiance to such concepts as country or social class. Individual members of such societies can usually satisfy their own needs best by acting in accord with the material, social, and spiritual values of the society, using established channels and approved procedures.

In periods of turmoil, such as exist today—when traditional values are questioned, political institutions are no longer trusted, and the power of institutionalized religions has eroded—society no longer provides adequate psychological support or behavioral guidelines to its members. Under such

149

circumstances, individuals indulge in a wide range of behaviors aimed at restoring a sense of meaning and personal security to their lives. These efforts can be crudely grouped as egoistic and altruistic—that is, self oriented and socially oriented. An urgent task today is to work out ways of preserving the most valuable features of both orientations while modifying them to accord with the conditions of contemporary life. Ideally, such an integration would promote vigorous social action guided by the deep insights and allegiance to the higher values fostered by certain forms of self-centeredness. As a modest contribution toward this goal, this essay seeks to describe and characterize primarily the forms of egoism that are dominant today, with a brief side glance at behavior guided by a sense of social responsibility to society as a whole or certain groups within it. In the process, features of life experiences and personality that may determine the balance chosen by individual members of society will be ignored.

Activities motivated by a sense of social responsibility include volunteer efforts such as participation on community boards, performances of specific good works such as those of the Gray Ladies in hospitals, or working for citizens' groups aimed at ameliorating certain social evils or increasing the power of certain groups without fundamentally challenging the structure of society; examples are Common Cause, New Directions, and the National Association for the Advancement of Colored People. In contrast, adherents of ideologically based responsible revolutionary movements believe that the political structure is beyond reform and seek to overthrow it, with the aim of superseding it with a more just one.

Several features of the American world view foster socially responsible behavior. One is the strong historical tradition of helping the underdog. A cynical view would have it that this is primarily motivated by the need to atone for the guilt created by the competitive nature of our society and the pursuit of what William James called the "Bitch Goddess Success," which has led to considerable oppression of the weak by the strong. Other more attractive values of American society, however, also play a part in altruistic activities. These include a view of humans as basically good, or at least as a mixture of good and evil, coupled with emphasis on doing rather than being, and an orientation toward the future rather than the past or present. In conjunction, these values imply that altruistic activities by individuals and groups can make a better world in the future. Finally, and this is perhaps another aspect of the emphasis on doing, because Americans view the proper role of humans as controlling or subduing natural forces rather than living in harmony with them, social evils are seen as part of the natural environment in this sense; thus the implication is that humans not only can eliminate them but are responsible for doing so.

A strong incentive to socially oriented activities is the perceived gross discrepancy between the expressed values of American society and the way its institutions actually function—for example, the high value placed on self-fulfillment of the individual contrasted with the exploitation or oppression of various groups, such as unskilled workers, children, women, and blacks. Which group is considered to be oppressed, of course, depends on the norms of the time. For centuries what today would be regarded as outrageous exploitation of children was simply taken for granted as a feature of the natural order.

A necessary impetus to constructive social action is hope. Reform movements flourish in relatively affluent societies that allow considerable social and economic mobility. Revolutionary movements emerge when this mobility is blocked, but only when hope is also present—that is, when a better society seems possible but there appears to be no hope of achieving it through reforms within the existing political structure. This may be why revolutionary movements flourish in times of rising prosperity—that is, when revolutionists see hope of bettering themselves and those for whom they are fighting.

Despite these forces impelling to social responsibility, we seem to be witnessing today a swing toward activities that are primarily egoistically motivated—that is, aimed at the enrichment or aggrandizement of the self, regardless of effects on the welfare of others. Such activities take one of two diametrically opposed forms: plunging into interactions with others in pursuit of power, wealth, or worldly pleasures, or withdrawing in order to focus on timeless verities behind appearances.

Egoistically oriented interpersonal behavior includes naked

exploitation of others, the pursuit of pleasure without regard for others, and activities with an altruistic component that remain basically exploitative. A typical justification for exploitation of others in the service of self-aggrandizement is well expressed in the following quotation from a best-selling book called *Winning Through Intimidation:*

> If there is something beyond our earthly existence, that will be just great: but analyzing the only facts I had at my disposal . . . I reasoned that I had better look at this time around as my only shot—just to play it safe—and consider anything that might come after as a bonus. . . . I decided that if I only had about thirty years left, I had better go after all the good things I could get as quickly as possible.
>
> And that's the essence of the Thirty Year Theory: to go after all you can get, as quickly as you can get it, because you acknowledge that your time for doing so is limited.[1]

This attitude is supported by the philosophy of free enterprise, according to which each individual's efforts to increase his own share of worldly goods leads to a rise in the prosperity of the society as a whole.

Another type of egoistic behavior is hedonism, the pursuit of sensory gratification for its own sake. This takes the form of over-consumption of material goods and excessive travel by those who can afford such luxuries, and also includes indulgence in the cheaper pleasures of sex, drink, and drugs.

An ethically more defensible form of hedonism centered on the immediate present is promulgated by the so-called human potential movement. Activities conducted in its name include a variety of sensitivity training and encounter groups that stress ways of enriching experience and achieving deeper awareness of oneself and others, culminating in "peak experiences." There is little doubt that such experiences can heighten feelings of energy, optimism, and group solidarity, at least temporarily. Unfortunately, however, their benefits are usually transitory. Moreover, although such groups pay considerable lip service to mutual concern, in actuality members more often than not use each other for their own gratification, and concern for the welfare of other members stops abruptly at the group's edge.

As philosophers have long noted, pursuit of pleasure is self-defeating because, although sensory gratification may temporarily anaesthetize deeper cravings for meaning and personal significance, they do not satisfy them. Thus the pursuit of pleasure, especially in an affluent society that offers an abundance of potential gratifications, in the absence of values to guide choices, contributes to what Viktor Frankl has termed "existential frustration": "Man is no longer told by tradition or by values transmitted by tradition what he must do. He no longer even knows what he wishes to do."[2] Moreover, at any given level of stimulation sensory pleasure eventually palls. Thus the pleasure seeker typically escalates the stimulation he requires. As the old saying has it, "What *does* one do for an encore?"

Greed for pleasure may also be reinforced by the consumer orientation of American society. This has had a high value because it keeps the wheels of industry turning. Advertising fans consumers' desires in order to increase producers' wealth so they can better indulge their own desires.

The search for ever increasing stimulation tends to eventuate in excesses of sex and violence, exemplified by the unspeakable "snuff" movie in which a woman is apparently (many believe actually) sexually abused, tortured, and murdered before the camera. Hedonistic indulgence eventually arouses revulsion and guilt, however, which, coupled with the failure of pleasure to satisfy deeper needs, results in periods of hedonism being accompanied or followed by swings to puritanism or asceticism in pursuit of transcendental experiences. One manifestation of this swing in contemporary America is the mushroom growth of evangelical Christian sects and Far Eastern–based cults such as the Hare Krishna and Transcendental Meditation movements. As Adam Smith wrote in 1977: "Neo-Oriental religions disappear into the astonishing American digestive tract like tin cans into a goat."[3] The popularity of transcendental cults may also be an oblique reflection of consumerism, in that it suggests a greed for spiritual experience analogous to greed for material objects.

Transcendental cults seek to provide their adherents with a sense of meaning and personal significance through direct expression of the godhead. In contrast to the exuberant sensuousness of sensitivity and encounter groups, most of these cults stress rigid self-discipline and an ascetic life style. Although their meditational rituals involve withdrawal, adherents depend heavily on group support. Their beliefs are inculcated through group activities under the guidance of a spiritual leader and are sustained by continual attendance at groups supporting their underlying philosophy.

A significant contributor to self-centeredness and the search for individual salvation is the weakening of the social fabric. The main glue that holds a society together is a common belief system embodied in institutions in which all its members have confidence. This has been badly shaken, in part because of the unprecedentedly rapid changes in the conditions of life that have made traditional values and goals maladaptive. When I was in college over fifty years ago, the philosopher Alfred North Whitehead told us that our generation was the first in human history that could not be guided by the precepts of its grandfathers. Since then, change has accelerated to the extent that one cannot be guided by the precepts of one's older brother or sister. To take just two examples, the advent of effective contraception and the successful treatment of venereal disease have profoundly altered the relations between the sexes and made chastity an unnecessary abstention from gratifying experiences. Analogously, thrift, which was a virtue in an economy of scarcity, is a vice in an economy of abundance where excessive consumption is necessary to keep the wheels of industry turning.

Although competitiveness, consumerism, and the weakening of the social fabric have contributed to the upsurge of self-oriented activities, I believe the major source may be the disillusionment resulting from the manifest failure of measures to promote social welfare embodying the values of future orientation, mastery, and doing. Despite decades of "progress," Americans have never been more aware of poverty, starvation, bloody civil and international wars, terrorism, and torture. Most of the socially oriented programs launched with so much optimism have fallen far short of expectations. One need only look at the shambles of the welfare program, the failure of rehabilitation programs for prisoners, and the abysmal state of public education. At least 30 percent of Florida high school graduates are reported to be functionally illiterate, and there is no reason to think that the level of education in most of the rest of the country is higher.

Modern medicine has occasioned perhaps the most severe disappointment, by what has been well characterized as the failure of success. To be sure, remarkable advances in diagnosis and therapy have helped or even cured many formerly doomed sufferers, but at the cost of producing a net overall increase in suffering and disability through keeping persons alive at both ends of life who would previously have died. Although some of the grossly damaged infants who are heroically resuscitated become happy children, many remain sources of misery to themselves and their families, while many of the elderly have been rescued from pneumonia and similar diseases to live on and decline into wretched senility.

Science and technology, through which Americans hoped to reach new levels of material well-being, have indeed provided it, but at a terrible cost, for they have simultaneously created by far the greatest and most immediate threats to humankind that ever existed, in the forms of poisoning of the biosphere and nuclear war. The damaging psychological effects of this betrayal have been aggravated by the fact that, unlike previous threats to human survival, these are potentially under human control. Threats to humanity have always existed. What is new is that they now are the consequences of our own choices. We know how to conquer pestilence, starvation, overpopulation, poverty, and industrial poisons and to stop building more and more terrible instruments of destruction. We know what needs to be done, and even how to do it, but we cannot act on this knowledge. We can no longer take refuge in a benevolent but inscrutable God who permits evil in the service of some unfathomable good.

Since today's major evils are created solely by humans, they can in theory be overcome by human efforts. This idea offers grounds for hope. On the other hand, our persistent failure to overcome the viciousness of humans to each other makes it increasingly hard to maintain the belief that humans are basically good. Moreover, failure to control man-made threats to survival, coupled with awareness of our potential ability to do so, probably contributes to the widespread malaise from which self-centered activities offer an escape.

Up to this point, I have considered egoistic and altruistic activities as if they were independent of each other. Actually, all except the most extreme forms of human behavior contain both egoistic and altruistic components. Even ruthless self-aggrandizers like Andrew Carnegie and John D. Rockefeller were partly motivated by the aim of contributing to human welfare. Altruistic behavior contributes to egoistic gratification from the gratitude of those who are helped, and the ability to help enhances the individual's sense of power. A common expression of altruism is shown by physicians, who willingly undergo enormous inconveniences to save a patient's life; yet there is nothing more gratifying than to succeed in such an endeavor, and the greater the personal sacrifice involved, the greater the personal reward. Transcendental religious sects are in one sense extremely altruistic in that members sacrifice their own welfare for the good of the group and attempt to convert others out of concern for their welfare. However, these activities have strong egoistic components. The altruistic desire to share a good thing, which I am sure motivates some proselytizing, fuses with the goal of increasing the power of one's sect by enlarging the number of its adherents. Also, much of the proselytizing drive is based on the desire to gain credits in heaven by the number of infidels one succeeds in converting. Finally, making converts is a powerful way of shoring up one's faith in the validity of one's beliefs. This has been beautifully demonstrated by a research study that found that—consistent with historical examples such as the Seventh-Day Adventists—a small modern sect that predicted the end of the world by a certain date started to proselytize only after the date had passed.[4] Until the prophecy fails, adherents of the religion feel secure in their beliefs. Its failure threatens these beliefs, and one way of strengthening them is to seek new converts.

Similarly, most revolutionist and terrorist groups ostensibly seek to create a better world—that is, they claim to be altruistically motivated. Yet certain recent terrorist groups, such as the Baader-Meinhoff gang and the Japanese Red Army, seem to be motivated primarily by diffuse rage and thrill-seeking. Their living quarters are said to contain no ideological literature such as characterized the libraries of earlier terrorists, and their ideologies consist of diatribes against an ill-defined imperialism. The only reason given by a wealthy German girl for murdering a banker friend of her father's was, "I'm tired of all that caviar gobbling." Like other self-centered zealots, their sense of personal significance seems to be derived primarily from intense identification with their group; thus, their chief motives for highjackings and kidnappings are usually to blackmail authorities into releasing imprisoned members.

It is obvious that the welfare of society depends on the proper balance of altruistic and egoistic activities. If carried to extremes either is destructive. This is obviously true of self-centered activities. Excessive competitiveness is incompatible with maintenance of the level of cooperativeness necessary to permit social institutions to function. José Ortega y Gasset pointed out that civilizations fall primarily because too many citizens want to enjoy their fruits without being prepared to undergo the self-discipline and effort required to maintain the society that provides them.[5] Finally, transcendental religions, by focusing on the afterlife, neglect the problems of this world, and those that preach exclusive salvation also foster intergroup conflicts that weaken the social fabric.

On the other hand, activities aimed at enhancing social welfare, if too extreme or based on insufficient analysis of the problem, can do more harm than good. Too often activists do not adequately envisage the potential social costs of the altruistic programs they advocate. A Hindu proverb, which social activists would do well to keep in mind, states that for every plus there is a minus. An example is the Quaker invention of the penitentiary, which, by providing opportunities and incentives for criminals to repent and reform, was promulgated as an advance over the previous way of dealing with criminals by immediate severe punishments. But it is questionable whether the penitentiary has improved or worsened the lot of the criminal and whether it has increased or decreased the incidence of crime. For another example: currently, too zealous efforts to preserve the environment by hampering full use of available sources of energy may create as great a disaster as the one environmentalists seek to forestall.

On the positive side, moderate or intermittent self-centeredness in the form of self-aggrandizement, hedonism, or pursuit of ultimate truths is essential for individual and social welfare. Some self-aggrandizing individuals provide the leadership necessary to prevent societies from falling apart. Some pursuit of pleasure is necessary to restore energy and enthusiasm. The flourishing of art, literature, and music depends on hedonistic values, while consciousness-raising and encounter-group exercises may enhance the sense of self as well as awareness of the feelings of others, thereby contributing to the effectiveness of community-oriented actions. Transcendental religions give meaning and purpose to their adherents' lives, which increases their self-confidence and may help to guide their socially oriented efforts in a constructive direction. Finally, new ideas and new values required to meet changing conditions seem to come primarily from those who are able to gain fresh perspectives by periodically withdrawing into prayer or contemplation.

The best exemplars of creative integration are those outstanding mystics, such as Mohandas Gandhi and Martin Luther King, Jr., who are at the same time holy men, great teachers, and effective social reformers. For those of us who cannot reach these heights, my own feeling is that if one is not sure what to do, one may do less harm by doing nothing than by rushing into social action. And even if one is sure, one may be wrong. I have always valued the adage that what gets you into trouble isn't what you don't know but what you do know that isn't so. It seems also probable that sustained modest efforts do more good and less harm than crash programs, because they permit modification of goals and activities in the light of preliminary results. A problem with such programs is sustaining motivation, for their visible consequences may be long delayed. It is therefore important to structure long-term efforts so they yield rewards for their participants along the way. In my own experience, it does not take much to keep hope alive—thus the delay in authorizing the B-1 bomber was enough to renew my vigor in working for disarmament despite endless discouragements. In this connection, the Indian guru Krishnamurti has offered a consoling thought: "A pebble can change the course of a river."

To conclude on a more general note, since we are social animals for whom the groups to which we belong are parts of ourselves, self-realization, fully understood, includes both egoism and altruism. Everyone's life contains episodes of conflict between what are felt to be one's own needs and the demands of others, and there are phases of society when such conflicts are especially salient, as seems to be true today. I believe, however, that most of the time the needs of the individual and group are mutually gratifying and supportive. Because the most powerful individual gratifications spring from the respect, approval, and affection of members of one's group, the individual usually satisfies his or her own needs best in accord with the material, social, and spiritual values of the society in which he or she lives.

11. Galloping Technology as a Social Disease

THE OUTSTANDING CHARACTERISTIC of our time is the headlong rush of technology and science. Scientists and engineers are prying new secrets out of nature and remaking our lives at a breathtaking and ever accelerating rate. The adverse effects on society of their efforts could be referred to as social diseases, although we have preferred the terms social issues or social problems. Our galloping technology has created or aggravated problems of unemployment, urbanization, racial and international tensions, war, overpopulation, and many others that have been the constant concern of many social scientists.

But "social disease" in my title refers to the other, old-fashioned medical meaning of the term—namely, illness caused by the conditions of social living. My particular training has made me sensitive to the direct effects on life and health of man's reckless conquest of the environment, a topic that has been largely neglected by social scientists. The most obvious reason for this neglect is that the problems present themselves as medical or technological. My thesis is that, although the new menaces to life and health may be caused by new machines and poisons, the remedies lie mainly in the realm of human behavior.

In its medical meaning, the term "social disease" referred to illnesses that are contracted, directly or indirectly, by misbehavior and that are therefore blameworthy. Most commonly, of course, it was a euphemism for venereal disease, but it was also used for illnesses like tuberculosis, presumably contracted by living under unhygienic conditions. These diseases were reprehensible because our forefathers blamed the slum dwellers for the circumstances under which they were forced to live.

Of the social diseases caused by galloping technology, those caused by air pollution might be thought of as analogous to tuberculosis, whereas injuries and deaths caused by reckless driving—a voluntary, pleasurable, but disapproved activity—would be analogues of venereal diseases.

Like their medical counterparts, technological social diseases can be acute or chronic. The most virulent and acute form, which fortunately has not yet broken out, would be modern war. The threat to survival posed by modern weapons is receiving so much agonized attention from most of us that there is no need to dwell on it. It may be worthwhile to point out, however, that modern weapons symbolize the reversal of man's relation to his environment. For the first time in human history, the chief danger to human survival comes from man himself instead of the forces of nature.

Historians have sufficiently described the horrors of war throughout the ages, but actually weapons were a trivial source of death compared to natural causes until very recently. Even when men tried deliberately to kill each other in war, they succeeded only sporadically and in localized areas. The influenza epidemic in 1918, by contrast, killed ten million people throughout the world in six months. Endemic diseases like malaria and tuberculosis took their tolls in millions every year, as did famine.

World War II claimed about sixty-five million lives in eight years, if one starts with the Japanese invasion of Manchuria, but in that war, as in all others, the majority of deaths were caused by disease and starvation resulting from the dislocations of society caused by the fighting. World War II was the first in which, even among the fighting men, more died of wounds than disease. As a great bacteriologist has observed: "soldiers have rarely won wars. They more often mop up after the barrage of epidemics. Typhus . . . plague, typhoid, cholera and dysentery (have) decided more campaigns than Caesar, Hannibal, Napoleon and all the inspector generals of history."[1]

Now, just as we have learned to master the major epidemic illnesses and to produce food in abundance for everyone, we have suddenly created a new, more powerful form of death dealing that can destroy tens of millions of people in minutes and, indeed, could put an end to mankind. If one were mystically inclined, one might suspect that there is some law of nature which states that the danger to human life remains constant, so that as one source diminishes another must take its place.

I shall assume, without any really valid grounds, that humans will shackle the self-created monster of modern weapons before it is too late. Otherwise there would be no point in continuing with this discourse, which deals with the causes and cure of chronic forms of technological social disease. These are the subtle, insidious dangers that are the unwanted and incidental by-products of fabulous achievements in raising the level of human welfare. These dangers are at present more apparent in the United States because our society is the most technologically advanced, but in due course they are certain to plague all nations.

The dangers can be grouped into three categories: pollution of the living environment, the biosphere; accidents; and drugs. Let me start with the only brand new danger, of small consequence at present but potentially one of the greatest—the pollution of the biosphere by radioactive products of nuclear power plants.

In 1962 nuclear power accounted for only one-half of one percent of the total power generated in this country, but it could be as high as fifty percent by the year 2000. And the growth rate is exponential. In absolute figures nuclear power plants produced one-half million kilowatts in 1960, 46.4 million in 1976, and an estimated 240 million by the 1990s.

Nuclear power plants present three types of danger. The first is a break in the protective casing that encloses the radioactive elements. Such an accident to the reactor in Windscale in England in 1957 is said to have released more radioactivity into the atmosphere than the explosion of an atomic bomb of the Hiroshima type. Another serious potential hazard lies in the possibility of a leak in the transportation and storage of high-level radioactive wastes that cannot be safely released.

The third source of potential danger lies in low-level radioactive isotopes. These are now released into the environment under carefully monitored conditions, to ensure that the dilution is sufficient to prevent any predictable human exposure above levels believed to be harmful. The trouble is that very little is known about these isotopes, since they have only existed for a few years. So far, none has approached the presumed maximal permissible concentration in humans. However, they raise uncomfortable questions. Even though traces of radioactive isotopes in our tissues may be harmless in the short run, we do not yet know enough about what long exposure to slight doses of ionizing radiation does to living systems to be sure that we are not suffering slow damage. In this connection, deaths from cancer in survivors of the Japanese atomic bombings have only now, after about twenty years, started to show a sharp rise.

A more serious problem is that some living creatures accumulate certain isotopes which become increasingly concentrated as they move up the food chain. For example, algae concentrate radioactive zinc to about 6,000 times that of the surrounding water. The algae are eaten by bluegill fish, in whose bones the concentration is about 8,700 times that of the water. Fortunately, humans do not eat bluegill bones, but who knows what edible tissues will be found to store other radioactive substances in the same way?

Dangers of the same type are created by pesticides. In terms of the amount of chemical per unit of body weight, most pesticides are equally toxic to all living creatures, though immunity for some can be built up in time. They kill insects and not men simply because the former receive enormously greater doses in proportion to their weight. The amount found in human tissues to date is far below the concentration that would cause immediate damage. But certain creatures we eat concentrate pesticides to a fantastic degree. The oyster, for example, accumulates DDT to a level some 70,000 times above that of the surrounding water. This happens because water-living creatures lack the enzymes, present in adult humans, that metabolize most of these substances into harmless wastes. It turns out—an example of an unanticipated danger—that babies also lack these enzymes, so that they would be damaged by much smaller amounts of pesticide than adults.

Furthermore, some pesticides, like radioactive isotopes,

cause cancer in animals on repeated exposure, and some are suspected of damaging the germ plasm, so that their deleterious effects, though long delayed, may eventually be very serious.

A more serious, immediate menace to health is atmospheric pollution from factories and automobiles. It is estimated that 133 million tons of aerial garbage are dumped into the atmosphere of the United States each year—more than the weight of our annual steel production. As to its effects on health, a cautious statement is: "A large fraction of our population is now being exposed to significant concentrations of a variety of toxic chemicals. These levels are often a substantial fraction of those which produce acute effects. There is a possibility that our people may be sustaining cumulative insidious damage. If genetic injury were involved, the results would be especially serious."[2] It is estimated that the chances of a man dying between the ages of fifty and seventy from respiratory disease are twice as great if he lives in an air-polluted area than in a clean-air area.

A particularly subtle form of air pollution, which may have the most inexorable effects, is the slow increase in carbon dioxide in the atmosphere produced by industrial use of fossil fuels. This blocks the radiation of heat energy back to outer space, so that the temperature of the earth is gradually rising. The average temperature is 8 percent higher than it was in 1890. This, of course, could be due to other causes. In any case, if it keeps up, among other unpleasant consequences, it will melt the polar ice caps, flooding the world's seaboards.

The social diseases considered so far have been analogous to tuberculosis—the individual cannot do anything about the noxious agents to which he is exposed. Now let us turn to those that are more analogous to syphilis—that is, they result from a person's own actions, whether deliberate or heedless. This category includes disability and deaths caused by accidents or by drugs. Accidents have become the leading cause of death from ages 1 to 37 and the seventh cause of death at all ages. Their prominence obviously results, in part, from the sharp reduction in natural causes of death, especially in the younger age group, but in absolute figures they claim an impressive toll. In 1975, they killed 103,000 people and injured 10,300,00. The worst offender, of course, is the automobile. On United States highways a death or injury occurs every 18 seconds. In 1976, 46,700 people were killed—or almost half of those who were killed in all accidents—and 1,800,000 maimed. I shall return to the question of the causes of this carnage presently, but for the moment wish to pass on to a brief look at the last category of new environmental hazards to be considered. Ironically, these are created by the medical profession or, more broadly, the life sciences.

The worst, fortunately, is only hypothetical so far. Now that biologists have been able to rearrange living molecules, they can create self-reproducing viruses that never before existed. Probably some are doing this in the service of biological warfare, but many are working on such projects purely out of that powerful human urge, scientific curiosity. A Nobel-Prize-winning biologist views such research with profound alarm. He speaks of the good possibility that these tinkerers will create a new poliomyelitis virus, for example, against which humans have built up no immunity. "Any escape into circulation . . . could grow into the almost unimaginable catastrophe of a 'virgin soil' epidemic involving all the populous regions of the world."[3] He concludes: "there are dangers in knowing what should not be known,"[4] a feeling shared by many atomic scientists. Apparently, splitting the molecule may have consequences as disastrous as splitting the atom.

To return to more mundane but more immediate hazards arising directly from efforts to prolong life and health, floods of new medications are being put on the market. Despite increasingly stringent laws, some that cause serious damage to health or even death get past the guards. Examples were the contaminated strain of polio vaccine and the malformed babies caused by an apparently harmless sleeping medicine, thalidomide.

Finally, there is the growing menace of drugs that alter states of consciousness, including sedatives, stimulants, mood-lifters, and drugs such as LSD. Most of these drugs were thought to be harmless when first introduced. Cocaine, barbiturates, dexedrine, and now LSD, to name a handful, were first viewed as great boons to man.

We should have learned by now that no drug powerful

enough to cause a change in psychic state is harmless if taken over a long enough period of time or in large enough doses. Barbiturates proved to be superb suicidal agents, dexedrine produces serious psychoses (in one series 83 percent of those who used this supposedly harmless pep pill for one to five years showed psychotic symptoms), and there have been many sufferers from the acute and chronic ill effects of LSD.

Hundreds of common drugs, moreover, impair driving ability. One physician found that a group of patients receiving a tranquilizer for ninety days had ten times more traffic accidents than the population at large. He concludes, glumly, "No matter how strenuously doctors warn patients about drugs and driving, the advice probably wears off faster than the drug."[5]

This reminder that our topic is people, not technology, may serve to conclude this very spotty survey of the new hazards to life and health created by man. I have not even mentioned, for example, water pollution by industrial wastes, the more than 150 poisons that can be found in any household, or the host of new industrial hazards.

The psychological questions I should like to raise concerning this new group of social diseases are, first, why do we not pay more attention to them and, second, why are our countermeasures so ineffective.

The obstacles are both perceptual and motivational. Perceptually, most of the dangers are remarkably unobtrusive. In fact, they are undetectable by the senses. Radioactive isotopes and pesticides in our tissues, and the slowly rising carbon dioxide content of the air cannot be seen, heard, tasted, smelled, or felt, so it is easy to forget about them. When they do intrude on consciousness, in the form of eye-burning smog or brown water, in the language of perceptual psychology, they are ground rather than figure. As an authority on air pollution says:

The private citizen is unaware of the fact that the substance he is inhaling may eventually cause cancer of the lungs. He does not associate a bad cough with atmospheric conditions. It may be only on days of particular wind direction that a housewife will be bothered by fly ash on her clothesline; immediately thereafter, she'll forget it. . . . The offensive odors of some industries, the dust on windowsills, the haze that obscures an otherwise beautiful day—all are taken as features of urban living about which nothing can be done. And when the air is clear, the facts of the matter might as well not exist.[6]

One is reminded of the old man in Arkansas whose roof didn't leak when it didn't rain.

Occasionally the dangers do spring into focus, as when at least 4,000 people died during a four-day London fog in 1952, or when traffic deaths hit the headlines on a holiday weekend, but these occasions are too brief and infrequent to sustain attention.

A further difficulty in identifying the damage to health caused by noxious environmental agents is that illnesses have multiple causes, so in any given case it is hard to single out what really is to blame. If an elderly man with chronic lung disease dies during a heavy smog, who can say for certain that the smog was the cause of death? In other terms, statistical variations in various environmental and internal factors are so great that the true noxious agents may be hidden by them. The problem is analogous to that of detecting evoked potentials on the electroencephalogram. These are spike waves occurring a fraction of a second after the stimulus. They can only be detected by superimposing hundreds of tracings so the random variations cancel each other out.

Finally, although the damage done by environmental poisons is constantly increasing, the increments are very small compared to the base level. So, in accord with a well-known psychophysiological law, they do not rise above the threshold of awareness. Humans may be in the same plight as a frog placed in a pan of cold water, which is very slowly heated. If the rise in temperature is gradual enough, it will be boiled without ever knowing what happened.

These perceptual obstacles to appreciating the dangers created by technological advances play into strong motives for not doing much about them. The major source of complacency, I believe, is that the new dangers to life and health are tiny compared to the benefits. For example, American industry, the chief source of pollution of the biosphere, produces half the world's goods in addition to a fabulous arsenal of weapons—a technological triumph that could, in a flash, nullify the gains produced by all the others. And our society could not function at all without that space-annihilator, the automobile. Pesticides are mainly responsible for enabling less than 10 percent of the American population not only to feed the rest too well, but to produce millions of tons of surplus food.

Medical science has prolonged the average length of life in the United States by about 50 percent in the last half century and has virtually conquered the major epidemic diseases, although this battle is never permanently won. And the lives of millions have been made more tolerable by relatively harmless sedatives and antidepressants.

Surely, it will be said, these huge gains in human welfare (and I have named only a few) far outweigh the relatively minute increases in illnesses and deaths that accompany them.

True, but in absolute numbers over 100,000 accidental deaths a year and the rising death rates from cancer and lung disease are far from insignificant. And even though the immediate danger to health and life may be small, some types of damage are cumulative and some may be irreversible. For example, no one knows how to restore to the water of Lake Erie the oxygen it has lost through a complex chain of biological and chemical reactions set off by industrial wastes, resulting in destruction of its edible fish.

In any case, the rewards yielded by our galloping technology are large, tangible, and immediate, and the penalties are remote and contingent. It does not take a learning theorist to know which will determine behavior. The pleasure of a puff on a cigarette far outweighs the possibility that it will shorten the smoker's life by a few years in the distant future. The increased risk of getting killed influences the automobile driver much less than the joy of speeding, especially after a few drinks. And, at the social level, the prospects of increased revenues to a community from a new industry dwarf the hazard to health it might create.

So, everyone is motivated to minimize the dangers, especially when taking them seriously might jeopardize some of the gains. Perhaps this universal underestimation also partly reflects the proverbial American optimism. Even scientists, whose sole task should be to establish the facts, seem to be affected. One is constantly running across news items like: "New tests developed at Pennsylvania State University reveal that pesticide residue in plants is fifty per-cent to a hundred per-cent greater than present tests indicate."[7] Or "Radioactive caribou and reindeer may pose a health threat to nearly all the residents of Alaska. Scientists previously had believed that only Eskimos living near the Arctic Circle were endangered."[8]

When profits, not merely truth, are at stake, optimism becomes literally blind. One example may suffice. Fluorides discharged into the air by phosphate plants in two Florida counties damaged citrus crops over a radius of about fifty miles, cut production in some groves by as much as 75 percent, and resulted in a $20 million reduction in property values. In the face of these facts a spokesman for the Florida Phosphate Council told local citrus growers: "Gentlemen, there's no problem of air pollution in this area that is affecting citrus groves. All you boys have to do is take better care of your groves and you will have no complaints about air pollution."[9]

Since local chambers of commerce wish to attract people to their localities, they join the creators of pollution in minimizing it, so whatever tendency the average citizen has to overlook his slow poisoning is aided by the absence of corrective information. A poll of the inhabitants of Nashville, where substantial numbers die every year from heart and respiratory diseases aggravated by heavy air pollution, found that 85 percent believed it to be a healthy place to live, and less than 3 percent suggested that measures be taken to reduce air pollution.

Despite these impediments, Americans have at least officially recognized the existence of the problems and taken action to solve them. Congress has appropriated funds for fighting air pollution, water pollution, and highway accidents. So, you may ask, what is there to worry about? Unfortunately, in comparison with the size of the dangers, the efforts to combat them are so small as to be pitiable, or laughable, depending on one's point of view. To quote an expert: "America of the near future will be filthy and foul, and our air will be unfit to breathe. Indeed, this dark, dangerous era ahead of us is inevitable."[10]

In short, so far, efforts to halt the diseases created by our galloping technology have been too little and too late. That this state of affairs is a pressing social issue seems self-evident, so it is appropriate to ask why it has aroused so little interest among social psychologists. The basic trouble may be that, in contrast to our other concerns such as war, poverty, and racial discrimination, this one has no focus and no villains. Ironically, the ills caused by technology are by-products of benevolent efforts to promote the general welfare. It is hard to get indignant over this, and indignation seems to be the initial goad to becoming concerned about a social issue.

Moreover, if one looks about for a focus, one can find only familiar and universal aspects of human nature—such as failure to appreciate the seriousness of dangers that are not in awareness, unwillingness to forego immediate rewards in order to forestall future disasters, and the general inertia of social organizations. We may be dealing with a new manifestation of the illness that, according to the Spanish philosopher Ortega y Gasset, afflicts all civilized societies and eventually kills them—the desire of the citizens to enjoy the fruits of civilization without putting forth the effort or accepting the discipline necessary to maintain it. Perhaps the last word was really said by Descartes over three centuries ago: "Defects are always more tolerable than the change necessary for their removal."[11]

Lest we throw up our hands prematurely, however, let me suggest some aspects of the problem to which social psychologists might be able to contribute.

One is the American faith in the quick fix. Our history of incredible inventiveness has fostered the belief that some new technological invention can always be devised to correct the evils created by the last one, without causing anyone too much cost or inconvenience. No doubt, new inventions will be required to help combat new dangers, and all of the diseases created by technology have partial technological antidotes. But right now we have the techniques to sharply reduce such evils as air and water pollution, if only we would apply them, and the most efficient way to relieve many other dangers would be through modifying the behavior of people, not machines.

Traffic fatalities are a case in point. When the disgraceful carnage of our highways finally passed the threshold of awareness, a great cry went up for safer cars, whereas what we need more are safer drivers. Certainly cars could and should be made much safer than they are today, but just consider a few facts. Twenty percent of drivers are involved in 80 percent of accidents. If they were all kept off the roads, accidents would be sharply reduced at one blow. Many studies have found that in about 50 percent of fatal accidents one or both of the persons involved had been drinking. And I have mentioned the tenfold increase in accidents found among one group of patients on tranquilizers.

Finally, speeding is involved in nearly two out of five driving deaths. No amount of tinkering with automobiles will change the fact that the human reaction time is about three-fourths of a second, which means that at seventy miles an hour a car will cover seventy-seven feet or about three car lengths before the driver can even press the brake. So if a driver is tailgating at that speed and the car in front stops suddenly, no safety devices on earth can keep him from crashing, although they could, to be sure, reduce his resulting injuries.

Nor are these considerations merely theoretical. The introduction of the nationwide 55 mile an hour speed limit was followed by a drop in traffic accidents. Three New England states have reduced their accident rate to about half the national average simply by enforcing laws against speeding and drunken driving. If to these were added universal driver education courses, and effective measures to keep accident-prone drivers permanently off the roads, traffic fatalities would drop to a negligible level without changing the design of a single car.

Insofar as improved safety features on cars are involved, the human problem has only been pushed one step back to the auto makers. It is much easier to invent safety devices than to get auto manufacturers to install them. No manufacturer can afford the additional cost of making his cars safer unless all his competitors do likewise.

This consideration calls attention to a broad social issue that creates serious impediments to combatting technological sources of damage to health—the competitive orientation of our society. The American social philosophy assumes that competition is the mainspring of social and economic advance. The general welfare is believed to emerge from the interaction of conflicting economic interests. Every American inevitably belongs to several overlapping interest groups, but, by and large, he assigns the highest priority to the one centering on his means of livelihood, whether it be producing or selling goods, working for wages, or selling services. Groups are formed to protect other interests than making money, to be sure, but they do not exert as powerful or pervasive an influence. If an interest does not affect income and offers no dramatic focus for attention, no group will form to protect it, regardless of how vital it may be. It is safe to predict that there will never be a National Association of Air Breathers or an Amalgamated Water Drinkers Union. As a result, efforts to combat the poisoning of the biosphere are bound to receive a low priority. Everybody's business is nobody's business.*

Another social issue implicit in technologically caused ills arises from the fact that they cannot be effectively combatted by local action. The dangers are seldom confined to political units. When they are, as when fumes from a factory pollute the air of a town, the industry involved is seldom locally owned, and so is relatively immune to local pressures. The characteristics of local administrative agencies also impede effective action. If the job of policing water pollution, for example, is assigned to an established agency like the Health Department, it must take its place at the end of the line behind the department's established duties, and must compete for funds and personnel that are usually already inadequate. If a new department is formed, it must battle established agencies, resistant to encroachments on their terrains.

Nor can local communities meet the financial burdens involved in adequate safety measures. A major reason for the success of the federal highway program seems to be that the federal government footed 90 percent of the bill. It will probably have to assume a similar share of the cost of combatting environmental ills, instead of the meager 40 percent it now offers.

And so we find ourselves once again facing in a new guise the perennial problem of the place of government regulation

*The upsurge of environmentalist groups in the 1970s has, I am glad to say, proved this analysis to be too pessimistic.

and control in a free society—a manifestation of the inevitable and universal tension between freedom of the individual and the welfare of the group.

In other words, it appears that technologically caused ills of individuals can be successfully combatted only by correcting the ills of society with which they are intertwined. At this point certain new tools that psychologists have helped to develop may come to our aid.

One is computerized systems analysis. The biosphere is a single system, of which human beings are an integral part. So attempts to modify any aspect of it may have repercussions on the rest, sometimes unforeseen. For example, the introduction of methods to control air pollution might affect patterns of mass transportation and employment, which in turn may influence rates of crime, alcoholism, and drug addiction. Computerized techniques of systems analysis, which enable rapid gathering of many types of data and analysis of their interactions, for the first time permit solution of such problems. They analyze the relationships of the different aspects, make it possible to anticipate the effects of various remedies before actually implementing them, and provide continuous feedback on the success of the measures finally undertaken. California has pioneered in a pilot application of systems analysis to problems of air and water pollution, mass transportation, and crime, with encouraging results.

To combat the ills caused by technology also requires bringing about major changes in the attitudes of the American people. We would have to learn to view our problems in a broader context—to realize that the quick fix will not work and that adequate solutions require consideration of the social and ethical implications of remedial measures. In addition, we shall have to learn how to cope with a constantly changing environment.

The achievement of both these aims would require drastic and large-scale changes in our philosophy and methods of education. There would have to be more emphasis on general principles and learning how to solve problems, and less on sheer information and development of technical skills. It would be necessary to introduce these orientations into the school curriculum from the earliest grades. Their implementation would require full use of new methods of teaching that eliminate the enormous waste motion of traditional methods.

A massive program of adult education along similar lines would also be necessary. Electronic communications media could be used very much more effectively for such a purpose than they are today. Many industrially backward nations are using radio and television to speed the education of their people, as well as for other less worthy aims. Today, educators, political leaders, and other molders of the public mind can drop in for a chat, via television, in over 93 percent of American homes. Attempts to use the educational potentialities of television more fully would run into the same obstacles as any other social innovation. The mere existence of television, however, gives grounds for hope that it will be used to speed the changes in public attitudes required by the changes in the environment.

Lurking behind all the problems I have discussed is a brand new psychological issue. It probably concerns philosophers, theologians, and poets primarily, but psychologists cannot be indifferent to it. Let me introduce the topic by taking as a text a comment of a State Conservation Commissioner defending a public utility, one of whose atomic power plants has caused an enormous fish kill by its effluent. He described this mishap as "almost in the vein of an act of God."[12] I do not think he really meant to imply that God is dead and has been replaced by Consolidated Edison. But such a proposition might contain a germ of truth. Our generation is living through the culmination of a struggle between man and nature that began when someone first resolved to sail into the wind, rather than letting currents and breezes carry him where they would. After he learned how to do it, he became able to choose his destination, so he had to develop navigational instruments to tell him where he was and how to reach his goal. From then on, step by step, man has gradually bent the forces of nature to his will, until today, barring only his inability to conquer death, he seems to be nature's master. But let us not become too self-confident. At first the benefits of our assault on the natural environment far exceeded the costs, but now the latter are rapidly mounting. Nature may simply have been biding its time.

The interesting psychological point is that our increasing

power over nature has been accompanied by growing despair about ourselves. Playwrights, novelists, poets, philosophers keep hammering away on the related themes that life is meaningless, absurd, a kind of bad joke, and that man is capable only of making himself and his fellows miserable. And these statements find a wide response. Could they spring, in part, from a feeling of terror at our inability to live up to the appalling responsibilities of our new power?

In the past, men could shrug their shoulders in the face of most of the evils of life because they were powerless to prevent them. A misfortune like a fish kill could be blamed on God or Fate. Now there is no one to blame but ourselves. Nothing is any longer inevitable. Since everything can be accomplished, everything must be deliberately chosen. It is in human power, for the first time, to achieve a level of welfare exceeding our wildest imaginings or to commit race suicide, slowly or rapidly. The choice rests only with us.

Perhaps we are realizing that no degree of control over nature can solve basic problems of social living. Our dazzling material triumphs are, rather, a warning that in the end, all depends on improving the quality of our relationships with each other. Without this, all our scientific and technological triumphs may only hasten our destruction.

Man has been characterized as the only creature with an infinite capacity for making trouble for himself, and we seem to be exercising that capacity fully today. It may be some comfort to recollect, with a student of man's origins, that "man is a bad weather animal, designed for storm and change."[13]

Today man is making his own stormy weather. Perhaps it is not too much to hope that the same qualities which enabled him to triumph over the destructive forces of nature will enable him to master those he himself has created.

12. *Psychological Challenges of the Nuclear Age*

MY PURPOSE in this chapter is not to offer solutions to the political problems of our times, since these must in the last analysis be devised by politicians, but to bring together information and ideas arising out of my own area of interest, which may stimulate thought and discussion about these problems. As a psychiatrist, I have been struck by an analogy between the behavior of policy makers today and the behavior of mental patients—that is, they see a problem or a threat and then resort to methods of dealing with it that aggravate it. The leaders of the world agree that nuclear armaments pose or soon will pose an insufferable threat to the existence of humanity. This is reflected in the unanimous United Nations resolution of November 2, 1959, that "the question of general and complete disarmament is the most important one facing the world today." Yet the preparation for war goes on feverishly.

The dilemma is sharply pointed up by two items which appeared in the same issue of the *New York Times*. The first was a statement by President Eisenhower:

> No other aspiration dominates my whole being as much as this: that the nations of the East and West will find dependable, self-guaranteeing methods to reduce the vast expenditure for armaments.

In the same issue appeared the following news item:

176

United States armaments manufacturers have begun to pour massive amounts of capital and technical experience into the reviving West Germany arms industry. The motive . . . is the widespread conviction that the Bonn republic is destined to become a major weapons producer.[1]

The psychiatrist will recognize here a pattern similar to that of the patient who has insight into his problems but is unable to act on it—for instance, the alcoholic who drinks in order to relieve himself of anxiety and depression, even though he knows that this will ultimately prove disastrous to him. He says, in effect, "I know this is killing me," as he takes another drink.

The psychiatrist must often first convince the patient that he is really ill; then try to help him understand the emotional blocks and faulty habit patterns which impede the solution of his problems, and even aggravate them; and finally help him to find more successful solutions. Applying the same approach to the predicaments of the nuclear age, I shall first try to demonstrate how mankind's present course leads inevitably to disaster, then consider some of the psychological blocks to finding a way out, and finally explore some possible solutions.

At this point an awkward question arises. To what extent is it possible to draw valid analogies from individual behavior to the behavior of groups of people? This question cannot be satisfactorily answered. All one can do is to point out possible analogies and try to test their usefulness. Certainly I do not believe that information about personality quirks and personal motivations of national leaders helps much to understand the behavior of nations. True, Hitler's personality had something to do with the excesses of Nazi Germany, but in a conflict situation between two groups those in control of each group are *usually* the most responsible, talented, and exemplary members, who can withstand the strains of the conflict situation, as Sherif and Sherif point out.[2]

Thus leaders of nations in their official dealings are primarily motivated by their concept of national interest and by the values of the groups they represent. Certain general principles of individual psychology, however, govern the behavior and attitudes of both leaders and followers and are, I believe, pertinent. Moreover, group psychological principles are obviously relevant. I shall try to call upon concepts of individual and group psychology where each seems most appropriate, while recognizing that it is not always possible to distinguish sharply between them.

THE NATURE OF THE THREAT

The core of the problem is that mankind is faced with a rapidly and drastically changing environment. More drastic changes in habits of thinking and behavior are required than have ever occurred in the history of mankind, and they must be made in a very short time. As Albert Einstein put it, "The unleashed power of the atom has changed everything save our modes of thinking, and thus we drift toward unparalleled catastrophe."[3] In a more erudite vein, Brewster Smith writes, "irrationality proliferates when the challenge to a person's adaptation is too severe, or too obscure, to be met head on with the resources then at his command."[4] The challenge of the nuclear age is at once too severe and too obscure to be met head on with the resources now at our command.

One facet of this challenge is the growing interdependence of the world through improved communication and transport. While war has sometimes been an agent of progress, as Margaret Mead has pointed out,[5] this cannot occur any longer, because humanity is now one interdependent web. The problems which this interdependence creates are immensely aggravated by the fantastic destructive powers of modern weaponry. Mankind now has the power to destroy itself in three entirely independent ways. The first is by nuclear weapons. A Committee of the National Academy of Sciences has calculated that a 10,000-megaton nuclear exchange between the United States and the USSR, less than half their current stockpiles, would, in addition to its direct effects, reduce the ozone layer by 30 to 70 percent, with disastrous long-term ecological consequences.[6] This conclusion is supported by a statement of the Federation of American Scientists, a highly responsible group: "With a stockpile . . . that now exists it is possible to cover the entire earth with a radiation level which for ten years would remain sufficiently intense to prove fatal to all living beings on land."[7]

The second means is by nerve gas; according to Representative Byron Johnson of Colorado there is now enough stockpiled in that one state to wipe out all of mankind and, of course, the Russians have at least as much, if not more.[8] Finally, bacteriological weapons of incredible virulence have been developed. A little more than a glassful of one strain of botulinus toxin would be enough to wipe out mankind if it could be distributed. While these chemical and biological agents are easy to prepare and are produced in many countries, for simplicity's sake I shall not consider them further, since the problems they present are no different in kind from those of nuclear weapons, and the latter are at the moment by far the most menacing.

There is no defense against these weapons, and it is highly unlikely that there ever will be, for the same thought processes which perfect a defense against a weapon at the same time devise ways of thwarting the defense. For example, we are now trying to develop a system for intercepting missiles through plotting their trajectories, and at the same time developing missiles which do not follow predictable trajectories. We boast of our means of confusing Russian radar, but they, of course, will be able to confuse ours equally well.

In the days of conventional weapons, a defense which worked reasonably well was good enough. Because of the massive destructive power of nuclear weapons, this is no longer true. Now a defense would have to be at least ninety percent effective—a level of effectiveness never achieved in history; and the likelihood of its being achieved when technology is advancing at such a fantastically rapid rate seems extremely remote.

And the weapons are getting more deadly and more effective all the time. According to Herman Kahn, right now it would be possible to build a "doomsday machine," capable of literally blowing the earth into little pieces, at a cost between fifty and a hundred billion dollars. This machine—the ultimate deterrent—would be set to go off automatically in the event of an enemy attack. It will become ever cheaper to make such machines, and small nations will have a particular incentive for building them, because this would enable them to blackmail large nations.[9]

While it is unlikely that anyone will build such a machine, and unlikely that the stockpiles of nuclear weapons will go off in such a fashion as to wipe out mankind, a nuclear war is not at all unlikely. The exact amount of damage it would do is uncertain, but the most optimistic estimate of American casualties, based on the development of a full-scale civil defense program, is around six to twenty million people. As Bertrand Russell says:

> The world which would emerge from a nuclear war would not be such as is desired by either Moscow or Washington . . . it would consist of destitute populations, maddened by hunger, debilitated by disease, deprived of the support of modern industry and means of transport, incapable of supporting educational institutions, and rapidly sinking to the level of ignorant savages.[10]

Some sophisticated defenders of nuclear armaments maintain that if certain drastic conditions are met—in itself highly unlikely—a country might survive a nuclear war with its social structure relatively intact. Perhaps this would be true during the next few years, but as an able expositor of this position himself writes, "It is most unlikely that the world can live with an uncontrolled arms race lasting for several decades."[11]

A final point about nuclear explosions is that they make the environment permanently more hostile to man. The increase in radiation alone after a nuclear war would cause higher rates of genetic malformations for at least ten thousand years.

In short, it is extremely unlikely, even today, that any country could win a war fought with modern weapons, and the likelihood of it becomes smaller with each increase in the accumulation of destructive power. In the next war all humanity will be the loser. There may be a few survivors, but the way of life for which they fought would not survive. They would mainly be preoccupied with trying to stay alive.

As a psychiatrist, I am especially impressed with the dangers inherent in the steady diffusion of power to fire modern weapons. The diffusion among countries is bad enough; even worse is the spread within countries. As nuclear weapons multiply and the warning time for retaliation decreases, the power over these weapons filters further and further down the chain of command. At this point individual psychology is certainly relevant. Every population contains a certain number of psychotic or profoundly malicious persons, and it can only be a matter of time before one of them comes into position to order the firing of a weapon which in a flash will destroy a large city in another country. This danger is aggravated by the fact that a large proportion of the generation now coming to adulthood spent its formative years under conditions of unprecedented chaos in refugee camps and the like. Disorganized conditions of living and unstable human relationships in childhood may leave serious scars in the adult in the form of anxiety, bitterness, and emotional instability. The conditions following the last war were worse than those in Germany following World War I, which produced Hitler's followers. It is persons like these who will have the power to set the world on fire.

Americans have nominal command of the weapons in the bases in foreign countries, but they are enormously outnumbered and could not prevent local soldiers' seizing the weapons if at some future time they wished to become independent of us. The British have, in fact, pointed out that under the present system American control over the warheads is an illusion. The only answer to this is, as an American Air Force officer said, "You've gotta trust your allies."[12] Personally, I find it difficult to trust an ally like Germany, for example, which twice in my lifetime has been our mortal enemy.

The increasing diversity of modern weapons offers an ever-widening choice of means of delivering them, including the holds of freighters and suitcases. Coupled with their widening dissemination, this means that the margin of error between us and catastrophe is steadily decreasing. If this process continues, I can see no escape from the conclusion that the disaster will certainly occur.

In concluding this sketchy review of the dangers to mankind created by nuclear weapons, let me point out that if there is anything certain in this world, it is that accidents will happen. Even if atomic energy is confined to peaceful uses, disastrous accidents will occur. For example, on December 12, 1952, a nuclear reactor in Canada burst. A 10,000-acre area had to be evacuated temporarily, and the reactor had to be buried. The AEC found that a single major accident near a city the size of Detroit could, under adverse climatic conditions, cause 3,400 deaths, 43,000 injuries, and property damage of $7 billion through radiation alone. It could require the evacuation of 460,000 people and restrict the use of 150,000 square miles of land.[13] A world at peace could cope with atomic accidents as it does with volcanic eruptions, earthquakes, and hurricanes. In a trigger-happy world, however, it is all too easy to envisage how such an accident could set an irretrievable chain of destruction in motion before its source was discovered.

THE EMOTIONAL BLOCKS TO SOLUTION OF THE PROBLEM

The responses of individuals to the threats of modern weaponry include all the reactions that people customarily show to massive dangers that exceed their powers of adaptation. One of these is a kind of apathy or fatalism, often coupled with a melancholy pleasure in contemplating one's inevitable doom. This is illustrated by the following quotation, written in the spring of 1959, when many people believed that Khrushchev had set a deadline for our evacuation of Berlin in May:

> Last week I was invited to lunch with a tall, smiling young man, happily married, who has risen in a very short time to one of the highest executive posts in American journalism. . . . "My wife and children know what to expect, and they've accepted it," he said. "I've told them that there'll probably be an exchange of hydrogen bombs before the end of June and I've explained to them that it probably means the death of all of us." His voice was calm . . . he was not arguing a case but regretfully defining a position.
>
> I said that while I recognized his right as an individual to commit suicide rather than live under alien rule, I could not understand his equanimity at the thought that the whole of mankind would perish with him. At this he smiled a deep, forgiving,

historian's smile. Other forms of life, he said, had been destroyed; what was so special about the human race, which was doomed to ultimate annihilation anyway, by the cooling of the earth?[14]

What is most disturbing about this anecdote is that the speaker has risen "to one of the highest executive posts in American journalism." If enough of our opinion leaders feel this way, we will go to our doom like cattle to the slaughter.

Somewhat similar in its effects on the person is habituation to the danger. Somehow we seem unable to sustain our feeling of fear in the presence of a constant, continual danger, and we lose our moral repugnance toward any evil which persists long enough. As Alexander Pope said of vice, "seen too oft, familiar with her face,/We first endure, then pity, then embrace,"[15] so David Cavers of the Harvard Law School says, "Habituation to the thought of nuclear war has blinded us to the realization that what we are discussing is the end of our civilization. Like Samson, we now have the power to pull the temple down upon ourselves and our enemies, but Samson, cycless in Gaza, knew what he was doing."[16] We now talk of being able, through a massive civil defense program, to limit our casualties to "only five million dead" and show no qualms at all about exterminating all of Russia. Such statements would have been unthinkable before the Second World War, and probably even a decade ago.

A more common maladaptive response to an overwhelming threat is the denial of its existence. Denial is not always pathological. For example, the inability of most humans to contemplate their own deaths is a healthy form of denial under most circumstances, since constant awareness of one's own inevitable dissolution would produce nothing except depression. But denial, in the form of minimizing the dreadfulness of modern weapons, seriously impedes our efforts to solve the terrible threat they present. For example, we assume that somehow our weapons can wipe out Russia but theirs cannot wipe us out. The *Wall Street Journal* once devoted four and one-half columns to our capacity to destroy Russia "in several ways and several times over," but included just two references to what Russia could do to us: "Even granting that Russia would have the advantage of surprise, U.S. officials reason that a first blow by the Soviets, although perhaps able to pierce this country's defenses in part, would not cripple Western power to retaliate. . . . either side certainly can inflict painful destruction on the other."[17] With nuclear weapons, piercing a country's defenses in part or inflicting painful destruction on it would mean the destruction of that country's social organization.

A more subtle form of denial is a fallacious appeal to history: With the advent of each new weapon alarmists prophesized that it would destroy mankind, and they were wrong; so those who say that nuclear, biological, and chemical weapons threaten the existence of humanity are probably also wrong. The fallacy lies in the proportionate increase in destructive energy made available by the splitting of the atom. At the dawn of history, when men killed each other with clubs and stones, a blow could scarcely kill more than one person. By 1944 mankind had so improved the destructiveness of weapons that an average firebomb raid on Japan killed four thousand. Thus the killing power of weapons increased by a factor of four thousand over half a million years or so. Today a moderate nuclear raid could kill fifty million people,[18] and nuclear weapons could be made in sufficient quantity to wipe out the entire human race. This represents an increase in destructive power over the most deadly nonatomic weapons by a factor of somewhere between 12,500 and infinity in a scant half-generation. Those who prophesy disaster, and their like-minded forebears, are in the position of the boy who cries "Wolf" too often, so that when the wolf really comes no one believes him.

Another form of denial is to believe that nuclear weapons will not be used just because they are so terrible. Those holding this viewpoint to the mutual restraint in the use of poison gas in the last war. This comforting fallacy can be exposed in a word. Our whole military policy commits us to the use of nuclear weapons. If we got into a major war, we would have no other alternative, since we no longer have sufficient conventional weapons.

A very important obstacle to facing up to the dangers of a modern world has been termed the insensitivity to the remote. Nuclear weapons are not directly present to any of our senses. A few miles from me there is an accumulation of viruses, bacteria, and toxins more than sufficient to wipe out the human race several times over, yet it gives most of us not the slightest concern. The principle operating here is, I think, similar to the gradient of reinforcement described by learning theory. This is, in essence, that the effect of a reward or punishment on a response diminishes very rapidly as the time between the response and the reward or punishment increases. While symbolic thought may bring the anticipated consequences of an act into the present, so that they can have an effect on present behavior, this is not always effective. To return to the alcoholic, he takes a drink to gain immediate relief from anxiety, even though he knows through his memory and powers of anticipation that the following morning he will feel much worse.

Transferred to the international level, this principle operates in both space and time. Thus the mother who cannot bear to see her child's cut finger is unmoved by the extinction of eighty thousand people in Hiroshima or twelve thousand in Agadir. A good example of the soothing effect of temporal distance is the fixation of Russia and America on the immediate danger each poses to the other and their neglect of the greater long-term danger to both resulting from future dissemination of nuclear weapons. The immediate mutual threat will pale when China, Israel, Egypt, and many other countries have such weapons, for then it will be possible for any country to trigger a war in such a way as to conceal the source of the attack. Yet such is the soothing effect of temporal distance that this dire possibility carries practically no weight, compared with each country's supposed need to remain strong vis-à-vis the other.

A final, subtle form of denial is the universal tendency to use reassuring words to describe our predicament, even though they are rapidly losing their meaning in today's world. People talk of defense when it is clear that there is no defense. They speak of national security when it is clear that no nation will be able to maintain even a semblance of security for its citizens at the expense of the security of other nations. One need only remember that there are satellites flying above the earth's atmosphere, quite oblivious of national boundaries, that can spy on any area in the world and that it may soon be possible to melt the icecap at the North Pole, flooding the seaboard cities of the whole world.

To the extent that we do not succeed in denying the dangers of modern weaponry, we are made anxious by them. Anxiety in moderation facilitates thinking and motivates a search for new and better solutions to the threat. However, if it gets too severe, it tends to make thought rigid and to paralyze initiative. This may have something to do with the repetition compulsion in neurotics, when they keep trying to solve current problems with solutions which may once have worked, but no longer do. It may be that the neurotic is too anxious and demoralized to try something else; he finds it better to bear the ills he has than to risk new ones.

At the level of group dynamics, emotional tension is most seriously reflected in the formation of the stereotype of "the enemy." Whoever we are and whoever the enemy is, we gradually assume all the virtues and they become the incarnation of everything evil. It is frighteningly easy to create the stereotype, as Sherif and Sherif have shown. They set up two groups in a boys' camp whose members did not know each other and arranged competitive situations in which one or both groups felt frustrated. Within a few days, each group had become a cohesive whole, bragging about its own virtues and having only contempt for the other group.[19]

Many psychological factors go into creating the bogey-man concept of the enemy, such as the convenience of projecting the sources of one's own dissatisfactions and justifying one's own aggressive behavior by use of a scapegoat.[20] Here I am more specifically concerned with why a stereotype of the enemy is so hard to break down, and what some of its consequences are. It seems to be a manifestation of a fundamental law of the human mind—that one's perceptions are guided to a large extent by one's expectations or assumptions. This has been demonstrated very nicely by an experiment in which by means of a stereopticon, different pictures are shown to the right and left eye simultaneously. When groups of Americans and Mexicans were shown by this device a bullfighter and a baseball player, the Americans tended to see the baseball player and the Mexicans, the bullfighter.[21]

Once we have cast another group in the role of the enemy, we know that they are to be distrusted—that they are evil incarnate. We then tend to twist all their communications to fit our belief.[22] If we meet individual members of the enemy group and find that they do not seem villainous, but appear to be ordinary, easy-going, fun-loving family men like ourselves, we preserve the stereotype by assuming either that they are diabolically clever at deceiving us or that it is their leaders who are villainous.[23] And all evidence indicates that the Russian view of the Americans is a mirror image of our view of them; that is, we—or our leaders—are war-mongering, untrustworthy, and dangerous, while they are peace-loving and honorable.

The following quotation from a letter I received recently indicates how disruptive the stereotype of the enemy can be to rational thought. From his choice of words, this correspondent is obviously an intelligent man, and yet he is able to write the following: "One cannot reason, bargain, or do business with a Khrushchev any more than with a Hitler, except possibly at the end of a long club. The intent of this maniac is to enslave forever, to 'robotize,' if you will, the *entire* human race. This fiend will consign humanity to an ant hill existence. Even the death of humanity is preferable to such an existence."

The mutual distrust of enemies has two dangerous consequences. First, it tends to disrupt communication between them. If a member of one group wishes to communicate with the other, this automatically subjects him to the suspicion of disloyalty. Even Senator Hubert Humphrey, who had maintained a steadfast anti-Communist position for many years, felt it necessary to reassure the public that his desire to talk with Khrushchev did not mean that he was favorable to Communists. Furthermore, since the enemy is viewed as so diabolically clever, each side fears that the other will be able to use improved communications to its advantage. In November 1959 the Senate Internal Security Committee called the Soviet-American cultural exchanges part of a "poisonous propaganda offensive."[24] Soviet hoaxers are playing us individually and nationally for suckers, the Committee said. At virtually the same moment, the Russian counterpart of this Committee was warning that the Americans might use this program as a "Trojan horse." Thus leaders on each side fear that their people are so naive and innocent as to be easily misled; that any favorable information about the enemy is bound to be false; and that their side could not use the contacts as effectively to further its own ends as the enemy could.

I am not suggesting that enemies do not deserve to be mistrusted. But disruption of communication prevents gaining information which would help to rectify any incorrect perceptions of one's opponent. On the other hand, increased communication, however desirable, does not in itself remove the causes of war between groups. No peoples communicated more completely than Northerners and Southerners in the early days of our country. Yet because they were operating under systems of value which were incompatible on one crucial issue, that of slavery, they wound up fighting the most deadly war in history up to that time.

The second and greatest danger of the mutual stereotype of the enemy is that it tends to make itself come true by virtue of the mechanism of the "self-fulfilling prophecy,"[25] which operates at both individual and group levels. We expect people to behave in a certain way and then behave in such a way toward them as to cause them to fulfill our prophecy. As an example at a group level, for many years psychiatrists expected patients at mental hospitals to be violent and unmanageable. They therefore put them in isolation rooms, locked them in chairs, and wrapped them in strait jackets. And, sure enough, the patients were violent and unmanageable. Recently psychiatrists have changed their prophecy and expected mental patients to be able to control themselves, and the patients have fulfilled these expectations.[26]

Unfortunately, with enemies the self-fulfilling prophecy tends to move in a malignant direction. Enemies may not be untrustworthy to begin with, but if the mutual posture lasts long enough, they eventually become so, as each acts in such a way as to justify the other's suspicion.[27] For example, for some time now Russia has been making conciliatory proposals and suggestions for disarmament which we consistently reject, or at least view with great suspicion. How does this affect their image of us? Since they are undoubtedly convinced of their sincerity, as we are of ours, our attitude can only serve to exasperate them. Constantly accusing someone of bad faith is scarcely the best way to win his friendship. Further, since they distrust us, they would naturally conclude that we are seeking excuses to continue arming, and the only possible purpose must be to attack them. The obvious next step is to conclude that their only hope for survival would be to attack us first. At this point, their disarmament proposals would indeed become screens for their own arming, heightening our fear that they would attack us, to forestall which we would have to attack them first. Each side now fears that the other side will strike, and each frantically builds up its striking force, so as to be able to retaliate if the other side should strike first. But this is not enough, because the side that strikes first has an enormous advantage. Therefore, each side must build up the capability of striking first if it sees that the other side is about to strike first. Thus each country's original policy, that under no condition would it strike first, begins to shift to the position that it must be prepared to strike first.[28]

CURRENT ATTEMPTS AT SOLUTION

If one's efforts to cope with a problem are based on false assumptions, one arrives at absurd solutions. So far our attempts to resolve the threat of nuclear weapons are based on an assumption which used to be true but no longer is—that possession of superior destructive force assures victory. The proposed solutions which follow from this are self-contradictory. We support the UN resolutions calling for cessation of the spread of nuclear weapons and for general disarmament. In practically the same breath we talk of giving nuclear arms to West Germany and Turkey, and of having to build up our armed strength before we can disarm.

The argument for this "realistic" solution goes something like this: Disarmament is certainly necessary, but bitter experience shows that you can't trust the Russians. The only thing they respect is force. Therefore, only by being strong can we give the Russians an effective incentive to disarm. To quote Nelson Rockefeller, "Successful negotiation with Russia will be possible only if the United States is in a position of maximum military strength."[29]

While this position has a superficial plausibility, just a little reflection shows that it is hopelessly self-contradictory. For a build-up of our armed strength practically compels our opponent to do the same, and both sides will have to reserve the right to accumulate those weapons which they believe to be the most effective. So they could negotiate only about relinquishing weapons that do not really matter, and negotiations would become merely a screen behind which the arms race would continue unabated. I think C. Wright Mills is correct in calling the policy of arming in order to disarm "crackpot realism."[30]

The military part of this argument has two interrelated aspects: the build-up of the capacity to wage limited wars, and the development of invulnerable or undetectable launching sites for deterrent weapons. The ability to wage limited wars requires an arsenal of conventional weapons and "small" atomic weapons, so that any aggression of the enemy could be opposed by just enough threat of retaliatory destruction to make it not worth his while. This would be a good scheme, except that it requires retention of weapons of mass destruction as well, because an enemy facing defeat might use them if we did not have them. Furthermore, each country must have enough destructive power so that even if most of its bases were destroyed what remained would be enough to wipe out the other's population. Thus the threat to civilization would remain. Human judgment is notoriously fallible at best and becomes especially so under conditions of war. It may be possible to limit a few wars, but sooner or later one would trigger off the holocaust.[31]

The second plan stresses the development of invulnerable retaliatory bases to eliminate the advantage of surprise attack. We are doing this now through the Polaris submarine and Minute Man missiles. By assuring each side that the other cannot wipe out its retaliatory force by surprise, this approach allows more time for deciding whether to strike back and so diminishes the danger of an accidentally started war. However, this is the most it can accomplish, and even this is questionable. In view of the rapid advances in arms technology, a base that is invulnerable today may prove very vulnerable tomorrow. One thinks of the Maginot Line.

But the most serious flaw in the doctrine of invulnerable bases is that it would cause an enemy to conceal the source of its attack. This will become ridiculously easy when many countries have nuclear weapons and as they continue to shrink in size. Right now an atom bomb can fit into a typewriter case. A country could smuggle atom bombs into all our major cities and arrange for them to go off through a timing device six months later. Against whom would we retaliate? Or if a country chose to be more diabolical—and small countries would certainly have the incentive to be so—it might arrange to fire a weapon at us in such a way that it would appear to come from Russia, and we and Russia would then fall on each other.

Finally, all policies based on maintenance of military strength accelerate the diffusion of nuclear weapons, with its attendant dangers. Neither Russia nor America can be prepared to fight limited nuclear wars all over the world without entrusting control of at least tactical nuclear weapons—of about the destructive power of the Hiroshima bomb—to their allies. The major antagonists in a showdown will not risk their own annihilation to protect these allies, so they must be given the power to "defend" themselves. And the countries to whom we or the Russians do not give nuclear weapons will be strongly stimulated to devise their own for the same reason.

Thus arming in order to disarm can only increase the world's insecurity; and, in addition, it places almost insuperable obstacles in the path of disarmament. As long as each side believes that it can negotiate only from a position of strength, the conditions for negotiations which are acceptable to one side are unacceptable to the other. When we had exclusive possession of atomic weapons, Russia was in no mood to consider disarming; now that we are behind in missiles, we show a similar reluctance. And, since each country is convinced that it must maintain a superior military force, "the true, if unavowed aim of every nation that goes into a disarmament conference is to increase its real or relative armament to the detriment of its rivals. Thus 'disarmament' turns out to be but one of the forms the armaments race can take."[32] As a result, all disarmament conferences have failed, with one or two minor exceptions.

There are two logical possibilities for disarmament—by agreement, or by unilateral action. Since we distrust the Russians and they distrust us, the fears of each create grave obstacles to disarmament by agreement. We demand an adequate inspection system to make sure that Russia is not cheating; but with the breakneck development of modern weapons, such inspection and control becomes ever less possible. An inspection system devised for today's weapons is obsolete for tomorrow's. Already it is impossible to inspect for stockpiles of atomic weapons, and we have been told that there can be no perfect inspection for underground explosions. But even if foolproof inspection could be achieved, the Russians would fear that they were being spied upon and we that we were being duped— both intolerable prospects to countries which view each other as enemies, because each contains the threat of the loss of national existence. Therefore, in a framework of reliance on superior force, disarmament by agreement seems almost impossible. Witness the fact that Russia and the United States were long unable to agree on something as simple as a ban on atmospheric tests of nuclear weapons, even after both countries stopped these tests.

Unilateral disarmament is even more difficult,[33] for any move of this kind would arouse initial suspicion by the other side, such as we have shown toward the Russians' announced decrease in the size of their conventional armed forces. To be convincing and to produce the hoped-for reciprocal step, disarmament would have to involve obvious weakening and to be persisted in long enough to convince the other side that it was genuine. But in the context of reliance on superior force, it would undoubtedly be viewed as surrender by both the side that did it and the opponent, demoralizing the former and perhaps tempting the latter to attack while it had an advantage.

But even if the world achieved some degree of disarmament by agreement or by reciprocal unilateral action, it would be faced with another problem. With conventional weapons, the lower the general level of armament, the more secure the peoples of the world could feel. But with nuclear weapons, the lower the general level of armaments, the greater the instability, because of the greater advantage to the side which, secretly or otherwise, maintained a slight preponderance. If the rest of the world were totally disarmed, the country that had withheld a dozen nuclear weapons could blackmail all the rest. Therefore disarmament will get more and more difficult as it proceeds.

THE ONLY ULTIMATE SOLUTION

The knowledge of how to make weapons of mass destruction, like the knowledge of good and evil, will never pass from the mind of man. Even in a completely disarmed world, any nation that was so minded could reconstruct these weapons in a few months. To be sure, it might be difficult to construct nuclear weapons secretly, but there would be no difficulty at all in brewing deadly toxins, because this can be done in any basement. Therefore, the only ultimate solution lies in creating world conditions which would inhibit a country possessing superior force from using it. In brief, this means the abolition of war.

Let me reinforce this conclusion by an appeal to authority. At a Pugwash Conference in 1959, twenty-six scientists from eight nations, including some of the world's leading experts in atomic, biological, and chemical warfare, who were trusted advisors of governments on both sides of the Iron Curtain—men who should know better than anyone else in the world the implications of modern weaponry—agreed unanimously on the following statement, which contains no qualifications or equivocation: "In the end, only the absolute prevention of war will preserve human life and civilization in the face of chemical and bacteriological as well as nuclear weapons. No ban of a single weapon, no agreement that leaves the general threat of war in existence, can protect mankind sufficiently."[34] In short, the drastically changed conditions of modern life produced by the shrinkage of the world and the advent of weapons of unlimited destructive powers mean that the two time-hallowed institutions—war and the nation state—have become threats to the continued existence of mankind and that new social inventions must replace them.

The relinquishing of war would require very drastic changes in human value systems and behavior, analogous to those produced by a religious conversion. The psychological challenge is to find means of persuasion which are more effective than the threat of violence or its actual use, or to create conditions such that the possessor of superior military force will be inhibited from using it. This will require overcoming the thought barrier which has been constructed over the thousands of years in which conflict was always settled in favor of the side with superior destructive power. It will require relinquishing a pattern of behavior as old as humanity and constantly reinforced by success, and adopting a new and essentially untried line of conduct.

Under these circumstances, it is not possible to prove that exclusive reliance on nonviolent means of resolving conflicts is feasible. If, however, one can show that it is not theoretically impossible, people may begin to take it seriously instead of dismissing it out of hand as a fine ideal but hopelessly impractical.[35] In beginning to think about this extremely difficult question, one must remember that the correct solution for an unprecedented problem is almost certain to appear ridiculous at first, for the habitual, and hence seemingly reasonable, solution almost by definition becomes maladaptive when conditions change drastically. Leo Szilard told how he and Enrico Fermi burst out laughing when they discovered the correct solution to a problem in atomic physics because it seemed so ridiculous.

It may help to clarify matters if I first discuss some common misunderstandings about nonviolence. Our language lacks a term to describe exclusive reliance on nonviolent means of persuasion. The usual terms, such as nonviolence, passive resistance, pacifism, and so on conjure up images of a person standing by with a holy look on his face while a soldier runs a bayonet through his sister. Actually, the aim of nonviolence is to prevent this situation from arising—to inhibit the use of destructive force by the person who possesses it. The achievement of this goal requires a very high degree of initiative, activity, and courage.

A second misunderstanding is that the reliance on nonviolence requires that conflict be eliminated from the world. On the contrary, it seems to me that conflict is not only a necessary but a desirable part of human existence. Life would be unbearably dull without it. The goal is rather to develop effective nonviolent means of resolving conflict.

A third common misconception is that nonviolence is offered as a simple, global solution to the dangers which threaten us. Actually it is an extraordinarily difficult one which incurs grave risks and demands the development of a wide variety of measures tailored to meet the specific requirements of different types of conflicts.

I shall not attempt to consider the religious and ethical arguments for the renunciation of violence. A psychological puzzle is why these arguments have motivated a small number of people so powerfully yet have left the great body of mankind untouched. Through the ages a few religiously inspired persons have kept the ideal of nonviolence alive, and in recent years two of them, Gandhi and Martin Luther King, have shown ways in which it might be practiced on a mass scale. Yet the doctrine of nonviolence has been in existence for two thousand years in the form of Christianity and for longer than that in other religions, without having the slightest effect on war. In fact, differences between religious doctrines both of which preach peace have been used to justify extremely destructive wars.

One reason for the ineffectualness of pacifist preachments today is that we agree in principle, simultaneously dismissing them as hopelessly idealistic—an attitude which renders them impotent. Thereby we put our consciences at rest and avoid having to think further about the matter. To forestall this response from you, without denying the force or relevance of the moral arguments for nonviolence, I shall try to examine it in as hard-headed and realistic a manner as possible. Let me tackle the most difficult problem first—the nature of man.

Many hold that it is absurd to expect man ever to renounce war, because he is by nature aggressive and self-aggrandizing—the very qualities that have enabled him to conquer his environment and are responsible for the forward thrust of his development. On the other hand, humans also show strongly affiliative and altruistic behavior. Students of human nature, depending on their philosophies, tend to view man as basically aggressive but forced to tame his hostile impulses by the necessity to live in close relationships with his fellows, or basically affiliative, becoming hostile only when frightened or frustrated.

Freud was an influential exponent of the former view. It has been said of his daughter, Anna Freud, "to hear [her] speak of the criminal tendencies of the one- and two-year old is to be reminded inevitably of the Calvinistic sermons on infant damnation,"[36] and her father writes:

> Under primitive conditions it is superior force—brute violence . . . that lords it everywhere. . . . Brute force is overcome by union, the allied might of scattered units makes good its right against the isolated giant. Thus we may define "right" (i.e. law) as the might of a community. Yet it, too, is nothing else than violence.[37]

Freud holds that in each generation the child painfully learns to hold his self-aggrandizing, destructive impulses in check, under the pressures of his parents and his group, since social survival would otherwise be impossible. But they are always just beneath the surface, ready to break forth under the slightest encouragement. Moreover, says Freud, the more elaborate and complex civilization becomes, the more it necessitates damming up man's hostilities, which then eventually break forth with even greater fury. Human existence is thus a race between love and destructiveness, with the latter more than likely to win out.

This pessimistic view of human nature is hard to refute. In situations of extreme stress there is no doubt that the veneer of civilization drops off many people, and they become savage beasts. They trample each other to death in panics; they murder and eat each other under conditions of starvation. The more civilized societies become, the more destructive are their wars; and highly civilized societies, such as that of Germany under the Nazis, perpetrate the most fiendish atrocities. This view of human nature may well be true; and if it is, mankind is doomed to become extinct, because there is a flaw in his make-up which is no longer compatible with survival.

Fortunately, there is evidence that man's affiliative drives may be at least as basic as his aggressive ones.[38] In infants loving as well as aggressive behavior appears spontaneously, and it gains a spontaneous loving response from the parent. Furthermore, for most people anger and hate are unpleasant emotions which they desire to terminate; whereas love is a highly pleasant one which they endeavor to prolong. Finally, just as aggressive drives can cause people to make heroic sacrifices, so can affiliative ones, which cannot be explained on the basis of self-interest, as when a person offers his life to save the life of a stranger. Gordon Allport, after an exhaustive study of the causes and forms of human prejudice, which is a gross manifestation of man's uglier side, is still able to write:

> Normal men everywhere reject in principle and by preference the path of war and destruction. They like to live in peace and friendship with their neighbors. They prefer to love and be loved rather than to hate and be hated. While wars rage yet our desire is for peace, and while animosity prevails the weight of mankind's approval is on the side of affiliation.[39]

The only reasonable conclusion concerning man's innate endowment is that he has both altruistic and self-aggrandizing trends, and that both are very strong. The elimination of war requires that the former be strengthened and the latter be inhibited or rechanneled.

The crucial point is that man is extraordinarily modifiable. His attitudes, feelings, and behavior are molded by the groups to which he belongs; his society transmits to him its values, standards, and ideals. Hunger may turn a man into a cannibal, but no purely personal drive will cause a Hindu mother to throw her infant under the wheels of a juggernaut or an SS man to roast little children alive on an open fire. It takes powerful group standards to cause such behavior. Mother love may lead a woman to give her life to save her child, but only dedication to a group ideal such as Christianity can cause a martyr to march singing to the stake.

In this fact lies the greatest hope for the renunciation of force. For war is a social institution, and the values and standards supporting it must be transmitted afresh to each new generation. It is conceivable that we can learn to adhere to a set of values which excludes the possibility of war. Anthropologists have described isolated societies which do not have the institution of war. For example:

> Among the Hopi competition is the worst of bad taste and physical aggression is rigorously suppressed. Outwardly a Hopi learned to smile at his enemies, to use "sweet words with a low voice," to share his property, and to work selflessly with others for the good of the tribe . . . but there remained another form of aggression open to him . . . with a tongue as pointed as a poison arrow, he carries on a constant guerilla warfare with his fellows.[40]

This example is instructive in showing that aggression does not disappear, but can be rechanneled into socially less destructive forms. The Hopi are prone to nightmares, but I think any of us would be willing to settle for a few nightmares in exchange for the removal of the threat of extermination.

Even more instructive is the case of the Comanche. As plains tribes, war for them was the be-all and end-all of existence. But initially the same people, as plateau tribes, were "completely without war patterns; they did not fight each other even over trespass."[41] This tribe passed from the most peaceful type of existence to the most warlike in a few generations—a striking example of the power of group standards.

Within civilized societies there has been a steady reduction of the kinds of conflict for which personal violence is sanctioned. A little over 150 years ago Aaron Burr killed Alexander Hamilton in a duel over a matter of honor, which was at least tacitly condoned by their society, but today would be unthinkable. In our courts people are daily waging bitter conflicts; the man who loses a lawsuit may commit suicide, but it does not occur to him to shoot his opponent. Only two generations ago industrial conflicts regularly involved the use of violence by both sides. Yet today, even in bitter and prolonged industrial strikes, neither side entertains the possibility of resorting to force. Why not? Certainly today's steelworkers and plant owners are not less belligerent as individuals than their forebears, nor are the police stronger in 1960 than in 1910 when industrial warfare was common. The most plausible explanation is that the standards of today's society condemn the use of violence to settle industrial disputes, so that each party realizes that resort to force would cost more than it would gain.

These examples indicate at least the possibility that mankind may eventually subscribe to a set of values which exclude war. But what about the present, when violence is still sanctioned as a means of settling disputes between nations? The heart of the matter is whether it is possible to win by nonviolent means against an opponent whose group standards sanction the use of violence. Almost everyone unhesitatingly answers "No" to this question, but I believe that there may be some room for doubt. At the level of the individual, as I have mentioned, a very important aspect of behavior is that it is guided by the responses of the person to whom it is directed. A person's response to what I do influences how I respond to his response, and this, in turn, influences what he does next. Violent behavior, like all other behavior, is not self-sustaining. Whether it increases or decreases depends on how the victim responds. It seems to be stimulated by counter-violence or by fear and inhibited by a calm, friendly attitude which implies that the victim is concerned about the welfare of the attacker as well as himself. For example, a missionary's wife in China, whose husband was away, learned that the inhabitants of the village in which they lived were planning to come and massacre her and the children because they blamed a drought on the anger of the gods at the presence of foreigners. When the armed mob broke into the house, she walked calmly up to the tall, surly leader and offered him a cup of tea. Nonplussed, he accepted the tea, and the others uncertainly followed his example. After this there was nothing for them to do but to leave peacefully. Fortunately for the sake of the story, the drought was broken by a rainstorm the following day.[42] This example may be exceptional. If an attempt to meet violence with nonviolence fails, there is no survivor to tell the story.

Yet if a person can find the courage to meet aggression with calm friendliness, this may have a powerfully inhibiting effect.[43] Only a rare individual has such moral strength in the face of threatened death for himself or his loved ones; but when very strong group support is forthcoming, nonviolent campaigns may be surprisingly successful—as in the examples of Gandhi in India and King in Alabama. Certain features were unusually favorable in both cases. The group using nonviolent methods was able to turn the values of the dominant group against them—that is, they could appeal in India to the British value of fair play and in America to the American values of the equality of all peoples and of individual freedom. In both instances the opposed groups were in close personal contact, so that the oppressors could not take emotional refuge in the insensitivity to the remote which I mentioned earlier. In each case, the oppressed group could use media of mass communication to sustain their own morale and to sway public opinion. But despite the favorable circumstances that can be seen in retrospect, no one would have predicted that the nonviolent campaigns could have succeeded, and one cannot exclude the feasibility of a nonviolent approach to some of the current conflicts in the world.

Scrutiny of these examples suggests certain conclusions which may have widespread applicability. First, the heart of nonviolent resistance is to fight the antagonism, not the antagonist. Gandhi makes a sharp distinction between the deed and the doer:

> Man and his deed are two distinct things. Whereas a good deed should call forth approbation and a wicked deed disapprobation, the doer of the deed, whether good or wicked, always deserves respect or pity as the case may be.[44]

That is, Gandhi rejects the stereotype of the enemy. He assumes that his opponents are acting righteously according to their own standards and tries to demonstrate how his position would achieve their aims better than their own approach. Second is his insistence that the conflict must be waged in a constructive way:

> In a group struggle you can keep . . . the ability to work effectively for the realization of the goal stronger than the destructive violent tendencies and the tendencies to passiveness and despondency only by . . . giving all phases of your struggle, as far as possible, a constructive character.[45]

Thus to oppose the salt tax he organized a march to the sea to make salt. Analogously, King named his organization of the bus boycott the Montgomery Improvement Association, implying that breaking down segregation in buses would be good for all the citizens of Montgomery.

A third important point to be gained from the experiences of King and Gandhi is that waging a nonviolent battle is not a simple or easy way of fighting and requires the highest type of generalship, with an extraordinary level of flexibility, courage, and organizational ability. The leaders must be able to activate the strongest type of group ideals and controls in order to hold despair and violence in check, despite provocations. These controls will differ in different cultures. Gandhi fasted as a means of mobilizing guilt in his followers when they strayed from the path of nonviolence, and King held nightly prayer meetings with hymn singing to maintain the morale of the Negroes.

Because it rests on group controls, successful conduct of a nonviolent campaign does not require that the individual members be saints, or even believers in nonviolence. Gandhi, with less than 200 disciples, was able to free a nation of 350 million. King's followers, as individuals, are considered to be among the most prone to violence in our society, at least according to popular stereotype. But nonviolent methods of fighting, like violent ones, require a willingness to stake one's life on the outcome. The English killed many Indians, and many Negro citizens in Montgomery owe their lives only to the ineptitude of white bomb throwers. The psychological problem is to create group standards which impel people to offer their lives in a peaceful battle with the same dedication that they do in war.

To try to sum up the essence of nonviolent campaigns, I would say that they abjure all behavior which stimulates the enemy to continue being violent, and exploit all behavior which tends to inhibit his use of violence. They avoid fear or counterattack or efforts to humiliate the enemy, while they treat him with respect and try to understand his viewpoint. They steadfastly look for a solution to the conflict which will satisfy his interest as well as their own.

While thus steadily inhibiting the aggressor's use of violence, they prove to him that he cannot gain his ends with it. In most battles destruction is not the primary end, but a means of coercing the adversary—except where the aggressive feelings have been very strongly fanned, or the group standards require the destruction of the enemy, as was the case with the Nazis and Jews. If the aggressor's violence continues to meet with no reinforcing response and if his destruction of members of the other group fails to coerce the survivors, then in time his violent behavior may grind to a halt as his own guilt feelings mount.

In trying to apply the lessons of Gandhi and King to present international conflicts, two cautions must be kept in mind. First, they are examples of the successful use of nonviolent means by one group against another within a single society, rather than between societies. Second, in each case the society was grounded on democratic values. One, therefore, has to ask whether nonviolent methods could work against a ruthless dictator, and whether they could solve international conflicts. Obviously I cannot give a completely satisfactory answer to either question, but I can at least suggest considerations to indicate that the answer might not be automatically negative.

The question of nonviolent conflict with a dictatorship arises in two forms. First, if a doctrine of nonviolence ever showed signs of winning the adherence of a majority of the American people, the remainder who still believed that force must be an instrument of policy would almost certainly attempt to seize power, to prevent the disaster that they feared. In this situation, as in India, most of the values of the ruling group and the opposition would be the same, and it would be possible to appeal to the ideals of the ruling group against itself. The outcome would depend on whether the proponents of nonviolence had been sufficiently trained in the use of nonviolent methods and were able to be steadfast in their purpose. A dictatorship from within could not maintain itself against a persistent refusal of the masses of the population to cooperate.

If our renunciation of force tempted an enemy to impose a military occupation on us, the question would be: Can nonviolent methods prevail against a dictatorship by a group which does not highly value human life? First of all, it is an oversimplification to say that Gandhi's methods worked in India because of the British attitude toward human life. When the Mau

Mau in Kenya used violent methods, they were met with extreme forms of violence by the very same British. But the most powerful argument, at least from an emotional standpoint, against the success of nonviolent methods opposing a dictator is the fate of the Jews in Germany. There are many flaws in this argument. First, there are some situations in which no method of fighting would work, and this was undoubtedly true of the plight of the Jews after World War II was under way. Incidentally, the murder camps were set up only after Germany was at war; whether even the Nazis could have perpetrated such atrocities in peacetime is problematical. The Jews had three choices, none of which could have saved their own lives: violent resistance, nonviolent resistance, and fatalistic acquiescence; and so all they could do was to die in the way most compatible with their own self-respect and most likely to win sympathy for them abroad. Most of them did not resist but simply acquiesced apathetically in their own destruction. There are many moving anecdotes of Jews who, having received a notice to report to the police station, would go to their non-Jewish friends and say farewell, without expressing any thought of attempting to escape. No one knows what might have happened had the Jews resorted to nonviolent methods of resistance early in the Nazi regime. Suppose, for example, in organized fashion they had refused to wear the stigmatizing armbands and forced the police to publicly drag them off to prison. This would at least have made it more difficult for the German people to pretend they did not know what was going on. One cannot know what effect this might have had.

The question really comes down to whether the group standards of the rulers are sufficiently strong to sustain indefinitely a program of slaughter and torture against a trained, undefeated people who steadfastly maintain a pattern of behavior which tends to inhibit aggressiveness. It must be remembered that the maintenance of a dictatorship requires constant personal contact between the ruling group and the oppressed. As a clinical example of the difficulty of slaughtering a personalized enemy, an artillery observer in the last war found great satisfaction in the impersonal game of directing artillery fire until, one day, a German officer surrendered to him, and, a few minutes later, saved his life by directing him away from a heavily mined area. From that point on, directing artillery fire became in his mind a personal assault on the bodies and lives of fellow human beings. He rapidly developed incapacitating emotional symptoms and had to be hospitalized.[46] It might be added that some Russian soldiers were shot because they refused to fire on the East Germans in the nonviolent revolt which broke out in 1953. Thus, although it is clear that a nonviolent campaign against a dictatorship might be very costly in lives and difficult to maintain, it is not a foregone conclusion that it could not succeed.

Whether nonviolent methods of fighting can be used successfully in an international arena is unknown territory. Nations have resolved many disputes through peaceful negotiation, but these have always been held with the knowledge that violence could be resorted to if the negotiations failed. All I can hope to do, therefore, is again to indicate that nonviolent methods need not totally be excluded as a possibility.

One advantage that a nation would have, in comparison with an oppressed group under a dictatorship, is its greater command of the instruments of mass communication. It could wage a massive propaganda campaign in favor of its view, and of a form which would tend to inhibit the enemy's use of violence.

The fragmentary experimental data on the resolution of conflicts between groups suggest that the most successful way to resolve an intergroup conflict is through the creation of goals of overriding importance to both groups, which can be attained only by their cooperation. For example, in the experiment in a boys' camp, which I mentioned earlier, the experimenters eventually tried to resolve the mutual antagonism between the two groups. Merely bringing them together in social and other activities had no effect. Antagonism was markedly diminished, however, by confronting both groups with urgent threats which could be overcome only by cooperation. For example, the counselors interrupted the camp water supply, creating an emergency situation which required the efforts of the entire camp to overcome. After a few such experiences, the boys began to choose friends from the other group as well as their own.[47]

On the international scene, there are many potential goals

which are analogous—for example, the exploration of the undersea world, the conquest of outer space, and cooperative efforts to speed the economic advance of the developing countries. Moreover, these activities would offer substitute goals for the satisfaction of drives which in the past have been satisfied by war. Many years ago William James pointed out that one of the major attractions of war lay in the opportunity it afforded for heroism, adventure, self-sacrifice, group solidarity, and so on. He called for the development of "moral equivalents for war"[48] which would meet similar needs. Modern technology has made such moral equivalents potentially available on a scale never before possible. This imaginative exploitation could lead to the redirection of much human energy now expended in warlike pursuits.

Let me in conclusion try to make this discussion of nonviolence more concrete. Suppose that America had committed itself to exclusive reliance on means other than military force for pursuing its aims and defending its values. It then would welcome the Russian proposal for complete disarmament in a given number of years—not out of fear but from the conviction that it would be to our advantage, because our goals can be achieved only through peaceful means.

In this connection, it should be stressed that commitment to nonviolent means does not require instantaneous total disarmament, any more than belief in the decisive power of superior violence requires the immediate launching of nuclear war. Actually, drastic disarmament by the United States without considerable advance preparation might plunge the world into chaos.

Ultimate values, however, guide day-to-day behavior, so renunciation of violence would be promptly reflected by a change in attitude at the conference table. If, instead of being trapped in the absurd position of having to rearm in order to disarm, we committed ourselves to the long-term goal of the nonviolent solution of disputes, at each choice point of negotiations we would select that line of action which would most foster the development of a peaceful world. We would be prepared to run risks in order to achieve this end, knowing that at worst they would be less than those entailed by the continual build-up of weapons of unlimited destructive power. We would, of course, try to establish such controls and inspection as the Russians would permit, but we would not make our disarmament contingent on having precisely the controls we desire. As we disarmed in accordance with a prearranged schedule, assuming that Russia was doing likewise, we would be taking certain other very important steps. That is, disarmament as a means of carrying out a program of nonviolence could not occur in a vacuum.

To abolish armies as well as war colleges and general staffs, as the Russian proposal requires, each country would have to wage a peaceful propaganda offensive within its borders as well as outside them; failure to do so would in itself be an evidence of bad faith. Therefore, a major task would be to change certain of our values. Although we give lip service to peace, we glorify violence, as our TV programs bear witness.[49] We would have to learn to venerate heroes of peace as we now do gangsters and desperados. This would require extensive changes in educational curricula as well as in programs of entertainment.

We would have to be prepared to make the necessary economic readjustment required by disarmament—remembering, as we did so, that arms contribute nothing to the national wealth and that if we hurled them into the sea as fast as we made them, we would be no whit poorer. The only problem would be to overcome the psychological barrier against making the necessary plans for conversion of the armaments industries to other types of production.[50]

Believers in nonviolence would have to learn the methods of nonviolence, for the most pessimistic possibility is that they might have to resist seizure of power by internal as well as external groups, or even that an internal group might try to foment a war in a desperate effort to keep control. The optimistic possibility is that the growth of a movement for nonviolence in any one country would encourage the like-minded in other countries, leading to increasing pressures on all governments to negotiate their differences peaceably.

Externally we would make every effort to expand peaceful communication, not only with Russia but with the rest of the world. We would especially emphasize cooperative activities toward the attainment of superordinate goals, such as the highly successful International Geophysical Year. The stronger habits of cooperation became, the more effectively they would inhibit a subsequent resort to violence. Along the same lines, we would work toward peaceful resolution of outstanding tension spots in the world, such as Berlin, Korea, and Taiwan. We could not expect to resolve all the disputes in our favor. We have gotten ourselves into certain positions which are untenable with or without war, and we would have to recognize this fact. We would in each case seek the solution which most furthers the cause of universal peace, rather than the one which seems to promote an illusory national interest.

We would launch an all-out effort to win over the uncommitted countries to allegiance to our way of life. This would involve measures to raise their economic level by self-aid, expansion of medical help, and so on. We would endeavor wherever possible to conduct these programs in cooperation with the Russians, rather than in competition with them.

Finally, we would work toward bringing about worldwide disarmament and building up institutional machinery for the peaceful solution of international disputes. This would, of course, require surrender of some aspects of national sovereignty. This may not be so difficult as we come to realize that the advent of modern weaponry has doomed unlimited sovereignty, in any case.

The most favorable outcome of this program would be that each successive disarmament step would become easier as its advantages to all countries became increasingly obvious, culminating in an increasingly prosperous world which contained strong inhibitions against resorting to violence and increasingly effective institutional means for peaceful resolution of disputes.

In such a world, any government that contemplated taking advantage of the general disarmament to blackmail another country through threat of force would face extremely unpleasant consequences. First of all, such a move would have a profoundly demoralizing effect within the country that made it. Even an absolutely ruthless dictatorship cannot make major changes in policy overnight without consideration of the feelings of the population. It can change it tactics, as the Hitler-

Stalin Pact shows, but it cannot swing instantly from a peacetime to a wartime psychology. Even Hitler, who probably conducted the most vigorous internal campaign to glorify war in the world's history, required several years to rouse Germany's martial fervor sufficiently to enable him to start the last war. Russian leaders would have a considerably more difficult time, especially if the liberalizing process in Russia had been accelerated by increasing prosperity, rise in educational level, and removal of the threat of war.

An even more serious consequence would be that every country of the world would rearm as rapidly as possible and the aggressor would be the enemy of them all. Since the countries would still know how to make weapons of limitless destructive power and since some of these weapons—notably bacteriological ones—are very cheap and easy to produce, the government which threatened violence would have to be prepared to police the entire world. Finally, she would know that she would meet stubborn nonviolent resistance in the countries she occupied.

But what if one country did announce, after the world was disarmed, that she had retained enough nuclear weapons to destroy America, and attempted to coerce us? To keep the discussion concrete, I shall assume that this country is Russia, although it could be any other country. America, if we continued to follow the policy of nonviolent resistance, would refuse to submit, pointing out that although Russia could destroy us, she could not coerce us. Three choices would be left to Russia—to exterminate us with a nuclear raid; to occupy us; or to use her superior force to weaken our influence internationally by threatening our allies and the uncommitted nations.

The first choice—a nuclear raid—would be unlikely, for the main incentive for such a raid—the fear that we would strike first—would be gone. Moreover, her aim would be coercion, not destruction, and she would much prefer to take over an intact country and make it work for her than to have to deal with a radioactive desert. Thus the risk of nuclear attack under these conditions seems worth taking in view of the infinitely greater risk of destruction through involvement in a nuclear war.

An attempt to occupy us would be more probable, but this would be difficult, for she would have to reassemble an invasion force. Meanwhile, we would use all possible means of mobilizing world opinion against her and of strengthening the will to resist of our own people by propaganda and refresher courses in nonviolent resistance. She would then know that if she did succeed in occupying us, she would be in for a long and difficult fight, while world opinion would become more antagonistic and the danger of other countries' arming would be steadily increasing. If she nevertheless occupied us, our nonviolent methods would probably be costly in lives, and they might not succeed. But even if they failed, it would be better to die in a course of action which held out some hope for the future than as part of a general holocaust. The cause of freedom might be set back for a time, but I am convinced that eventually it would prevail, for the only sure way of extinguishing the spark of liberty is through the destruction of the human race.

More likely than outright occupation would be the effort by Russia to use her superior force to overcome our influence in doubtful areas of the world and to gradually encroach upon us in this way. But she would have to be prepared to cope with the disillusionment of her own people and to face the reinstatement of international anarchy and resort to arms all over the world. If, nevertheless, she persisted, we would have to rely on the determinations of the peoples involved to resist because they had been convinced of the superiority of our way of life. Obviously, we would lose in some areas, as we will if we rely on force. But again in the long run the future for humanity would be much brighter.

It therefore seems possible that, having considered nuclear blackmail, Russia would decide that the game was not worth the candle, and would commit herself to the peaceful competition she already professes to want.

This analysis of the renunciation of violence does not mean failure to appreciate the evils of communism, or underestimation of the Communist drive for world domination. It does imply recognition of the fact that the values we believe in can be promulgated only by peaceful means. Commitment to winning through possession of superior destructive power leads further and further along the road to a garrison state at home and tyranny abroad. At home we are witnessing a steady erosion of freedom. Dissent becomes ever more dangerous. Not long ago, some Baltimore high school students mobbed a young man who was merely trying to peddle a Socialist newspaper. We are told that technology has become so complicated that decisions concerning the life and death of mankind can be made only by experts, unharrassed by the pressures of public opinion. A short time ago our President rebuked no less a person than the Chairman of the Senate Foreign Relations Committee for daring publicly to question our China policy on the ground that this endangered our will to resist. Abroad, by compelling countries to assume large, uneconomic arms burdens we hinder their development and heighten international fear.

I believe it safe to assert that all human beings aspire to freedom. The common denominator of all psychiatric illnesses is that they impose limits on the patient's freedom, and his longing to be free of the tyranny of his symptoms is a very strong motive for accepting the work and suffering often entailed by psychotherapy. At the level of societies, men have always striven for freedom, even though poverty, ignorance, and fear have sometimes made them willing to accept tyranny as the price of food and safety. As Gandhi said: "For the starving men and women, liberty and God are merely letters put together without the slightest meaning; the deliverer of these unfortunate people would be the one who brought them a crust of bread." A rising level of education and prosperity in a world at peace is regularly accompanied by a growth of freedom. In this connection, evidence of the growth of individual freedom in Russia is overwhelming; only those completely blinded by the stereotype of the enemy can fail to see this. And our commitment to the renunciation of force, far from being a surrender to communism, might be the most effective way of fighting its tyrannical aspects and fostering a growth within Communist societies of the values in which we believe.

What are the chances that conversion to abandonment of force as an arbiter of international conflicts could come about? As I have already suggested, this would involve a change in attitudes of the magnitude of the religious conversion of an individual or a major revolution inside a country, such as took place in Russia with the overthrow of czarism. Not much is known about the conditions fostering either individual or group conversions, but it must be confessed that the little that is known is not encouraging. Individual conversions may be the result of a long, gradual process of education and indoctrination, or they may be precipitated suddenly by a catastrophic psychic experience. Sudden religious conversions occur typically in persons who have undergone a long period of desperation, hopelessness, or panic. To use a phrase of which alcoholics are fond, they have "hit bottom."

But sometimes the alcoholic "sees bottom" before he hits it; the disastrous ultimate effects of the course on which he is embarked become very vivid to him before they actually transpire, and he is converted to abstinence. Perhaps it may be possible for the peoples of the world to renounce violence if they see the "bottom" to which modern weapons are leading them before it actually comes to pass.

While even less is known about the conversion of groups than of individuals, there are some hints that it may be easier to change group standards than to change those of individuals. Witness the fact that Germany and Japan changed in our eyes from diabolical enemies to trusted allies in about a decade.

In all honesty, the most likely source of a conversion of mankind to renunciation of mass violence would be a nuclear accident which would bring home the horrors of modern war. We must, however, bend every effort to develop group standards of nonviolence through intensive educational methods. It may be hopeful that America, in contrast to many European countries, has glorified nonmilitary figures, such as Benjamin Franklin, Thomas Jefferson, and Thomas Edison. Even Abraham Lincoln and Woodrow Wilson, although they became war leaders, might be included in this category. Perhaps we can exploit the potent TV image of the heroic cowboy who throws away his gun and faces down the villain by sheer will power. To be sure, this scene usually culminates in a glorious fist fight, but basically it is a situation in which the person who possesses superior destructive power is inhibited from using it.

In view of the present grave and entirely unprecedented threat to survival, it is important to examine all our patterns of behavior to discover which are still useful and which must be modified. Then we must fully exploit those which still work and endeavor to change the others. Among patterns of human interaction which undoubtedly still are valid are certain features of internal organization of societies, such as relations of larger to smaller units of governments and of governments to individual citizens, the role of the legal system in a society, and so on. Certain patterns of negotiation and diplomacy at the international level are probably also appropriate to present conditions. But the time-hallowed institution of war must eventually be abandoned if the human adventure is to continue.

As an eminent German scientist, C. F. von Weizsacker, has said: "The renunciation of war is no longer a pious hope but a necessity. The only question is whether mankind will arrive at it before or after a catastrophe."[51] It seems to me that the necessary first step toward achieving this goal without a catastrophe is to combat the world-wide hypnotic fixation on superior violence as the ultimate arbiter of conflict. This would release the imaginations of the world's intellectual, moral, and political leaders to devise constructive alternatives for war. If this can be accomplished, it would liberate man's energies to create a world of unimaginable plenty in which humanity, freed at last from poverty and war, could develop its full potentialities. One may hope that the human mind, which has proved capable of splitting the atom and putting satellites in space, will also prove equal to this supreme challenge.

13. Psychologic Aspects of
International Negotiations

WAR HAS ALWAYS BEEN the ultimate means for settling international disputes, but many international quarrels have been settled by other methods, among which are bilateral negotiations between representatives of the contending parties. As war becomes increasingly unworkable, the new conditions of life must be exploited to make these and other methods of nonviolent conflict resolution more effective and to create new ones.

In limiting myself to a consideration of bilateral negotiations, I fully realize that, no matter how skillfully conducted, they are merely a means to an end. In themselves they cannot ensure a world of enduring peace, which requires a system of international institutions for adjudicating disputes and enforcing their judgments. Moreover, they represent only one type of negotiation. The reason for excluding other procedures such as mediation, arbitration, and, above all, continuing international forums like the United Nations, which offers diplomats new opportunities for creating flexible patterns of negotiation, is partly limitation of time and knowledge but mainly because bilateral negotiations have been the object of more empirical and experimental studies that highlight some of their psychologic obstacles and how they might be overcome.

To avoid misunderstanding, let me state at the outset that the main determinant of success or failure in negotiations is, of course, the nature of the issue itself. The more the negotiators desire an agreement on an issue and the greater the relative rewards for reaching one and the penalties for failing, the more likely it is that an agreement will be reached. Furthermore, it is easier to reach agreements about matters that do not involve very high stakes and in which gains and losses are immediate and obvious. An agreement for scientific cooperation in the Antarctic, for example, was considerably easier to negotiate than would be one to halt the arms race. In the former, life and death were not at stake and the potential rewards for agreeing were clear and immediate. In the latter, the stakes are astronomically higher, and both the gains from a disarmament agreement and the penalties for not agreeing are unclear and hard to place in time.

What psychologists are interested in are aspects of negotiations that operate more or less regardless of the substantive questions involved and that, therefore, can impede or facilitate negotiations about any issue.

Often the influence of these features on the outcome is only marginal, but since they may influence the very definition of the issue to be negotiated and the participants' perceptions of the potential rewards and punishments for different outcomes, they may be more important than appears at first glance.

The outcome of negotiations is undoubtedly affected by the personal attributes of the negotiators, including their sensitivities, momentary emotional states, and conditions of health. One cannot help wondering, for example, what effects Franklin Roosevelt's moribund condition at Yalta had on the agreements reached there. The present state of the art, however, does not permit the development of a systematic body of knowledge about the effects of personalities of negotiators on the outcome of negotiations, so I shall move promptly to features of the negotiating process itself.

A pervasive obstacle to international negotiation is sheer difficulty in communication arising from differences in language, cultural background, and habits of thought of the negotiators, and especially mutual mistrust. The latter looms large when the countries represented at the negotiating table have a history of mutual hostility. As a diplomatic historian has put it with respect to the United States and Russia:

For Moscow to propose what we can accept seems to us even more sinister and dangerous than for it to propose what we cannot accept. Our instinct is to cast about for grounds on which to discredit the proposal instead of seizing it and making the most of it. Being distrustful of the Greeks bearing gifts, we are afraid of being tricked.[1]

The Russians no doubt feel the same way about us.

Mutual distrust is also justified by certain dynamic properties of the negotiating process itself, to which I shall return, but first let me discuss briefly the communication problems created by differing cultural backgrounds of the negotiators. Wedge and Muromcew have analyzed the transcripts of the first 116 sessions of the eighteen-nation disarmament conference and reached some conclusions about the background assumptions of the Russians.[2] (As Americans, it was naturally easier for them to see the Russian preconceptions than the American ones.)

Behind all the obstacles to agreement on specific issues or modes of procedure was a difference in the way Americans and Russians habitually tackle problems. The latter's approach is universalistic and deductive—they want to start with the general principle and deduce the specific case from it. Americans, on the other hand, are pragmatic and inductive. They prefer to take one step at a time and decide on the next step after they see how the last one has worked. Appeals to reason or principle work best with Russians; appeals to fact and concrete details carry most weight with Americans.

These traits are reflected even in the language used to characterize negotiating proposals. The Russians use words like "correct" and "incorrect," the Americans "acceptable" and "unacceptable." The Russians look for the "right" solution, the Americans for the "preferred" one.[3]

For a long time American and Russian disarmament proposals reflected this difference in approach. The Americans proposed proceeding step by step, checking how well each had worked before moving on to the next. The Russians insisted that the Americans commit themselves at every step to total and complete disarmament before starting. Perhaps the Americans feared to accept the general principle in advance because they could not foresee all its consequences, and some of these might prove to give the Russians an advantage. The Russians, on the other hand, might have feared that unless the Americans committed themselves to the whole process, they might refuse to go on if any step turned out to give them an edge.

That culturally determined differences in outlook also complicate the carrying-out of agreements reached through negotiations has been shown by Wedge's study of the vicissitudes of the Russian-American student exchange program. The Russians saw this as an agreement between governments which make decisions and speak for their citizens; the American government saw itself as the agency of the Inter-Universities Committee on Travel Grants, which represented individual students who wished to study in Russia. The Soviet ministry expected that the American universities would accept its nominees without question and that it would supervise the study programs of the American students. When the American committee requested more data to determine where the Russian students could best be placed, and finally rejected a few on the ground that they were insufficiently qualified, the Soviets took this both as a politically inspired capricious rejection of official judgments and a derogation of Soviet academic degrees.

On the other hand, Americans, raised in the tradition of free scholarship, were resentful when they found that they were expected to accept programs given them by the Soviet educational authorities and that they would not be permitted to study certain subjects ideologically distasteful to the Russians.

> Each side felt the other was sabotaging the agreement and each was trying quite vigorously to impose its standards on the other. . . . There could be no doubt of the sincere efforts of each side to make the program work, to be maximally accommodating to the other, and there could be no doubt . . . each side believed the other to be deliberately obstructionistic.[4]

Fortunately, the exchange program has managed to limp along despite such misunderstandings, and perhaps the experience gained in circumventing them will make more far-reaching agreements easier to arrange when the time is appropriate.

Turning now to the effects of structural properties of the negotiating situation that influence outcome regardless of the issues involved, the personal attributes of the negotiators, or cultural differences in the groups they represent, an illuminating series of experiments has been conducted by Blake and his co-workers.[5] Taking advantage of the setting of training laboratories in group development, in which persons live together for several days, they formed groups of adults who met together for the first three days in five or six sessions, each lasting two hours, to study, on themselves, the process of group formation. At the end of this time they had become real groups with a sense of identity, cohesiveness, and a rudimentary group structure. Each group was then given a type of problem familiar to them, such as one concerning the operation of a business firm or the handling of a deviant student in college, and told to prepare and type up a solution in three hours. In any one experiment, all groups received the same problem.

The solution of each group was then distributed to the other group or groups involved in the experiment. Each was asked to familiarize itself with the solutions of the others, either by studying them separately or listening to discussions among the captains elected by each group.

After the groups signified that each fully understood the other's solution, the captains met in the presence of their groups to try to agree on which solution was the better. The members of each group were permitted to communicate with their captains privately but could not enter the discussion.

The confrontation of the group captains resembles international negotiations in that negotiators come to the table as representatives of groups that already have their own proposed solutions to the problem. It differs from international negotiations in many ways, among them that the negotiators cannot modify their groups' solutions, and that a neutral individual or small panel makes the final decision if the negotiators cannot agree.

The central finding was that sixty of sixty-two negotiations ended in deadlock. By contrast, the uncommitted judges easily picked the better solution every time.[6]

The reason for this unhappy outcome was, of course, the

commitment of each group to its own solution. As a result, whenever a team captain showed signs of yielding, his fellow group members demanded that he stand firm. The two captains who did give in were severely criticized by their team mates. This phenomenon has been termed the "traitor trap."[7] A negotiator who yields always runs the danger of being accused of betraying his group.

Another relevant finding was that, despite the conviction of the members of each competing group that they fully understood the proposal of their rivals, actually they did not. This was demonstrated by giving each participant, before the start of the negotiations but after they had indicated that they had fully understood their rival's proposal, a list of 40 statements, 10 contained in the proposals of both groups, 10 not contained in either, and 10 each in the proposal of a member's own group but not in that of the other. They were asked to classify these statements in their appropriate categories. Twenty out of 20 groups and 165 out of 195 group members identified correctly more items from their own group's position than from their competitor's.[8] They identified items from both groups' proposals much more often as in their group's only than as either absent from both or exclusively in the opponent's.[9] Needless to say, groups who simply studied the proposals without a competitive "set" showed no such distortions.

Along with inability to hear what the adversary was saying or identify its source correctly when they heard it, went an overvaluation of the solution of one's own group. In one experiment, of 48 possible comparisons, 46 groups thought their own solution to be superior, and the remaining two were tied.[10]

If artificially composed groups dealing with hypothetical problems regularly developed this much distortion of memory and perception and rigidity of behavior when in conflict, it is a wonder that international negotiations over vital issues are ever successful.

Dynamics of international negotiations have also been illuminated by the study of so-called mixed-motive games. (The term "game" in this sense has nothing to do with amusement, but describes a type of interaction in which the moves of each participant are influenced by the moves of the other.) In mixed-motive games, as contrasted to games like chess or poker in which the interests of the players conflict, participants have some interests in common and some opposed, and the best outcome for both sides can be obtained only if each takes the other's interests into account as well as his own. If each considers his own interests only, both wind up with an outcome neither prefers.

Russian-American disarmament negotiations afford a good example. For both parties, an agreement that slowed or reversed the arms race would be preferable to no agreement. To this extent their interests coincide. But their interests also conflict in that each wants to achieve or maintain superiority in armaments. So each is torn between the desire to reach an agreement that gives him the advantage and the fear that if he is too adamant no agreement at all will be reached.

This kind of bargaining situation has certain obvious implications for negotiations. First, the more disadvantageous the failure to reach agreement is to both sides, the more likely they are to arrive at an agreement. Thus industrial strikes seem to have to go on until both labor and management are hurting sufficiently, so that the disadvantages of a contract containing concessions to the adversary outweigh those of continuing the strike. This dynamic is apparent in the delay over the ratification of the nuclear nonproliferation pact. Whether the hold-out powers will ratify or not depends on the relative weights they assign to the drawbacks of surrendering certain potential advantages of the present anarchic state of affairs, as compared to their fears of the alternative—the continued unrestricted spread of nuclear weapons. As the dangers created by the latter mount, chances for ratification increase.

Another implication of mixed-motive games is that the player who appears more anxious to reach an agreement is immediately at a disadvantage, because this implies that he fears failure to reach agreement more than his adversary so that he is willing to make more concessions. In negotiations to end a war it therefore makes sense to continue fighting during negotiations to increase the cost to the adversary of continuing to fight and convince him that he cannot gain his ends this way, thereby heightening his incentive to seek agreement.

I believe that much of the haggling over apparently irrelevant matters in international negotiations such as order of agenda or place of meeting is really motivated by the determination of each party to show that it is in no hurry to negotiate. Also, each fears that yielding on an apparently minor or irrelevant point will encourage the other to push for further concessions.

But the chief psychologic obstacle to reaching a solution in mixed-motive games is the temptation it creates for both players to cheat on any agreement they may reach. To continue with the arms race, assume that two nations, Neptunia and Plutonia, have signed a disarmament agreement, which, like all agreements, is not completely immune to cheating.

> "If Plutonia does not cheat," the Neptunia strategist reasons "then clearly it is in Neptunia's interest to cheat; for then we shall be ahead of Plutonia in our research on nuclear weapons. If, on the other hand, Plutonia does cheat, this is all the more reason why we should also cheat; for otherwise we let them get ahead. Consequently, regardless of whether Plutonia cheats or not, it is in our interest to cheat. We must therefore cheat in order to serve our national interest."
>
> The Plutonian strategist, being in exactly the same position, reasons in exactly the same way and comes to the same conclusion. Consequently both countries cheat and in doing so are both worse off than if they had not cheated, since otherwise there was no point to the agreement (which presumably conferred benefits on both countries).[11]

The crucial psychologic dilemma of mixed-motive games is that, while mutual trust yields the best outcome for both players, each player is tempted to try to double-cross the other. That is, the best strategy for each player would be to convince his opponent that he would cooperate and then defect. In the example, each nation would gain the most advantage if it could convince the other that it would not cheat (so that the other would not) and then cheat. Each contestant is torn between the contradictory goals of winning the other's trust and betraying it, and between his desire to trust the other and his fear of being betrayed.

Thus the success of negotiations depends not only on reaching a resolution of the issues acceptable to all concerned, but on methods of enforcement in which all sides have confidence. This does not present much of a problem within organized societies which have established and tested institutions for enforcing agreements but can be a huge obstacle in international negotiations since no analogous international institutions exist. So agreement banning underground nuclear tests is still stymied by inability of the nuclear powers to agree on methods of inspection and enforcement.

If this analysis is valid, disarmament negotiations will have some hope of success only when national leaders become willing to run risks to obtain disarmament agreements comparable to those they now run in pursuit of illusory security through armaments. For disarmament negotiations to succeed, the participants would have to be convinced that the risk of no agreement outweighed the risk of being cheated by the adversary. In the past both risks were familiar—the latter is as old as human perfidy and the former simply meant continuance of an old-style arms race which each side hoped to win. With the advent of modern weaponry, the first risk has changed drastically. An uncontrolled nuclear, chemical, and biologic arms race cannot be won and is something humanity has never experienced before. A major psychologic obstacle to success in disarmament negotiations seems to be the underestimation of this brand-new danger in comparison with being cheated, a familiar, highly unpleasant, and dangerous experience. So even though the arms race presents an enormous risk in the long run, the risk that an adversary might gain a small temporary advantage by cheating on an agreement is psychologically far more potent, and so no agreement is reached.

Empirical and experimental studies of negotiations confirm the obvious fact that, regardless of the issues, a successful outcome is impeded by absence of mutual trust and lack of full and accurate communication between negotiators, and by certain structural properties of the negotiating situation. These studies also offer certain leads as to how negotiations could be improved.

It is reasonable to assume some potential basis for mutual

trust in almost all international negotiations. Thus one important way of improving the chances for the successful outcome of negotiations, regardless of substantive issues, would be to pinpoint and combat sources of mutual mistrust that may obscure underlying bases for trust. For example, participants in all negotiations could well make special efforts to bring into the open psychologic sources of mutual misunderstanding and mistrust that are out of awareness. These include conflicting habits of thought and ways of proceeding and, above all, the universal difficulty in really hearing what the other fellow is saying. Adlai Stevenson's quip "I sometimes think that what America needs more than anything else is a hearing aid" applies to all countries. If it could only be enforced, a splendid ground rule for all negotiations would be that bargaining could not start until each party could express the position of the other to the latter's satisfaction.[12] Unfortunately, as the experiments on understanding the adversary's position demonstrate, this is much harder to do than might appear at first glance. I urge everyone to try it the next time he finds himself in disagreement with a friend or colleague. It is amazing how one's own thoughts keep intruding. Merely striving for this goal, however, even if it is unattainable, would improve the atmosphere of all negotiations. As all psychotherapists know, the best way to get someone's favorable attention is to listen to him, not talk to him. To feel that a person, especially one you believe to be hostile or indifferent, is trying his best to understand you creates a very favorable impression of his good sense, intelligence, and good will. You are then in a much more receptive frame of mind for his ideas.[13]

From the structural standpoint, the goal would be to set up conditions that foster a cooperative rather than a competitive stance in the negotiators. The aim would be to reduce the barriers between the groups by making each feel, at every step of the way, that it is working on a joint enterprise. For example, instead of negotiators being selected by each group separately, they could be chosen jointly from a panel of names put up by each. This "criss-cross" panel would weaken the "traitor trap" because the negotiators would consider themselves as representatives of both groups, who would have implicitly committed themselves in advance to accept the outcome of the bargaining.[14] While this procedure is hardly feasible at the moment in international political negotiations, it could perhaps be used to improve cultural, economic, and scientific ones.

Pursung this same line, at every step of the way it might be possible to involve both groups in selecting problems to be discussed and devising alternative solutions, thereby taking advantage of the greater readiness of persons to accept innovations when they feel they have participated in planning for them.[15] The crucial importance of this principle has become increasingly apparent in negotiations to develop programs to improve Negro-white relationships, and there must be a way of applying it to international problems as well.

While procedural suggestions like these would increase the likelihood that negotiations over any particular issue would be successful, the most important single determinant of success remains the degree to which both sides believe that the other will adhere to any agreement reached, which brings me back once again to the theme of mutual trust. In concluding, therefore, I would like to widen the frame of reference to consider two new conditions of modern life, one of which creates new opportunities to penalize the breaking of agreements, the other new incentives to hold to them.

In a world full of nuclear weapons, it is probably impossible to enforce agreements by military sanctions, since a very small nation with a few nuclear weapons at its disposal could defy the world. The nuclear bomb plays the same role on the international scene as the pistol did in the wild West; it is the great equalizer. Modern electronic mass communications, however, especially communication satellites like Telstar and Early Bird, do seem to be creating a world public opinion which in time may eventually exert considerable constraints on national leaders. I cannot but wonder whether the strong emotional reaction of American leaders at the thought of a war crimes trial of American fliers in North Vietnam may not have reflected this new concern. Apparently some twelve fliers had been quietly executed, but this created no uproar. What apparently upset American leaders was the prospect of a public trial in which the actions of American soldiers would be displayed before the world as crimes.

An imaginative proposal that dramatizes the potentialities of a mobilized world public opinion is that for a "Court of International Delinquency."[16] Such a court would be empowered to try individual national leaders for offenses against the peace and security of mankind, as defined by the International Law Commission of the United Nations. If they refused an invitation to appear before it, they could be tried *in absentia* and without the consent of their governments, if necessary.

The court would have no power to impose sanctions on states, thereby circumventing one of the main current obstacles to an effective World Court. Nor could it punish the accused, if found guilty, by imprisonment or fines, so there would be no problem of trying to enforce its decisions if a nation backed the accused leader. If a national leader were convicted of violating a treaty, for example, the court could hold him up to public disgrace. It could recommend that other nations treat him as *persona non grata* by refusing to recognize his credentials of office, to grant him a visa, and the like. In the extreme case this would amount to banishment, not from his own country but from the world community. The convicted leader would be a prisoner within the borders of his own nation. A leader held up to international obloquy would have trouble maintaining his position at home. Even today national leaders make great efforts to appear in a good light, not only before their own countrymen but before the rest of the world. In short, the sanctions at the disposal of such a court might be considerably more powerful than appear at first glance.

On the positive side, modern science and technology have opened many new fields for international cooperation to achieve goals that no nation can achieve alone—that is, they can be reached only by nations working together. The incentive for adhering to such agreements is not the fear of punishment for breaking them but the rewards for keeping them.

One such undertaking has been running smoothly for some years—the cooperative exploration of the earth's crust and the oceans instituted by the International Geophysical Year. The treaty demilitarizing the Antarctic, which safeguards this activity, has not caused a particle of trouble because it is self-enforcing. That is, it is to the interest of every nation not to violate it because the gains from respecting it outweigh any gains that might result from attempting to militarize their zone at the cost of destroying the agreement. Scientists have outlined literally dozens of similar international projects that would have enormous pay-offs.[17]

Perhaps the most hopeful area for cooperative international research is outer space, including the moon and planets. The pay-off in terms of gains and knowledge, and therefore inevitably in human welfare, would undoubtedly be enormous, and the resources required to do an adequate job are beyond the reach of even the richest nation. The area is new, so it is not yet cluttered up with vested interests. To be sure, gains in knowledge about outer space do have military implications, and this is the most serious obstacle to international cooperation. But so far at least, nations seem prepared to forego possible military advantages, as the unanimous United Nations resolutions against the orbiting of weapons bears witness. And so far the potential military implications have not prevented the favorable reception by all countries of the space triumphs of Russia and the United States. The conquest of space is essentially an undertaking of all mankind. When Gagarin or Grissom is lost, the whole world mourns; and when either the United States or Russia achieves a new space triumph, people everywhere share the feeling of pride. Americans and Russians can sincerely congratulate each other on a new space feat, a response that would be unthinkable to an improved nuclear missile.

Although only a minute number of persons is involved in such activities, thanks to the human capacity for identification, all members of a group can participate vicariously in the acts of its representatives. Entire student bodies of colleges and large segments of the citizenry of cities become emotionally involved in the fortunes of their athletic teams, and the hero's receptions accorded to astronauts and cosmonauts indicate that the public at large shares the thrill of their achievements.

These considerations suggest that for cooperative international ventures to have the greatest beneficial effect on international attitudes, it would be important to dramatize the fact that the persons involved are participating as representatives of their nations, not as individuals.

·Successful international projects that benefit all mankind would facilitate international negotiations in several ways. Through working together nations strengthen patterns of cooperation and generate mutual trust, which would gradually extend to other areas. The international agencies required to conduct these projects create precedents and procedures for international conflict resolution that could and would be applied to other fields. As beneficial results accumulate, they increase incentives for international cooperation in ever widening areas of mutual interest. In these ways international scientific projects could create the atmosphere and lay the necessary institutional groundwork for eventual adherence by all nations to international institutions for preserving peace.

14. Behavioral Scientists and International Affairs

WE ARE LIVING in a time of the most rapid and drastic changes in the conditions of human life that mankind has ever known. These changes, brought about by science and technology, are creating new hopes and new dangers. For the first time we can realistically envisage a world without poverty, hunger, ignorance or chronic disease, closely knit by communication and transportation, in which the brotherhood of man could become a reality. At the same time, humanity has at last achieved the power to exterminate itself. The challenge to our generation is to change ingrained patterns of perception and behavior swiftly and drastically enough to overcome the dangers and realize the hopes. As Kenneth Boulding has said: "If the human race is to survive it will have to change its ways of thinking more in the next 25 years than it has done in the last 25,000."[1]

As so often seems to be the case in human affairs, the threatened evil is imminent, the hoped-for benefit problematical. The world of human brotherhood and enduring peace lies in the distant future; the suicide of mankind can occur any day.

President Kennedy put it metaphorically: "Every man, woman, and child lives under a nuclear sword of Damocles, hanging by the slenderest of threads, capable of being cut at any moment by accident, miscalculation, or madness."[2] In more prosaic terms it has been estimated that the United States and the Soviet Union have in deliverable form about one-eighth of the amount of fissionable material required to wipe out life on earth, and all signs point to further increases as other nations begin to make their own nuclear weapons.

Political and military leaders and scientists agree that the unlimited destructive power of modern weaponry has made the eventual elimination of war necessary for human survival. Since war is woven into all aspects of modern society and has afforded a way of satisfying all sorts of human drives, both aggressive and altruistic, eliminating it will require an immense effort. Not only must we forestall its outbreak, but for the long pull we must find other means of satisfying human needs that war has met in the past and develop new methods of resolving international conflicts that are suited for the nuclear age. This task can be accomplished only by massive, concerted, and persistent efforts of experts in human behavior, along with those in many other fields.

To be sure, determinants of war and peace lie primarily in the realms of politics, economics, and military science, as do hopes of finding substitutes for war and creating an enduring peace. However, national leaders, not nations, interact, and weapons do not fire themselves, unless men finally decide to abdicate this function to computers. Considerations of national policy, military and economic strength and the like determine the behavior of leaders to a large extent, but psychological factors may also powerfully influence their decisions.

Elimination of the ever growing threat of extinction posed by nuclear weapons will require drastic changes in those traditional attitudes and modes of behavior that were once adaptive but were rendered maladaptive by these weapons. These include such deeply ingrained and virtually universal patterns as resort to war to resolve international disputes, or the conviction that national security is a function of the size of the weapons stockpile a nation possesses. To break away from such fallacies and develop new patterns of behavior compatible with survival requires the best efforts of experts in all fields of knowledge, including specialists in human behavior and communication.

The successful application of psychological knowledge to foreign affairs requires mutual education. The politician must be educated to see the relevance of these concepts, and the psychiatrist must become informed about the details of the specific problems to which he tries to apply them. In the meanwhile, I believe psychiatrists can make most headway by fully acknowledging the limitations of what they can offer, while making every effort to make their analyses as specific as possible.

As a contribution toward improving communication between behavioral scientists and makers of foreign policy, this paper lists some obstacles to acceptance of efforts to apply psychological insights to international affairs and one or two examples of contributions that seem to have gained a hearing, based largely on personal experience.

Efforts to bring psychological principles to bear on international relations in a systematic fashion are novel, and therefore run into certain obstacles that retard the acceptance of any innovation.

One obstacle is erected by the people whom behavioral scientists are trying to reach. Many psychiatrists have become concerned about problems of war and peace because they recognize that modern genocidal weapons for the first time threaten the survival of the human species and that these weapons have invalidated the time-hallowed conviction that a nation's power and security is primarily a function of the size of its stockpile of weapons. They may be more sensitive than the average citizen to the tendency to cling to ingrained patterns of behavior that have become maladaptive because they see this so frequently in their patients. Psychiatrists know only too well how tenaciously patients resist abandoning behavior on which they have relied for security, however self-defeating it may become. Politicians also mobilize their defenses against abandoning maladaptive behavior, the most usual one being to dismiss those who point to the futility of achieving national security through arms in a nuclear world as idealists who do not understand reality. A politician with whom I have had many fruitless interchanges, for example, persists in seeing my position as advocating disarming ourselves unilaterally and trusting the good-will of the Russians. By this means he manages not to listen to a rather complex argument concerning the importance of developing other ways of maintaining national power and security, as weapons cease to serve this purpose.

But serious obstacles to communication are, I believe, created by psychiatrists themselves. One of these may be termed psychological imperialism. The heady realization that one's area of knowledge and expertise may be applied to another field, especially one concerned with human survival, is apt to generate uncritical enthusiasm, with overvaluation of the importance of the new insights, and attempts to apply them indiscriminately. One gains the impression from reading some of the early psychiatric literature on international affairs, for example, that international conflicts are caused primarily by unconscious perceptual distortions and motivations of national leaders which would dissolve if they could all be psychoanalyzed. Yet it is quite clear that in the realm of arms control, for example, the main obstacles to progress are genuine clashes of interest and realistic fears of the opponents' capabilities and intentions. Mutual distortions can aggravate these to be sure, but they do not create them, nor will exploring the distortions automatically resolve the issues in dispute.

Furthermore, most of the data from which psychiatrists try to extrapolate to international affairs come from the clinic or the couch. Amazingly, insights derived from these sources sometimes do seem to be relevant to international behavior, but it is well to be ever mindful that, as Winston Churchill said of Clement Attlee, psychiatrists in international affairs have a lot to be modest about.

A second barrier to communication created by psychiatrists, which is, I am glad to say, rapidly diminishing, is the temptation to resort to clinical generalities that seem to be explanatory but really serve only to obscure a simple point with irrelevancies. To quote an example from a statement by a psychiatrist concerning chemical-biological weapons:

> Certain specific features of chemical and biological weapons, such as their invisibility and modes of action, are particularly likely to revive and intensify anxieties, fantasies and conflicts dating back to childhood which, although outgrown by many people, often remain buried in the irrational depths of the mind.[3]

God knows that the human mind has irrational depths and that we all have anxieities; but what is the relevance of their having been incurred in childhood and why is the invisibility of chemical and biological weapons more apt to stir them up than the visible explosion of a bomb?

In this particular example, the simple and well-established psychological principle that a perceptually ambiguous threat is especially frightening is needlessly obscured. Incidentally, the point, although valid, is unfortunately irrelevant in that the fact that chemical and biological weapons frighten their victims would hardly be regarded by their proponents as an argument against their use.

In short, a lot of psychiatric and psychological writing on international affairs falls into the same category as the all-purpose political speech or the daily horoscope. By using concepts into which people can read whatever they like and which are appropriate to almost any situation, one gives the appearance of having explained something without really doing so.

To turn from problems of style to those of substance, one area in which psychiatry might be supposed to have something to offer would be the prediction of behavior of negotiators and national leaders from systematic analysis of their personal characteristics. In the conduct of foreign affairs mutual appraisals of each other's personalities by diplomats and heads of state have always played an important if nebulous role. The experienced, skillful negotiator senses the strong and weak points of his opposite number, when it is appropriate to bluff, when to compromise, when to stand firm, and so on; and leaders often base decisions of national policy on implicit psychological evaluations of leaders of other nations. One would like to think that the application of psychiatric knowledge could improve the accuracy and reliability of these assessments. Unfortunately, however, partly because leaders will not submit themselves to depth interviews and partly because concepts relating personality to behavior are still very crude, it will be a long while before the appraisals of the clinician will surpass in accuracy the intuitions of the experienced negotiator.

In the present state of the art, perhaps the chief contribution behavioral scientists can make is, as experts in communications, to call attention to common problems of international communication that may cause difficulty regardless of the individuals involved. As Senator Fulbright has put it, we can "articulate concepts which politicians often sense but cannot readily explain."[4] By reminding politicians of some general psychological principles related to their thinking and behavior, we may perhaps enable them to escape the traps into which they have repeatedly fallen. A good example is the characteristic underestimation of the enemy's will to resist. Despite the fact that the Battle of Britain failed to break the British fighting spirit and massive bombing of German cities likewise failed to bring Germany to its knees in World War II, American military leaders assumed that bombing North Vietnam would cause the North Vietnamese resistance to crumble.

Let me turn now to a few examples of the kind of psychological insights which have been relatively well received by politicians and diplomats. One, which has been the most completely documented, is that a person's perception of events is always colored by the culture in which he lives and that there is a universal tendency to assume that one's own world-view is the true one and that those who hold other views must be stupid or wicked. When two groups clash, these misperceptions rapidly escalate into the mutual development of the image of the enemy, which then further exacerbates fears and suspicions. In making this point, of course, one must emphasize that the enemy may indeed be as bad as he is painted. The crucial consideration is that perceptual distortions created by the mutual enemy image may obscure possibilities for reduction of tension, or even for agreement.

Along the same lines, psychological analyses of aspects of the negotiating process itself, as contrasted to the issues that are being negotiated, also seem to get a receptive hearing. These include data on how differences in habits of thought and world-views of the negotiating parties may create communication problems that have nothing to do with the points at issue. The psychiatrist Bryant Wedge has supplied concrete illustrations through his analysis of the transcripts of Russian-American disarmament negotiations.[5]

Finally, those concerned with arms control are interested in the psychological analysis of the policy of deterrence, which is the principle on which the nuclear arms race is based.

The success of deterrence depends on a rational calculus

of the risks and gains involved in yielding to the threat of punishment or defying it, and this, in turn, depends on an estimate of the adversary's capabilities and intentions—that is, in large part on an estimate of the credibility of his threat. With conventional weapons, capabilities could be roughly estimated, and since in a war one nation was always victorious, each could make its threat credible by convincing the other that it believed it could win. As many have pointed out, however, once both sides have accumulated enough nuclear weapons to be able to destroy the other after being hit first, calculations of relative power become meaningless, since a nuclear exchange would destroy both sides. In this situation the only way to maintain credibility is to convince the adversary that one would prefer to exterminate him and oneself rather than let him carry out the act one wishes to deter. Perhaps this is indeed credible— Bertrand Russell has remarked that humans would rather kill their enemies than stay alive themselves—but it does call attention to the irrational aspects of the policy of deterrence, about which psychiatrists may have something useful to contribute.

In any case, although the nuclear deterrent may possibly have prevented a nuclear exchange so far, it certainly has not reduced international tensions or the threat of a nuclear holocaust. All the stockpiling of nuclear weapons has accomplished is to increase the likelihood that when the exchange does occur, it will be maximally devastating.

The problem of understanding the fundamental alterations wrought by nuclear weapons in the concept of deterrence may serve to call attention to a psychological principle that is perhaps the biggest obstacle toward making headway with arms control: the difficulty of adjusting one's thinking to the drastic changes in time-hallowed notions of power, defense, and the like created by the rapid and enormous changes in the conditions of life that have occurred during the past few decades. Leaders in power today have all grown great by acting on the belief system that prevailed while they were climbing to the top. They will, therefore, inevitably resist facts and concepts that cast doubt on the validity of these beliefs. And the older the leader, the less the likelihood that he will be able to change his behavior and ideas to fit the new conditions, or, put in more hopeful terms, the younger the leader, the more rapidly he should be able to see that times have changed. A test of this hypothesis is afforded by the age distribution of U.S. senators who voted for and against deployment of the Safeguard antiballistic missile system in 1969. To oversimplify a good bit, the major argument against deployment of the ABM was simply that it would not work, because with nuclear weapons, in contrast to conventional ones, attack can always overwhelm defense. The main argument for deployment was that the Russians are doing it, so we must also. The pros relied on the wisdom of the past; the antis recognized that security solely through arms is no longer achievable and that a new approach was therefore necessary. If my supposition is correct, the older the senator, the more likely he would be to vote for deployment; the younger the senator, the more likely he would be to vote against it. In actual fact, the age distribution of the crucial vote on the Cooper-Hart amendment (which failed by one vote) was quite striking.

The mean age of the Senate was 57. The five senators who were 57 split 3 to 2 for and against. Of the remaining 95, the 46 under 57 voted 17 for and 29 against. The 49 senators over 57 voted 30 for and 19 against. That is, senators younger than mean voted almost 2 to 1 against ABM, while two-thirds of those older than the mean age voted for it. The relationship between age and vote is even stronger for the oldest and youngest senators. Of the 17 senators 69 or older, 14 voted for and 3 against (about 5 to 1 for). Of the 15 senators 40 or younger, 3 voted for and 12 voted against (4 to 1 against). These differences, incidentally, are all significant at the .01 level. This bit of evidence that our younger lawmakers are at last beginning to grasp the implications of nuclear weapons suggests that, unlike many psychiatric patients, they can abandon early patterns of behavior when they cease to be adaptive. It also suggests that the psychiatric concepts on which the prediction of the age distribution of the vote was based may be validly applied to the behavior of politicians. It thereby affords some encouragement to psychiatrists to continue their efforts to bring psychiatric insights to bear on problems of international conflict.

15. Deterrence—For How Long?

MODERN WEAPONS of mass destruction have forced into military thinking the new concept of weapons constructed for the purpose of preventing rather than winning certain types of war. The central power conflict between the major nuclear powers—the United States and the Soviet Union—currently is in the form of a competitive accumulation of arms that each views as the only way to forestall aggression by the other.

Unfortunately, unless nations stop building nuclear arsenals a major nuclear exchange seems inevitable—and the only questions are how and when it will be precipitated. It is safe to make this flat statement because nothing is more certain and inexorable than the law of chance. Present policies involve the continuing risk of nuclear war; the longer the risk continues, the greater the probability of war; and if the probability continues long enough, it approaches certainty. Despite its professed aims, therefore, I believe that the policy of deterrence, including civil defense, should be viewed as an aspect of preparation for war.

As far as can be foreseen, two paths to a nuclear holocaust are the most probable. One is the final step in a long series of small wars between nonnuclear nations that have involved nuclear powers more and more deeply, until finally one or the other believes it can do nothing except to press the button. It could start in Rhodesia or South Africa, where local racial struggles could expand to a racial war involving all of Africa, or it could start in the Middle East, as the major nations line up behind Egypt or Israel or the warring Arab nations. Alternatively, a nuclear holocaust may reflect the sudden failure of deterrence—that is, one of the powers, mistakenly led to believe that the other is about to strike, thinks it will have more chance of survival if it seizes the initiative.

General nuclear war will come in either case at the end of a period of intensifying mutual hostility and emotional tension that increases the chances for accident or failure of judgment.

Deterrence strategies are intended to achieve a posture that without heightening international tensions or provoking the adversary into further arming, clearly signals determination to retaliate if he attacks. Once this happy state of affairs has been achieved, the argument goes, nations could proceed gradually toward disarmament.

BUILDS UP TENSION

Inherent in policies of deterrence, unfortunately, are components that aggravate tensions and lead to a permanent state of instability, creating irresistible pressures for weapons proliferation. The more widely nuclear and other genocidal weapons are diffused, the greater the degree of randomness introduced into the situation. The resulting heightened emotional tension is further increased by the fact that as long as "defense" really means "retaliation," a distinction cannot be maintained between offensive and defensive weapons. The Russians insisted that the missiles they tried to install in Cuba were defensive, but the United States certainly reacted to them as if they were offensive; the United States claimed that similar missiles it had installed in nations bordering the Soviet Union were defensive, a view the Russians did not seem to share.

The strategy of deterrence relies on the rationality of the opponent, and its success depends on the deterrer's ability to convince his adversary that an attempt to gain his objective would cost more than it is worth and that the cost to the deterrer of applying the deterrent would be less than conceding the objective. Emotional tension impedes this type of rational calculation of relative costs and gains, increasing the likelihood that deterrence would fail in a crisis.

Two other destabilizing features of deterrence—the problem of credibility and the pressure toward research and development—require more extended comment.

Since strategic nuclear weapons can have only one purpose—deterring their use by other nuclear powers by threatening to use them oneself—the nuclear powers find themselves in the absurd predicament of trying to convince each other that they are spending huge sums to accumulate and perfect weapons that will not be used. This paradox leads to the kind of doubletalk well illustrated by the following news release:

> Adm. Arleigh A. Burke, Chief of Naval Operations, told the crew of 100 (of the nuclear-powered submarine "George Washington") in a radio message they will have proved the deterrent value of their task only "if the need to fire your missiles never arises."
>
> He added that if the need to fire should arise, "your ship and the missiles it carries will contribute to the salvation of civilization, for you man the most powerful weapons system ever devised."

Similarly, the statement of a high government official some years ago resulted in the absurdity that to defend human dignity and freedom, we must be prepared to risk wiping out Western civilization, if not mankind: "credible deterrence in the nuclear age lies in being prepared to face the consequences if deterrence fails—up to and including all out nuclear war."

In short, each nuclear power is faced with the extraordinary task of convincing the other that in a showdown a nuclear exchange would be preferable to yielding, while at the same time knowing, and knowing that the other knows, that after a nuclear exchange each would probably be worse off than if it had yielded. Thus, the problem posed by the policy of nuclear deterrence is how to make credible an essentially incredible threat.

Since in all conflict situations the worst thing one side can do is show irresolution or weakness, because this stimulates the other to increase his pressure, each side seeks to intimidate the other while simultaneously demonstrating that it cannot be intimidated. The more the threat's inherent incredibility, the greater the need to make this posture convincing, leading the United States and Russia to indulge in essentially irrational gestures in the effort to demonstrate their resoluteness.

Two examples may serve to illustrate this point. After Russia's verbally belligerent reaction to the U-2 incident in April 1960, a House Appropriations Committee subcommittee reauthorized previously canceled funds for a nuclear-powered bomber, giving the reason that it would be a psychological mistake not to do so. What they had in mind is only conjecture, but it is reasonable to suppose that the counterthreat response was an attempt to show the Russians that their bluster did not intimidate the United States. In any case, no more has been heard of the nuclear-powered bomber. Psychological motives must also have contributed to Russia's building and detonating a 50-odd-megaton bomb. Expert opinions lead to the conclusion that from a strictly military standpoint, the same resources invested in a number of smaller bombs would have made more sense; in addition, in announcing its detonation, Khrushchev said, "We will not be intimidated."

A reviewer of two biographies of President Kennedy states that in his dealing with Russia, he was preoccupied with the need to avoid giving the *appearance* of weakness, and that many of his moves can be interpreted in this way. One of his main reasons for resuming atmospheric tests after the Russians did (which his advisers had told him were not militarily essential) was that he feared that the Soviets would be likely to attribute to weakness rather than good will a decision not to do so. Similarly, he regarded it as vital to force Russia to remove her missiles from Cuba, even though their presence would not have markedly changed the military balance of power (which depended on the ICBMs in both countries) because "it would have appeared to, and appearances contribute to reality."

If pushed to its extreme, this logic asserts that the effectiveness of deterrence depends entirely on the adversary's belief in the opponent's weapons and will to use them. Cardboard ICBMs would be as effective as real ones if the enemy believed that they were real and would be used under certain provocations.

If all nuclear powers were content to accept being deterred by each other's stockpiles, some stability might conceivably be achieved. But each nation is impelled to try to free its own hands by simultaneously developing a defense that will escape the adversary's deterrence by intercepting his missiles and an attack that will keep him deterred by penetrating his defenses. Each contestant is spurred on by fear that the other might succeed even temporarily in the same endeavor and thereby achieve an opportunity for a knockout blow without danger of successful retaliation.

The devotion of the nuclear powers' major scientific and technological resources to weapons research and development has resulted in a rate of innovation vastly more rapid than ever before. Despite strong motives for improving weapons, the state of the art in the past was such that there were never major revolutions in weaponry more than once in a generation. Today the development of weapons partakes of the general acceleration of technological advance, with the result that in the two decades since Hiroshima there have been three weapons revolutions—the atom bomb, the hydrogen bomb, and the guided missile—and more are predicted for the near future.

The runaway development of weapons technology may create the chief danger of a major nuclear exchange, for if either side believed itself or its adversary to be on the verge of a major breakthrough in attack or defense, *both* would be strongly tempted to launch a preemptive strike. Nation A, fearing that Nation B had achieved or was about to achieve a decisive advantage, would be strongly tempted to strike before Nation B could exploit it; Nation B would be tempted to strike while it had a chance or more probably because it feared that Nation A might strike in fear that it would do so.

DOES DETERRENCE DETER?

Despite the built-in sources of instability in mutual deterrence, it is possible that the power of the United States and the Soviet Union to inflict huge destruction on each other has had a stabilizing effect on the international scene—there has been no nuclear exchange so far, and the prospect of one may have prevented the escalation of the smaller struggles in which they have been directly or indirectly involved. On the other hand, in the past, even without nuclear deterrence, some intervals between major wars have been longer than the time elapsed since the end of World War II.

All programs designed to prevent an event from occurring have properties that tend to perpetuate them after they are no longer necessary. The resulting major psychological problem arises because the programs provide no way of determining whether the action supposedly being deterred would have occurred in the absence of the deterrent or if a threat that existed when the deterrent was established has ceased to exist.

In an important respect deterrence resembles aversive conditioning—teaching an animal to perform an act to avoid an undesirable stimulus. Animals must first actually experience the stimulus in order to learn to forestall it; humans need only imagine it. For example, a dog taught to press a lever every five minutes to avoid an electric shock will continue to press the lever at just under five minute intervals almost indefinitely after the shock has been turned off—that is, by continuing to forestall the shock, he cannot discover that it no longer exists. The deterrent acts in somewhat the same way, for it is based on the assumption that the other side would attack if there were no deterrent. Many hard-headed and well-informed students of foreign affairs are convinced that Russia's occupation of the satellite countries and her other belligerent acts were responses to fear of the West, not precursors of an intended attack on Western Europe, but the United States could find out for certain only by removing the threat of retaliation, and this it is afraid to do.

Unnecessary deterrents are maintained not only because of continuing fear of a no longer existing threat, but equally or more important, because of the need to justify one's act by believing in its efficacy. When someone does something to prevent an undesired consequence, he is strongly motivated to regard its nonappearance as evidence for the correctness of his action, for if it really was unnecessary, it would have been foolish. There is an old story of a man who, when found busily tearing up newspapers and scattering the pieces about in a railway car, was asked what he was doing. He replied, "I'm keeping the elephants away." To the observation that there didn't seem to be any elephants about, he answered, "You see, it's working already!"

The greater the commitment to deterrent action, furthermore, the greater the reluctance to abandon it—once a belief has been made the basis for a public act, admission of error would be humiliating, so the leader or nation clings to it all the more strongly. That public approval of a policy rises after it has been put into effect is a regular finding of public opinion polls.

This can be seen as a manifestation of what has been termed the strain to consistency. If actions deviate from beliefs, one or the other must yield; often it is the belief. One starts doing something under external compulsion or on the basis of an erroneous judgment, and then the fact of his doing it becomes evidence that it must be right.[1]

If a course of action has been embarked upon in response to perceived threat, the greater the commitment to it and the sacrifices made in its behalf, the more its correctness must be defended. The very costliness of the nuclear deterrent thus becomes a strong motive for believing in the reality of the danger it is built to prevent.

The ultimate cost of deterrence to society as a whole has been a gain for certain of its influential segments. Deterrence has increased the wealth and influence of the American military establishment and that segment of the economy dependent on it, and since their position and affluence depend on the reality of the communist threat, they have a strong vested interest in continually affirming and even magnifying it. Similar vested interests in deterrence have presumably developed in the Soviet Union.

SELF-FULFILLING PROPHECIES

If the threat of nuclear attack were nonexistent, the dynamics of the deterrence process would still have generated a belief in its reality, for unfortunately they eventually make the threat real, whether or not it originally existed. This irony reflects the operation of a self-fulfilling prophecy, a familiar concept worth considering in some detail. Human behavior is a process of interaction—one person's acts influence another's, which in turn influence his—but actions depend in part on expectations, and these affect what actually occurs. Sometimes they lead to actions that prevent their realization. If everybody expects the beach to be too crowded on a Sunday, for example, they will all avoid it and the beach will be empty. In the area of our interest, a similar self-disconfirming expectation that a nuclear weapon would go off accidentally led to intensive efforts to improve their safety devices, thereby reducing the danger of accident. Conversely, some prophecies are self-fulfilling. The predictions of depositors in 1929 that their banks would fail, for example, led them to withdraw their funds, bringing about the very catastrophe they had expected would occur.

Deterrence policies grow out of mutual distrust and increase it every step of the way. In an effort to counteract the other's supposed hostile intentions, each side acts in such a way as to confirm the other's fears and thereby his hostility. Because the United States fears Russian attack, it rings Russia with nuclear bases, which increase Russia's fear that the United States will attack it, and so it tries to plant missiles in Cuba as a deterrent, which only serves to confirm American fears of Russian hostility and treachery. Enemies finally become what they imagined each other to be, whether they started out that way or not; some enemies are warlike and treacherous to begin with, but all become so in time. Despite an undoubtedly genuine distaste for this sort of thing, the United States has performed its full share of skulduggery in the back alleys of the world, has broken its solemn treaties (as in the invasion of the Dominican Republic), and has murdered the enemy on as large a scale as any other nation, perhaps larger. None of these actions indicate that the United States is more wicked than other nations—in fact, Americans generally deplore such actions if they penetrate the domestic information filter. All nations are forced to be wicked by the dynamics of international conflict.

So far we have dwelt mainly on the intimidating aspect of deterrence—the effort to prevent another country from attacking one's own by threatening to destroy it. The success of such a threat depends on its credibility, and one set of measures for increasing this is to convince the opponent that our side is more foolhardy.

But a better way to preserve the credibility of deterrence would be to build an effective defense against his weapons, so that our side would survive his retaliatory nuclear strike if we had to make good our threat. An effective defense system, moreover, would reduce tension by diminishing the fear of another nuclear power's surprise attack or his opportunities for nuclear blackmail—that is, it would make the threat of nuclear attack less effective. Such considerations may lie behind both the USSR's apparent decision in 1966 to deploy antimissile missiles around its larger cities and the growing pressure in the United States for embarking on a multibillion-dollar antimissile program.

Defensive measures have an active and a passive component: the antimissile missile and shelters to protect from the blast, fire, and fallout of nuclear explosions. Neither is much use without the other, and certain psychological considerations strongly suggest that both are unworkable.

Since there is no upper limit to the potential power of a nuclear attack, it would seem that building antimissile missiles would only impel the enemy to increase the size of his attacking force and that the attacker would always have the last word. American proponents of a massive antimissile program agree that this is theoretically correct but pin their hopes on building so extensive and effective a defensive system that the cost of building enough nuclear missiles to overcome it would be prohibitive for other nations. Perhaps, but considering human ingenuity, the many ways of delivering nuclear warheads, and the decreasing cost of missile production, this seems a rather shaky hope, especially since the United States is prone to underestimate other nations' technological capacities and the amount of sacrifice they are willing to make.

There are two major psychological obstacles to the creation of an effective active defense to nuclear weapons. First, as a result of the fantastic pace of weapons innovation, defense systems are obsolete almost before the ink is dry—Sage and Nike-Zeus, for example, were obsolete even before they were fully installed. Furthermore, since the designer of a defense cannot start work on it until he has some idea of the nature of the attack, he starts a lap behind the attacker.

But the main psychological reason for skepticism about the antimissile is that the very mental processes that devise defenses against a weapon simultaneously devise means of circumventing it. As two leading nuclear scientists put it: "Work on defensive systems turns out to be the best way to promote invention of the penetration aids that nullify them," and one secretary of defense observed that our missiles could penetrate our own defenses. As a result, no defense against a weapon has ever been very good, although this hasn't mattered too much because of the inefficiency of past weapons—after 500 years no one has devised a very good defense against the bullet, but one bullet can kill only one person; British air defense gained the victory even though no more than ten percent of the Luftwaffe was intercepted. But since a single nuclear warhead can wipe out a large city, a useful defense would have to be virtually 100 percent effective.

If these considerations are valid, nations will continue to be able to build missile systems that can penetrate each other's defense. And the efforts to achieve a defense against the other's missiles will keep the deterrence system from stabilizing while constantly increasing its cost.

EFFECTS OF SHELTERS

Since some enemy missiles would be bound to penetrate any antimissile defense and some of the defending nations's missiles might explode over its own territory, an antimissile program would have to be coupled with a large-scale civilian shelter program.

Most proponents of such programs agree that while no society could survive the largest conceivable nuclear attack, a shelter program might save lives that would otherwise have been lost in the event of a smaller attack. Shelters are said to be like insurance, but this attractive-sounding analogy is weak in several respects. An effective shelter program offers protection, while insurance, which merely indemnifies against loss, does not—life insurance does not postpone death and a fire insurance policy will not put out a fire.

On the other hand, insurance does not ordinarily increase the probability of an event against which it is taken out (although, to be sure, fire insurance sometimes tempts a person to burn his property). Serious doubts can be raised about this aspect of shelter programs. Even reading a government pamphlet about shelters has been shown to increase the proportion of people who believed a nuclear war would occur, and a group of shelter builders were more certain than a matched group of non-shelter builders that a nuclear war would come. Will a shelter program prove to be another example of a self-fulfilling prophecy?

American society has never really faced up to the vast changes in social organization that would be necessary if any shelter program were to have a reasonable chance of success, for merely to get people into them quickly would require regimentation to a degree far beyond anything America has experienced. The carnage that can ensue after someone stumbles on the exit steps when there is a sudden shower during a baseball game or when a theater exit door sticks during a fire scare would be multiplied many times. Actually, the shelter system might be feasible only if at all times a portion of the population lived in shelters in rotation. And the suggestion was not entirely facetious that they should be reserved for honey-mooning couples, so that at least some of the breeding population at any given time would escape destruction.

In the event of a nuclear attack those able to reach shelters would have to live in them until the radioactive fallout level had lessened to a point that permitted survival on the earth's surface. Conditions of life would be so unprecedented that no one can be sure how the shelter dwellers would fare. Londoners' reactions to their brief sojourns in underground shelters during World War II air raids, for example, cast no light on the psychic effects of a long and indeterminate period of underground living, under conditions of high emotional tension and with the prospect of eventually emerging to an environment changed beyond recognition.

Crowded together for an indefinite period in a confined space under conditions of mounting discomfort, those in community shelters would be for the most part strangers to each other or fragments of families (even for those with family shelters the odds are slim that the whole family would be present and could get in at the time of an alert). To these stresses would be added the anxiety and grief induced by separation and by fear of radiation sickness. An imperceptible threat or danger—like ionizing radiation—is particularly anxiety producing; and radiation sickness, real or imagined, causes vomiting and diarrhea. Added to these miseries and anxieties, the shelter dwellers would face uncertainties as to when they could safely emerge and anticipations of returning to a world whose desolation was indeterminate.

No real-life or experimental situation has ever remotely resembled this combination of stresses. Isolation is known to reduce a person's capacity to adapt to his environment, and if prolonged, even to precipitate psychotic states in some, but most shelter dwellers would not be alone. Experiments on shelter living have used volunteers, who have lived in a shelter in no danger and for predetermined periods of confinement. For example, one family—parents and two boys in their late teens—spent thirteen days in a fallout shelter; they were in constant contact with a local radio station, and the wording of one passage in the report implies that their words were broadcast, indicating that psychological isolation was far from complete. Yet even under these relatively ideal conditions they became increasingly depressed, and on emerging, "the family mood . . . [was] characterized by a depressive bleakness and a diminution of vitality."

In weighing the effectiveness of civil defense, it is necessary to evaluate the survival prospects of those who eventually emerge from the shelters. The effects of a nuclear strike on the physical and biological environment would be compounded by the concomitant psychosocial disruption.

Among the many historical accounts of catastrophes, the Black Death of thirteenth-century Europe is comparable to a nuclear strike in the deaths it caused, although it was not as sudden and did not also destroy the physical environment. According to one historian, "the horror and confusion . . . brought general demoralization and social breakdown. [The period after the crisis was marked by] a mood of misery, depression and anxiety."

In short, from the psychological standpoint, life in the shelters would be replete with emotional stresses. Many of those who finally emerged would be emotionally as well as physically ill-equipped to cope with the unpredictable stresses of the anarchic postwar environment. Civil defense might reduce casualties during the attack and the immediate post-attack periods, but the number of deaths would be far greater than is suggested by estimates based on blast, fire, radiation, starvation, and disease—for to these lethal agents would have to be added hopelessness (which can be literally fatal), suicide, homicide, and panic.

A PESSIMISTIC CONCLUSION

The pessimistic conclusion to which this analysis of psychological factors in the nuclear arms race leads is that although it is motivated by the desire to prevent nuclear war, deterrence creates conditions that increasingly favor its outbreak; the process is self-aggravating and contains few features that could lead to its abandonment. At best it affords a reprieve of uncertain duration during which national leaders may still have time to devise new, more hopeful means of achieving national security, appropriate to a world bristling with genocidal weapons.

ON BELIEF SYSTEMS AND
THE HUMAN PREDICAMENT

16. *Religion and Psychiatry*

BY WHAT RIGHT does one presume to bracket such divergent
spheres of human thought and activity as psychiatry and religion? At first sight they appear to deal with entirely different
realms and to use totally different means of reaching their conclusions. Religion is at once a way of life and an organized body
of thought and experience concerning the fundamental problems of existence: the nature of the universe and man's relation
to it. It reaches its conclusions initially through the revelations
experienced by its prophets, then by deducing the logical consequences that follow from these revelations.

Psychiatry is merely a branch of medicine—the one concerned with studying and treating a group of patients characterized as being mentally ill. It does not presume to state fundamental truths. Rather it tries to develop a set of tentative
working hypotheses, arrived at by painstakingly and systematically accumulated observations about its subject matter, the
mentally ill patient. It must be ever ready to abandon a
cherished notion if new evidence makes it untenable. Like all
arts and sciences, it invites trouble if it states its conclusions too
sweepingly or dogmatically. Neither revelation nor deductive
logic play any part in its development.

Psychiatry and religion do converge in one area, however,
and that is the nature of man, and it is in this realm that their
teachings can be compared. This convergence is firmly rooted
in history. Medicine and religion were once undifferentiated.
Temples were hospitals, and priests were physicians. The care

of the mentally ill remained under the aegis of religion long after bodily ills were separated out as the province of the physician. Mental illness was viewed as possession by evil spirits and therefore a problem for the priest, not the physician, to be treated by exorcism. Though this treatment was often fatal to the victim, it may be that mental patients were better off while demons prevailed than they were in the subsequent age of enlightenment. As harborers of demons the mentally ill were at least objects of serious, if hostile, interest to others, and so possessed a certain status. To be the focus of real concern, even if it expressed itself in brutal form, must have been some support to the self-respect of an insane person, and this may have accounted in part for the occasional success of exorcism.

With the decline of demonology, however, priests lost interest in the mentally ill before the medical profession accepted responsibility for their plight. During this period the insane sank to the level of beasts who were regarded with a mixture of horror and amusement. They were chained in quarters that were little better than dungeons, were treated abominably, and were exhibited for the entertainment of the curious and sadistic. This state of affairs prevailed in the Western World for centuries, and some hangovers still remain.

It is interesting that what might be called the rehabilitation of the insane was accomplished by a fusion of religious and medical motives. The religious one took the form of insisting that the insane were still human beings with souls who would respond to kindness and moral suasion, the medical one that the insane showed a fascinating set of behavioral phenomena, which warranted scientific study. These motives fused in the minds of a few great men, chief among them the French psychiatrist Pinel, culminating in the reinstatement of the idea that the insane were sick people who would respond to kindness and moral suasion. Thus, the territory of mental illness was rewon for medicine, starting about the turn of the nineteenth century.

Then an odd thing happened—the pendulum swung too far. With the enormously rapid rise of scientific medicine in the early years of the twentieth century, psychiatrists forgot that mental patients were people and saw them only as specimens of disease. They studied "mental diseases" to the best of their ability, delineated their manifestations in the living, and pored over their brains after death. But interest stopped there; and since there were very few doctors compared to the number of patients, those patients not under direct study were again left to rot in the back wards of mental hospitals. With this development, despite the rapid increase of medical knowledge, the cure rate of patients in mental hospitals went down. We were actually doing better in 1850 with moral suasion than in 1920 with modern medical science. Fortunately, in recent years the balance is being slowly restored, under the influence initially of the development of the private practice of psychiatry brilliantly pioneered by Freud. The psychoanalysts could not forget that their patients were people with wishes, hopes, fears, and ideals, and a generation of psychiatrists trained in this way inevitably began to look at the insane in the same light.

The concern with the patient as a person is the fortunate heritage of the fusion of psychiatry and religion. There is, however, also an unfortunate aspect of this heritage. This is that mental illness is still regarded to some degree as a moral weakness, rather than as on a par with other diseases. Several decades of public education have done little to remove the stigma from insanity, and the insane are still viewed with fear and horror by many. In this sense we have not yet fully escaped from demonology.

So the situation as it exists today may be summed up like this. As long as psychiatrists study their patients solely from the standpoint of their biological or biochemical make-up, they operate strictly as medical scientists. As such, they need not be concerned with ethical or religious matters. One need not bring religion into a consideration of the response of the brain to electroshock treatments or chlorpromazine, for example.

As soon as the psychiatrist turns to the study of man as he functions in his social environment, however, and he must do this in the practice of psychotherapy, he cannot avoid infringing on the territory of religion. He must be concerned with the nature of man, including the values man lives by. His beliefs, including his religion, are facts which the psychiatrist cannot avoid. That is, a man's feelings and behavior are to an important degree determined by his values, a matter to which I shall return presently. His religious beliefs are just as much facts about him as are the biochemical processes in his nervous system, and may be more important for an understanding of his behavior.

So the psychiatrist, whether he wants to or not, must think about human nature and values in the broadest sense, and also about the nature of the religious experience. In doing so, he inevitably poaches on territory traditionally staked out by religion and philosophy as their exclusive domains. I should now like to consider briefly what he has found on his forays—or better, what he has glimpsed, for he has done little more than that—with respect to two topics: the nature of man, and determinants of the religious experience.

The psychiatrist, with his background as a physician primarily trained to treat men's bodies, tends to view human nature first of all from a biological standpoint. When he does so, he is struck by the fact that man is both a highly aggressive, self-aggrandizing creature and a gregarious one, who functions most effectively as a member of a group. Depending on his own philosophy he sees man as basically aggressive, but forced to tame his hostile impulses by group pressures, or basically affiliative, becoming destructive only when frustrated.

The German philosopher Spengler summed up the former view by making a simple analogy. He noted that vegetable-eating animals like deer and cows have eyes set on the sides of their heads, so they can encompass as much of the environment as possible and so be able to spot the lurking predators. Carnivores like lions and wolves have the eyes placed in the front of the head. This gives them stereoscopic vision, which assures maximal accuracy of depth perception, which they need in order to spring accurately on their prey. Man has eyes in front of his head; therefore, Spengler concludes, he is basically a carnivore—that is, an aggressive creature. There are expectations to Spengler's generalizations—for example, the great apes who have stereoscopic vision but are *not* meat eaters—but it serves to point up one of the dominant psychiatric views of human nature.

Freud was perhaps the most influential exponent of this view. For him man is a battleground of life instincts and death instincts, the former working towards affiliation with others, the latter toward destruction of others and oneself. Freud seems to imply that the destructive, self-aggrandizing drives are primary:

> Under primitive conditions it is superior force—brute violence ... that lords it everywhere.... Brute force is overcome by union, the allied might of scattered units makes good its right against the isolated giant. Thus we may define "right" (i.e. law) as the might of a community. Yet it, too, is nothing else than violence.[1]

The superior might of the community becomes internalized in each individual, leading him to cooperate with others. In each generation the child painfully learns to hold his self-aggrandizing, destructive impulses in check, under the pressures of his parents and his group, since social survival would be impossible if we gave free rein to our aggressive drives. But they are always just beneath the surface, ready to break forth under the slightest encouragement. Moreover, says Freud, the more elaborate and complex civilization becomes, the more it necessitates damming up our hostilities, which then eventually break forth with even greater fury. Human existence is thus a close race between love and destructiveness, with the latter more than likely to win out, leading to extermination of the species.

It seems to me that aggressiveness, or the tendency to self-aggrandizement, as described by the psychiatrist, is very similar to the hubris of the Greeks or spiritual pride of the Christians. This is characteristically viewed as man's greatest curse, and it certainly has brought him to the brink of destruction. At the same time, one would have to admit that it is his greatest source of strength. It is this quality which has enabled man to bend the forces of nature to his will, and to reach great heights of scientific and artistic achievement, with all the richness of experience to which this leads. So in some ways the problem of aggressiveness may be insoluble, in that man would not be man if he did not possess this quality.

Whether or not this is so, it is fortunately possible to make out a strong case for the viewpoint that man's strongest drive is not to aggrandize himself but to live in harmony with his fellows. According to this view, he becomes hostile and aggressive only when thwarted. It can be maintained that this description does not gainsay the view of man as an essentially selfish creature. All it states is that he cannot satisfy his own basic needs except through cooperation with others. A good case can be made, however, for an extension of this viewpoint. This is that man is an essentially altruistic creature who finds his greatest satisfaction and fulfillment in the emotion of tender love and the behavior arising from it. Loving behavior appears in children apparently spontaneously. If it be argued that they learn it from their parents, this just pushes the problem back a generation, without refuting the idea that it is a primary aspect of human nature. Further evidence for its primacy is that it regularly exceeds the bounds of necessity, which it would not do if it were dictated purely by self-interest. Parents give up their lives for their children, and friends for their friends, so that love seems stronger than self-preservation. Moreover, in contrast to hostility, which for most persons is an unpleasant sensation, tender love is a self-reinforcing emotion—we enjoy it and strive to prolong it. Even Heinrich Himmler was said to be a devoted husband and father; and the disasters which bring out the beast in people also spur them to magnificent self-sacrifices for the sake of others. Think of all the bystanders who have risked and sometimes lost their lives in an effort to save a drowning stranger, or to extricate a few more people from a burning building. Such acts are done automatically, without any feeling of obligation or thought of reward and in the teeth of self-interest.[2]

From the biological standpoint, then, man's nature is clearly two-sided, and whether one prefers to emphasize the evil, selfish, destructive side or the good, loving, altruistic side is a matter of choice. In this the psychiatrists are like the theologians, some of whom promulgate the doctrine of original sin, while others stress "that of God in every man."

So far, I have discussed man as a biological organism with drives toward both ruthless self-aggrandizement and altruistic love. But to view man solely as a member of the animal kingdom obviously misses his most important characteristics—those in which he differs uniquely from all other living creatures.

The unique characteristic which I think is central to all the others is his capacity to form abstractions. This makes it possible for him to develop symbols. Through symbols he can communicate to others, guide his present conduct by memories of the past and anticipation of the future, and, above all, guide his life by values, ideals, and faiths.

The important point is that our conduct is influenced much more by these abstractions and their symbols than by our bodily needs. In making choices, a person is often guided more by which alternative is more consistent with his picture of himself than by which most meets his needs. When "basic instincts" and the abstractions we live by conflict, the abstraction often wins. A man will go to extreme lengths to maintain his picture of himself in his own eyes, and may kill himself if this picture cannot be maintained. The multimillionaire stockbroker kills himself after losing a few of his millions through an error of judgment, not because he is faced with starvation but because he cannot bear to see himself as less than infallible.

Other abstractions are equally potent—witness the murders in the guise of saving heretics' souland the suicides called martyrdom that have been motivated by differences about highly abstract concepts such as the nature of trinity or, in our day, communism and free enterprise or integration and racial purity.

Abstractions guide our lives to the extent that we have made an emotional investment in them. This investment goes by the name of faith. I should now like to turn briefly to some of the conditions which predispose to the development of faith in its most dramatic form: the *religious experience*, which seems common to all religions. I gather that this experience, which I have not had myself, is a sense of oneness with the universe, often with a feeling of absorption of one's personal identity into a larger whole. This experience may or may not be accompanied by visual and auditory hallucinations. After undergoing it one may feel himself to be, in a deep sense, a different person, with a greater feeling of personal security and peace of mind, a condition referred to in some Christian sects, I believe, as being "saved." Worldly matters seem less important and spiritual ones have gained a new significance.

A certain state of mind seems to predispose to this experience, as to the development of any other faith, namely an inner feeling of conflict or anxiety. It often seems to the individual before he has a conversion experience that everything is confused, and he is depressed, frightened, or otherwise upset. The situation seems to demand some action from him but he does not know what it is. Such a state of affairs can arise from the individual's inner conflicts, or from his environment. It is no coincidence that Billy Graham and the fundamentalist religions flourish in confused and dangerous times like these, when all of us feel insecure and are seeking guidance.

Given this state of mind, there seem to be two diametrically opposed routes to the emergence of a conversion experience—either intensive interaction with other persons, or drastic withdrawal from them. The first route is more common in our society and easier for us to comprehend. Faith is usually catalyzed and maintained by another person, or more often a group, which seems to the anxious person to know what it is about, to have an answer, and also to be functioning more successfully than he is. In psychiatry, the young psychiatrist usually develops and maintains faith in his particular brand of treatment through allying himself with a university, or an institute. It is through his identification with his colleagues and superiors in such a group that he develops his self-confidence. Similarly, in America, we worship in groups, and religious faith is sustained by identification with the minister and other members of the congregation. An additional group factor which predisposes to the awakening of the religious emotion lies in the contagion of feeling which evangelists are so expert in evoking. It may be not too far fetched to say that a man's feeling of oneness with the universe in these circumstances is really an extension of his feeling of unity with the group. From this standpoint religious faith rests on man's affiliative tendency which I have described above.

This view as a fully adequate explanation for the experience of unity with the world breaks down in the face of the hermit, who achieves his religious experience by drastically cutting himself off from others. To be sure, many mystics do not achieve the mystical experience until after a long period of close association with a religious teacher or group. But prolonged meditation in isolation is, in many religions, the means of achieving a mystical experience of direct relationship with the universe. In this sense, the American Indian going off alone into the wilderness to find his Manitou, his personal guiding spirit, the Christian monk in his lonely cell, and the Hindu fakir sitting immobile on the mountain top are using the same means to achieve salvation. The same type of religious experience has been reported by persons making long solitary sea voyages.

Keeping in mind the part played by isolation in facilitating the religious experience, let us now turn to some laboratory studies of the effects of isolation. The central purpose of these studies was to cast light on fundamental questions about the nature of the nervous system and the part played in its functioning by stimuli from the outside world. Unexpectedly, and quite incidentally, the experiments seemed to cast a little light on the conditions predisposing to a mystical experience.

In one series of experiments, college students were placed alone in a chamber with frosted glasses over their eyes, earphones over their ears, cardboard cylinders over their hands and wrists, and heavy felt slippers on their feet. In this way all *patterned* stimulation (except the occasional voice of the experimenter coming over the earphones) was shut off. Under these circumstances the students had many fascinating and scientifically illuminating experiences, of which two are relevant to our topic.

After several hours many students began to hallucinate— that is, to see things that were not there. These visions progressed from vague forms to definite geometrical shapes then to animals and persons. They were not under the subjects' voluntary control. Usually, the subjects found them merely entertaining, but sometimes they carried a strong emotional charge.

In addition to hallucinations, many subjects experience feelings of loss of personal identity, sometimes with disintegration of the body image. One man reported that he felt as if he were literally sitting beside himself. This state was sometimes accompanied by oceanic feelings of oneness with the universe.

On emerging back into the world after several days in the isolation room, some students felt for a time that things appeared distant and trivial in comparison to the rich experiences they had just been through.

Another researcher did the same type of experiment except that he reduced outside stimulation much more drastically. He suspended himself in a tank of lukewarm water in a pitch black room, so that the only sensations he received from the outer world were those produced where the edges of the breathing mask touched his skin. He experienced hallucinations and something similar to a mystical experience within two hours, whereas the students, in a less drastically deprived setting, required at least a day.

Though it would be dangerous to push the analogy too far, the isolation produced in these experiments seems similar to that achieved by the religious mystic, and at least two of the types of experience reported in the experiments are similar to those of the mystical experience. These are visions and the sense of loss of personal identity and fusion with the universe. The "real" world seems less real afterward. (Incidentally, the experiments support the view that the nervous system is a "self-starter" and that the purpose of outside stimulation is not so much to supply it with energy as to guide and pattern the energy it generates spontaneously.)

The fact that scientists seem to have stumbled on some of the conditions facilitating mystical experiences does not, of course, have any bearing on their objective validity. Perhaps all they have shown is that any man can establish contact with God if he excludes the distracting bombardment of daily life experience. I mention it as one interesting and unexpected way in which psychiatry may have relevance for religion.

In summary I should like to reemphasize that whether we try to define the nature of man from the nature of God, as religion does, or on the basis of systematic observations of his functioning as the psychiatrist does, we arrive at the same complex picture. Both the theologian and the psychiatrist find man to be a mixture of good and evil and in the same culture both tend to agree as to which predominates. Freud's spiritual kinship to the Jewish prophets found expression in his own rather dim view of man. In America today, the liberal religions, which are most interpenetrated by contemporary ideas, and psychiatry both prefer to stress the affiliative and loving aspects of man's nature. Psychiatry and religion both agree, furthermore, that faith in the broadest sense—that is, emotional commitment to an abstraction—is a very powerful motivating force.

That a person's faith is often strengthened by his identification with individuals or groups sharing his beliefs is in accord with psychiatric knowledge about man's nature. The recent finding that some aspects of the religious experience of revelation can be duplicated by creating extreme isolation under laboratory conditions is a bit more startling.

Perhaps the main upshot of this review is that psychiatry, a very recent newcomer, really has little to add to the basic insights about human nature developed over centuries by the great religions. At best, it has been able to reformulate some of them so that they are more accessible to scientific study.

17. Sources and Functions of Belief Systems

IN ORDER TO SELECT among and make sense out of the welter of experiences, humans need a moral and cognitive map of the universe. Such maps may be termed "belief systems," and they include beliefs as to the nature of reality and of causality, the nature of knowledge, and codes of ethics—that is, descriptions of valued and disvalued behaviors. Ultimately, all belief systems rest on premises which are not open to question and which cannot be demonstrated empirically—that is, they are articles of faith. This is as true of the scientific-humanist as of the transcendental world-views. They vary widely in extent, explicitness, the intensity with which they are held, and their power to influence behavior of individuals who hold them. In this presentation I shall consider some descriptive characteristics of belief systems, their sources and modes of transmittal, and their psychological functions, concluding with some problems involved in attempting to do psychological research on phenomena that cannot be reconciled with the cosmology of science. Attention will be confined to two all-inclusive world-views representing polar extremes: that of scientific humanism and that underlying transcendental religions.

Since a person's own outlook inevitably colors his efforts to describe and evaluate belief systems, let me start by briefly stating my world-view to enable the reader better to evaluate what follows. I am an agnostic. It seems to me incredible that, tiny, fleeting creatures as we are, we could grasp the nature of the universe. I do have a faith that my life is part of some unfathomable purpose and also suspect that the universe may have a moral structure, just as it has a physical one, but that humans can have only the most fleeting and vague ideas of what it might be. I would not mind having transcendental experiences, whatever their ultimate meaning, but do not feel moved to make the effort required to achieve them. However, I am quite prepared to accept the possible existence of realities or planes of being in addition to the world of sensory phenomena. My view has been well expressed by William James in a letter:

> The fixed point with me is the conviction that our "rational" consciousness touches but a portion of the real universe and that our life is fed by the "mystical" region as well. I have no mystical experience of my own but just enough of the germ of mysticism in me to recognize the region from which their voice comes when I hear it.[1]

To come to the business at hand, the humanist-scientific[2] belief system which has dominated the American scientific community assumes a single reality existing independently of the observer and consisting of objects and events anchored in a space-time continuum, which relate to each other according to laws of cause and effect. It can be perceived correctly only by the waking, unintoxicated brain and is to be comprehended by the intellectual analysis of sensory data. According to this view, the ultimate test of the validity of any phenomenon is its ability to meet the criteria of the scientific method, including replicability and the use of controls. The scientific-humanistic world-view dismisses as illusory all experiences that cannot meet these criteria.

The mystical or transcendental world-view, in contrast, assumes the existence of one or more realities that are accessible only to states of consciousness other than the ordinary waking one. It recognizes that persons can live in these other realities only temporarily but regards sensory reality, in which everyone must live most of the time, as ephemeral and philosophically unimportant.

It must be added that many scientists are able to maintain

both a scientific-humanist and a transcendental belief system by adhering to the scientific one only with respect to those aspects of reality which are the objects of their scientific efforts. That is, they demand the most rigorous scientific validation of one class of experiences while disregarding such validation altogether with respect to other experiences.

Transcendental belief systems, in contrast to the scientific-humanistic one, vary widely in metaphysical content and in the extent to which they seek to control all aspects of an individual's life. Underlying all transcendental dogmas, however, is the conviction of the existence of what Aldous Huxley has called the "Divine Ground." As he describes it,

> The phenomenal world of matter and of individualized consciousness—the world of things and animals and men and even gods—is the manifestation of a Divine Ground within which all partial realities have their being, and apart from which they would be nonexistent. Human beings are capable not merely of knowing about the Divine Ground by inference, but also of realizing its existence by a direct intuition.[3]

Belief systems seem to differ much less in their ethical than in their metaphysical content. Scientific-humanists as well as most transcendentalists espouse essentially the same ethic—that embodied in the Golden Rule or a variant of it.

Belief systems vary widely, however, not only in their metaphysics but in their tolerance for alternative world-views. Holders of the scientific-humanist world-view, consistent with their assignment of the highest value to the search for truth, tend to be tolerant, if condescending, toward transcendentalists, but only as long as they do not claim scientific validity for the phenomena in which they believe, a point to which I shall return. Transcendental belief systems range in tolerance from Hinduism, which accepts the validity of all religions as expressed in the phrase "all rivers lead to the sea," to fundamentalist Christian sects that assign all nonbelievers to Hell.

With respect to the origins of belief systems, scientific-humanism seems to have been gradually articulated on the basis of accumulated systematic observations of physical-chemical and biological phenomena and of human behavior. It has strengthened its hold through its remarkable success in enabling humans to understand and gain control of the physical and biological environment, thereby contributing enormously to health, material well-being, and the general excitement of living. It has made possible the creation of nuclear power, the invention of movies, television, and the automobile, the synthesis of penicillin and tranquilizers, the placing of humans on the moon and a space probe on Mars. Recently we have begun to suspect that material well-being is a will-o'-the-wisp, the pursuit of which is luring humankind to destruction in the bogs of nuclear catastrophe or ecological disaster. This recognition is, I believe, a major reason for the recent proliferation of transcendental, antiscientific belief systems.

In the West these characteristically stem from a revelation experienced by a single individual, which frequently includes vivid sensory experiences such as a blinding light, visual or auditory images, or the experience of a powerful blow and is characteristically accompanied by an overwhelming emotion such as exaltation, terror, or a combination of these. Other transcendental belief systems seem to emerge from widely shared experiences occurring in states of disciplined meditation. These lack the dramatic quality of revelation and may be essentially contentless.

Belief systems are transmitted from one generation to the next as an aspect of the process of acculturation. They are both expressed and reinforced by recurring group activities such as religious rituals or by repeated demonstrations of their validity such as scientific discoveries and technological inventions.

To turn to the functions of belief systems, from the standpoint of human psychology, humanistic and transcendental ones share certain functions but also differ in their particular strengths and weaknesses. To consider their shared functions first, the cognitive and moral map supplied by a belief system orders experiences in terms of importance. It thus provides guides as to what to select and to attend to out of the welter of experiences. Furthermore, by representing an orderly, self-consistent universe, it enables the believers to predict and control physical events and to evaluate the behavior of others as well as their own from an ethical standpoint. Control of physical events may be illusory—a rain dance may not actually bring the rain—but for the believer this does not disconfirm the belief system because it has ways of accounting for failure.

A major function of all belief systems is to bind the believers to each other. Indeed, a shared belief system is essential for the maintenance of a cohesive group. Much of the travail of American society today could well be related to the erosion of a previously widely shared belief system—a fusion of liberal Christianity and science.

Finally, a major purpose of all belief systems is to counteract what has been termed "ontological anxiety," the prospect of disappearing into nothingness, which all humans must face. Rollo May states it well: "Anxiety . . . is the subjective aspect of a being facing imminent nonbeing, that is, facing the dissolution of . . . himself as a self. Anxiety is the inward state of my becoming aware . . . that I can lose myself and my world, that I can become 'nothing'."[4] Ontological anxiety has been expressed most succinctly by Lewis Carroll in "The Hunting of the Snark": "If ever I meet with a Boojum, that day, in a moment (of this I am sure), I shall softly and suddenly vanish away—and the notion I cannot endure!"

All belief systems try to counteract this intolerable feeling by linking individual existence to something larger and more permanent, a goal transcending not only the individual but society itself. For the scientist-humanist it is the search for truth, linked to the enrichment of human life; for others, the service of God. As already indicated, these need not be incompatible.

The major shortcoming of the scientific-humanist belief system is that it offers no final answers to the riddles of existence. Some do not need these answers, but those who do are left dissatisfied. While scientific humanism supplies a justification for seeking the good things of life in both a material and ethical sense, it offers no satisfactory explanation of frequent triumphs of evil over good or the existence of injustice and needless suffering, and it provides only an unsatisfactory antidote to ontological anxiety. This is that we live on through our influence on the lives of our descendants. Considering the brevity of human life, this is small comfort. Our ancestors who lived only a hundred years ago are no longer real to us in any psychological sense. Moreover, the prospect of nuclear destruction takes away even this consolation. Death in a nuclear war would be like the death of a colony of ants. The ongoing network of human relationships on which the humanistic philosophy relies to give meaning to individual existence would be destroyed in the process.

Transcendental world-views excel in their antidotes to ontological anxiety. Many transcendental religions promise the individual eternal existence in the afterlife. Others, especially Eastern ones, elevate the merging into nothingness to the ultimate goal, the final stage of the mystic's quest. By being absorbed into the world soul, the individual achieves ultimate significance.

Because they hold out salvation as the reward for good behavior, transcendental belief systems exert much more power over the conduct of their members than scientific-humanistic ones and they have a variety of ways of accounting for misfortunes and evil. For them, suffering becomes meaningful or even desirable as an expression of God's will or the fulfillment of an individual's karma.

In this connection, by emphasizing the spiritual as opposed to the mundane world, many transcendental creeds supply little motivation for the relief of misery or suffering in this world. By contrast to scientific humanism, which places a high value on attempting to improve the human condition, transcendental religions cover every possible orientation with respect to this activity. Their adherents run the gamut from dedicating their lives to the relief of human suffering to total indifference toward the plight of others, especially if they are not fellow believers. Even the Protestant ethic, which stresses service to others, by viewing worldly success as a sign of Grace can easily be perverted into the view that being poor is evidence of wickedness and therefore a deserved punishment.

Many transcendental religions provide their adherents with a great sense of peace and happiness, especially if the adherents come to the religion through a conversion experience after a period of despair. Others, however, instill tremendous fear and guilt by stressing hellfire and damnation. A master of eliciting these emotions in his followers was Jonathan Edwards. Most instill a strong sense of group cohesiveness and solidarity, but, unfortunately, this is too frequently coupled with hatred or contempt for those who do not accept the same revelations. In fact, ruthlessness toward the out-grouper seems to be the other side of the coin of group solidarity. No treachery is so base, no cruelty so barbarous when applied to the infidel or heretic as not to be justifiable by some transcendental belief system, so such acts are accompanied by a sense of righteousness rather than guilt. Torquemada was a deeply religious man. Violence toward the adherents of a rival belief system is intensified by the fact that they represent a psychological threat. Their very existence implies that their beliefs may be valid, and this shakes both the personal security and group solidarity of holders of incompatible beliefs.

Let me turn finally to the problem of how transcendental experiences may be incorporated into the world-view of psychology and their possible accessibility to psychological research. There are great obstacles on both sides, primarily because, as already mentioned, holders of any world-view are made uncomfortable by phenomena that cannot be explained in its terms, and scientists are no exception. In this connection, I cannot resist quoting from William James:

> Of all insufficient authorities as to the total nature of reality, give me the scientists. . . . Their interests are the most incomplete and their professional conceit and bigotry immense. I know no narrower sect or club, in spite of their excellent authority in the lines of fact they have explored, and their splendid achievement there. Their only authority at large is for *method*.[5]

The sense of outrage and indignation with which many scientists greet even the faintest suggestion that paranormal experiences such as telepathy, precognition, and mystical experiences could be valid supports James's statement.

The scientist's first recourse in coping with paranormal phenomena is to dismiss them as psychotic or as biographically determined psychodynamic phenomena, but in any case as having no real existence—that is, as based on fraud, coincidence, or illusion, hence unworthy of their attention. Many adherents of transcendental belief systems are equally reluctant to expose their beliefs to scientific study. Their attitude is antithetical to research. Since research is based on doubt and they know their revelations to be true, most take the position that the effort to apply scientific method to transcendental experiences is irrelevant or that only trivial aspects of the experiences can be subjected to scientific study.

Thus the psychologist who wishes to study transcendental experiences must be prepared to cope not only with research problems presented by the nature of the material but also with the mistrust and scorn of many of his colleagues. Since the scientific establishment controls allocation of most research funds, furthermore, support for such research is hard to find. Despite these difficulties, it is now clear that scientific methods can help to illuminate some aspects of transpersonal phenomena, while admittedly not being able to penetrate to their essence. To consider only the mystical experience, the claims of Transcendental Meditation have led to studies of the physiological changes accompanying meditation. As Benson has shown, most of its bodily concomitants can be reproduced by relaxed attention to an imagined visual or auditory stimulus, such as hearing or visualizing the number one.

More direct approaches are efforts to chart states of consciousness including mystical ones and studies of the effects of LSD. A pioneer in describing the mystical consciousness is, of course, William James. Recently this effort has been carried to new heights of sophistication, including the linking of states of consciousness to states of the nervous system by Roland Fischer.[6] Another approach is study of the experiences occurring under the influence of psychedelic drugs such as LSD. The argument that such experiences reflect nothing more than a toxic condition of the brain probably does not hold. As Aldous Huxley has suggested, it may be that the healthy brain has to protect itself from being overwhelmed by the flood of stimuli impinging on it by shutting out large segments of reality. These can only penetrate into consciousness when the brain's "reducing valve" is paralyzed by metabolic disorders, drugs, or special meditative exercises.[7]

This hypothesis is consistent with the observation that, having had transcendental experiences under the influence of drugs, many persons can then evoke them without such aids, suggesting that the drugs are no more than facilitators. Grof, who has intensively studied LSD experiences, concludes:

> The experience of death and rebirth, union with the universe or God, encounters with demonic appearances or the living of "past incarnations" observed in LSD sessions appear to be phenomenologically indistinguishable from similar descriptions in the sacred scriptures of the great religions of the world and secret, mystical texts of ancient civilizations.[8]

In closing, I would like to speculate about an apparent paradox that could concern psychologists with respect to the role of transcendental experiences in human affairs. Although the essence of the mystical experience is that there is a fundamental unity to all things, yet this experience gets translated into the mutually incompatible, clashing dogmas of various religious sects. Perhaps the differences in function between the right and left hemispheres of the brain may be relevant to this strange state of affairs. The transcendental experience is basically indescribable, perhaps because it is mediated primarily by the right hemisphere, the one concerned with patterns and emotions in contrast to the analytic and verbal left hemisphere. Dogmas may be attempts to translate a fundamentally nonverbal, nonconceptual experience into words. As such, they are necessarily only partial renderings of the experience. Moreover, the process of translation would be subject to distortions by the beliefs and values of the group to which the promulgator of the dogma belongs, leading to wide differences in formulations of what may be essentially the same experiences. An additional trace of support for the assumption that transcendental experiences are mediated by the right brain is that the visual and musical representations of religious beliefs elicit similar emotional responses regardless of creed. The sacred music of many religions is deeply moving. Tibetan mandalas, images of Buddha, Krishna, and the Virgin Mary all elicit a powerful sense of the forces of harmony in the universe, while

Kali, Uitzilopochti, and some portrayals of the crucifixion are terrifying to persons regardless of their beliefs. In these realms our right brains appear to be in closer agreement than our left ones.

For me at least, it is not possible to deny the existence of phenomena that require the postulation of a reality or realities other than the sensory one and operating by different laws. In principle the scientific and mystical realities cannot be completely reconciled. However, they may have areas of overlap, in particular that of subatomic physics. It is interesting that the subatomic physicist describes his reality in terms indistinguishable from those the clairvoyant uses in describing his.[9] Furthermore, the scientific method can be applied to some conditions and characteristics of the mystical experience. Granted that the scientific-humanist and transcendental world-views must remain fundamentally apart, they can enrich each other. To end with a quotation, "The solution cannot be found either in deriding . . . spirituality as impotent or by mistrusting science as a destroyer of humanity. We have to see that the spirit must lean on science as its guide to the world of reality and that science must turn to the spirit for the meaning of life."[10]

18. Conscience and Moral Law

ONE WIDELY HELD concept of morality may be termed the social utility theory.[1] It holds that morality is identical with social usefulness and that the individual's conscience represents the internalized standards of the group to which he belongs. Today when values are in flux, such a position has undoubted appeal; but it may yet be that the other, less fashionable, view comes closer to the truth. According to it the universe moves in accordance with moral laws "as permeating and indefeasible as the physical laws of nature"; and conscience, at least in part, is man's glimpse of them. Conscience, in this view, is as much the sense organ for detecting manifestations of moral laws as the five senses are for detecting manifestations of physical laws. Without hoping to add anything new to the age-long debate between these views, this paper proposes to review some inadequacies of the first position and present some reasons to believe that the second may be at least as sound.

The social utility theory holds that man, like all biological organisms, continually strives to restore and maintain a state of equilibrium. At the psychological level this takes the form of striving to achieve pleasure and avoid pain. Man's nature is such that he can do this more successfully by cooperating with his fellows than alone. So he forms societies. Each society through trial and error develops certain forms of social behavior which yield its members the most pleasure and least pain. These behaviors are considered good and may differ from one society to another. They are instilled into each member of the society through his parents, from whom the child soon learns that certain acts receive approval and others punishment. In time such parental approval and rejection become internalized as the voice of conscience. Says Gregg, "Conscience is the feeling, or emotion, accompanying a social act that is either approved or disapproved by the social group one cares for supremely." It follows that by comparing different societies, we can eventually single out those forms of behavior which yield the most satisfaction for the most people, and so gradually arrive at a code of ethical conduct applicable to all mankind.

This is a persuasive view and undoubtedly casts light on many aspects of ethical behavior. It accounts, for example, for the fact that behavior considered good in one society may be seen as bad in another and that in each group, behavior deemed good will seem in accord with the dictates of conscience. The conscientious Spartan stole; the conscientious Inquisitor tortured the heretic; the conscientious Hindu turns the starving beggar away from his door so as not to interfere with the beggar's karma.

WHERE "SOCIAL UTILITY" FALLS SHORT

This theory of morals, however, leaves certain important questions unanswered and significant phenomena unexplained. If social utility is the sole criterion of good behavior, we are forced to accept as good the behavior which anyone would judge to be bad by almost any other test. Ruthless Genghis Khan, for example, after rounding up all the inhabitants of a town he could catch, would murder all but a few. These he would compel to run through the streets announcing that the invader had left, which would bring the other inhabitants out of hiding to be slaughtered. Yet his life was certainly successful from his standpoint, in that he died in bed after a life replete with satisfactions. The empire he founded probably gave his subjects a more satisfying life than the societies it destroyed. If it be objected that his behavior was moral for his time but would not be so today, one need only point to Stalin who acknowledged that his policies led to the deaths of some ten million peasants. From the social utility standpoint, whether this behavior was moral or not would depend on whether the Russians are better or worse off as a result, a question which would be answered quite differently on the two sides of the Iron Curtain.

As bad persons have been strikingly successful, so persons we intuitively regard as good have led miserable lives, even been martyred; and the social worth of the events they set in train cannot be shown to be any greater than those caused by men seen as wicked. There is no question as to the supreme moral value of the teachings of Jesus; yet disagreements as to their interpretation brought religious wars which wracked the Western world for centuries. How can such instances be reconciled with the view that the moral value of a doctrine is the same as its social usefulness?

One way might be to assert that the ethical value of an act is determined by its ultimate social utility in the light of *all* its consequences, good and bad. But this makes it impossible to express moral judgments at all: The final consequences of any act cannot be known until the Last Judgment; and by then so many other acts with their consequences will have become interwoven with the one whose moral worth is to be judged that its individual contribution could not possibly be disentangled.

Besides failing to supply an ultimately valid basis for moral judgments of acts or persons, the social utility theory of morals leaves certain important phenomena unexplained. Turning from man's behavior to his ideals, we find that though the former differs widely from society to society, the latter are remarkably similar. The Hindu lets the beggar starve; and the Inquisitor burned the heretic, out of the same concern for the victim's ultimate welfare. A value analysis of the speeches of Hitler, Stalin, and Roosevelt, who were trying to influence members of very different societies, showed that they all appealed to peace, friendship, nondomination, truthfulness, and justice. Regardless of the circumstances of his particular culture, man pursues the good; and he perceives it as essentially the same even though the ways he tries to attain it may differ.

Another such manifestation is the tendency of men in all

cultures and times to invest their leaders with the same qualities such as courage, probity, compassion, and love for the people, regardless of the actual attributes of the leader.

The social utility theory of conscience does not account for the fact that persons completely governed by the conscience representing the internalized code of their society are seldom seen as truly good but are apt rather to be regarded as timid, conforming, lacking in noble spirit. Our greatest admiration is reserved for those great souls, like Socrates or Jesus, whose societies destroyed them because their consciences were so at odds with current social mores, yet who eventually were accepted by most of mankind as promulgators of valid ethical truths. Moreover, despite the vast differences in the codes and customs of the societies from which such persons came, the ideals they advocated are remarkably similar.

NEGATIVE CONSCIENCE AND POSITIVE

Many problems inherent in the social usefulness theory of morals can be resolved if one follows Erich Fromm in distinguishing two kinds of conscience, a negative and a positive one. The former fills us with guilt when we transgress the code of our society; and it is adequately accounted for by the theory outlined above. The positive conscience makes us feel guilty when we fail to live up to the best that is in us. It is the glimpse of what we might be, and so, perhaps, a glimpse of the "moral manifold" as manifested in us. Fromm gives an example, a man with musical talents who went into business at his father's insistence, was unsuccessful, and then overcome with guilt feelings. At first these seemed to spring from realizing that he had failed to live up to his father's expectations. But after a dream in which, as a very successful business man praised by his parent he was suddenly overcome with panic and the impulse to kill himself, he came to realize that the core of his guilt feeling was not the failure to satisfy his father but, on the contrary, his obedience to the parent and his failure to live up to his own true potentialities.

The main distinguishing feature of this positive conscience is that, when it operates strongly, its dictates are so compelling that the individual is indifferent to social pressures. Whether his contemporaries praise or revile him or even put him to death, he is unmoved. Socrates in his immortal Apology said "Wherefore, O Men of Athens, acquit me or not; but whichever you do, understand that I will never alter my ways, not even if I have to die many times." And William Penn in the Tower of London, even more dramatically: "My prison shall be my grave before I will budge a jot; for I owe my conscience to no mortal man." Such positive conscience, whose dictates may be completely opposed to the society in which its owner lives, obviously cannot be accounted for as the internalized code of that society. It might of course be claimed that Socrates' conscience was out of step with that of his group because his parents had instilled socially aberrant views in him; but this just pushes the problem back a generation without bringing it nearer solution. What made them deviate? An alternative, as already suggested, is that the universe contains moral forces subject to their own laws, and that the positive conscience is our means of sensing them. From this viewpoint the social code of a given society is a mixture of components found empirically to promote the welfare of its members, and components based on their positive consciences.

Presumably man's nature is such that rules of conduct dictated by moral law often coincide with those based on expediency. When they diverge, only the former endure and become incorporated into later social codes.

WE NEED MORE LIGHT

Two obvious objections to this view may be briefly considered. The first, implicit in the preceding discussion, is that individuals' consciences tell them to do all sorts of acts, some of which later generations perceive as clearly wicked. How is this possible if conscience is our intuition of moral law? I believe the answer is that moral laws are revealed to us only piecemeal and that conscience is still a rudimentary and unreliable sense. Physical laws, also, are only slowly revealed to us. It was not so long ago that heavy objects were thought to fall faster than light ones and combustion to result from releasing phlogiston. Furthermore, like moral laws, physical laws are initially discovered by intuition. The only difference is that intuitions as to physical laws can be verified by scientific method, and there is no such tool for verifying intuitions about moral law except, perhaps, the slowly and painfully accumulating experience of mankind.

This point may be worth dwelling on. Intuitions may be very wrong. One of Pythagoras' intuitions was the theorem about the relations of the hypotenuse and sides of a right triangle, an immensely powerful insight. Another, held with equal conviction, was that it was wicked to eat beans. But the fact that an intuition can be wrong should not obscure the fact that it can also be right, nay more, that intuition is the major source of genuinely new knowledge. If it can be verified by experiment or observation, so much the better; but it can be right even if we cannot test it. Many great scientists have enunciated propositions, later verified, which they could not prove and which remained undemonstrated for decades. Nor would it be surprising if the light of intuition in moral matters were so often dim and uncertain. Man emerged into an awareness of moral values only an instant ago, evolutionarily speaking, so that his moral sense would be expected to be still rudimentary.

The second objection asks, "If there is a moral law which increasingly manifests itself in human behavior, why does man's behavior towards his fellows seem to be no better now than it was at the Stone Age? Indeed, in some ways it may be worse. Instead of killing individuals, we now wipe out whole societies." Several considerations weaken the cogency of this objection. Perhaps acts we now see as immoral will eventually prove to have been in the service of a higher morality beyond our present comprehension. Or, if our present appraisal of morality is correct, it may be that on balance there is more good in the world than before. Moral behavior may also be increasing, and perhaps at a faster rate. Or even if evil behavior has relatively increased, the significant fact may be that our moral sense has become more refined so that we are now outraged by acts and institutions which even our recent forebears took for granted, such as slavery and the public torture of criminals. Eventually this increase in moral sensitivity would seem certain to affect our behavior beneficially.

To sum up: The dictates of an individual's conscience may be completely opposed to the mores of his society yet later may be generally accepted as correct. Moreover, despite wide differences of behavior in different cultures, the values accepted by the members of these cultures are remarkably similar. The social utility view of ethics and conscience, while containing much truth, cannot explain these facts. Nor does it yield a valid basis for distinguishing right from wrong though it may appear to do so. These considerations are no less well accounted for by the hypothesis that the universe contains moral as well as physical forces, whose laws are revealed to us through conscience, however imperfectly. It is this moral aspect of the universe which gives dignity and meaning to human life. Physically we are unimaginably fleeting, trivial, and fragile organizations of matter. As the highest expression of moral law yet realized on earth, our lives may have immeasurable significance: "The power that stirs in you, if you will let it, is competent to produce results far beyond those you personally attain. . . . You are but a tiny estuary; but when the tides enter your being, you will feel the pulse of the infinite sea."

19. *The Challenge of Nuclear Death*

THE PROBLEM OF how to meet death has to be faced by everyone whom death does not seize by surprise, but until the recent past one could postpone coming to grips with it until one had reached old age. Now suddenly death may be equally imminent to everyone at every age and station of life. Although there are some hopeful developments, the hard fact remains that nuclear weapons are continuing to proliferate and are becoming more powerful. The destructive power of a single bomb has increased geometrically since 1945. That is, it has just about doubled every year. The largest H-bomb exploded by the Russians was about 3,000 times as powerful as the Hiroshima bomb which the Japanese call "the original child bomb." Until this process is halted, the probability that we shall all die in a nuclear war has continued to increase, and annihilation may come at any moment unannounced.

As the danger of destruction of our society through nuclear war looms ever larger, there are three alternatives available to us. The first is flight, and I really urge every one to take this seriously. It is conceivable that if one lived in the Southern Hemisphere, and if a nuclear exchange were not too heavy, one might survive the effects of radiation spread around the earth. However, as one thinks about this, there are certain great drawbacks. First of all, the security may be illusory. When one thinks of how Americans are disliked in all the countries of the south, one wonders what the chances would be for Americans to survive in case the United States were suddenly destroyed. One would expect chaos everywhere, and I expect many Americans would be victims. One is reminded of the old parable "Appointment in Samara," about the servant, who rushed to his master from the marketplace very frightened and begged for a horse because he wanted to ride to Samara since in the marketplace he had seen Death, who had looked at him threateningly. So the merchant gave him the horse, and off the servant went. Then the merchant went to the marketplace (this was one of those Arabian countries where one can speak to Death) and found Death. He reproached him for frightening his servant. And Death said, "Oh? Did I frighten him? I did not mean to. My look was one of surprise. You see, I have an appointment with him tonight in Samara." This parable has settled the question of flight for me. There is a deeper reason, of course, why flight is unacceptable to most of us. It means tearing oneself from the web of human relationships, from everything that gives life meaning. After one passes a certain age, it is ridiculous to think of prolonging one's life a few years at the expense of everything that really matters. So, for me, this particular escape is excluded.

The next possibility is to resort to what has been called denial. This is the mechanism by which one simply pretends the danger isn't there. This is something we all do and have to do to stay alive. No one can contemplate his own death steadily and remain sane. So all of us are very able to deny the prospect of our own personal deaths. One cannot quarrel with those who take refuge in this solution, but many will find it unacceptable also. For one thing it is an uncertain thing, for it is apt to give way at any time, leaving one unprotected from chaos. The head-in-the-sand posture is not a comfortable one, and it is hard to maintain indefinitely. Denial is also unacceptable to many because it reduces the incentive to continue to try to avert the catastrophe. "Don't pay any attention to him, and he may go away," may work for an importunate child, but it does not help much against the mounting danger of nuclear war. Like flight, for many denial is also incompatible with self-respect. We hope we are manly enough to face dangers squarely.

This leaves the third alternative, which is acceptance. If we face the possibility of an early death squarely, then we look to religion for help in reconciling ourselves to it. One of the main purposes of religion has been to help people cope with the prospect of their own dissolution. Yet religions in America, and especially liberal ones, seem to pay little attention to this problem. It is often not even indexed in books on ethical religion, as if it were taboo. We have a lot to say about bereavement, the death of someone else, but very little to say about our own death. Before considering how humanist religions view death, let us consider the traditional religious answer: the mystical one. According to this view, life is a preparation for the hereafter. Death is the beginning of the path to heaven. The chief evidence that a hereafter exists is that the mystical vision, the picture of heaven, is the same in almost every culture. Here is one of Dante's magnificent descriptions of heaven:

> We have now issued from the largest sphere
> Into that heaven of purest light composed—
> Light intellectual, with love transfused;
> Light of true good, transfused throughout with joy;
> Joy that surpasses every sweet delight.
> Much as a sudden lightning flash darts forth
> Which overcomes our sight, so that the eye
> Loses its power to see the clearest objects:
> Just so a vivid light shone round about,
> And left me veiled in such a dazzling glare
> That nothing else was visible to me.
> The light I saw as like a blazing river
> A streaming radiance set between two banks
> Enamelled with the wonders of the spring
> And from the stream proceeded living sparks
> Which set themselves in flowers on every side,
> And glowed like rubies in a golden setting
> Until, as if o'ercome by that sweet scent,
> They plunged again into the gleaming flood,
> Whence others issued forth to take their place.[1]

Now this picture of heaven has been described in almost identical terms by mystics in every culture. Its salient features are brightness, jewels and flowers, feelings of joy, brotherhood, and that all is right with the world, no matter how evil the world may seem to be and how much one has suffered. The experience always seems to be true. It has the stamp of verisimilitude upon it. What is particularly fascinating to psychologists and psychiatrists is that the mystical experience can now be produced almost at will by certain drugs, notably psilocybin, extracted from the "magic" mushroom of the Mexicans; they use it in their religious rites. If one takes the drug in the proper setting, one usually has visions of brilliant light, sparkling jewels and flowers, and feelings of joy, and brotherhood. If the environment is threatening, the same experience is hellish, the light becomes diabolical, and the vision becomes extremely frightening. How can one reconcile the fact that one can produce this vision with a toxic agent with the belief that it is true? This is not difficult for Aldous Huxley. He does it by the assumption that we could not stand the full force of this experience all the time and therefore our brains have what he calls a "reducing valve," which cuts down the strength of the outside stimuli. These drugs paralyze the reducing valve, and we experience reality.

It is interesting to think about the social conditions on earth when this kind of religion thrives. Life on earth is an inferno. There is death around every corner. Disease, misery, poverty, and distress are everywhere, and everyone is equally threatened whether he be master or slave. Furthermore all one's knowledge and energy cannot change the state of affairs. There is nothing a person can do to relieve his own lot or that of other people so he naturally looks to an afterlife. He can say to himself, "The more I suffer in this world, the more this will prepare me to enjoy the next one." Furthermore in a world where there is no reward for good deeds, and they cannot be assumed to be helpful to others, there has to be some kind of sanction for morality, since there was no evidence that what one did made any difference. This sanction could be found in the afterlife. Finally the very hardships of life fostered the mystical experience, which as I mentioned is fostered by a toxic state. Aldous Huxley, in a fascinating book called *Heaven and Hell*, describes how the mystics starved, flagellated themselves, and mistreated themselves in other ways and were probably full of infections, so that they were predisposed toward mystical experiences.[2]

The humanistic religions reject, or at least are unwilling to affirm, the existence of a hereafter. But they also recognize that every human being needs to feel that his existence contributes something to a larger purpose, and that his death, like his life, is part of it. The consolation they offer, which at first glance seems more rational than the mystical one, is that the individual continues to live through his influence in society. The ethical leaders have all expressed themselves on this point. I happened to have picked a quotation from Jerome Nathanson:

> It is not *that* we are, and shall *not* be that counts. . . . It is *what* we are and what we *might* continue to be in the lives of others that counts objectively. To keep one's mind nailed to this fact is I think the transcendentally important thing in the contemplation of one's own death: that relationships do endure in this living sense, and that they eddy far out beyond anything that any of us can imagine.[3]

Humanistic religions flourish in times when human misery is spotty, is not constantly before us, and can in principle be largely alleviated through the expenditure of enough energy, intelligence, and good will. We know *how* to bring about a heaven on earth if we only want to do so badly enough. In such a world moral behavior can be relied on to bring rewards. The individual *does* have the power to better himself and increase his own sense of self-fulfillment, directly as well as indirectly through the satisfaction he gains from the knowledge that he has been able to help others achieve richer lives. Thus a belief in human potentialities is reasonable and both a valid basis for morality and a way of coping with death. Unfortunately the advent of nuclear weapons changes this consolation and perhaps even abolishes it. Hans Morgenthau has recently expressed this point with great force, and although this is a rather painful passage to read, it makes the point well:

> Nuclear destruction is mass destruction, both of persons and of things. It signifies the simultaneous destruction of tens of mil-

lions of people, of whole families, generations, and societies, of all the things they have inherited and created. . . . This nuclear destruction destroys the meaning of death by depriving it of its individuality. . . . Man gives his life and death meaning by his ability to make himself and his works remembered after his death. Patroclus dies to be avenged by Achilles. Hector dies to be mourned by Priam. Yet if Patroclus, Hector, and all those who could remember them were killed simultaneously, what would become of the meaning of Patroclus's and Hector's deaths? Their lives and deaths would lose their meaning. They would die, not like men but like beasts, killed in the mass, and what would be remembered would be the quantity of the killed—six million, twenty million, fifty million—not the quality of one man's death as over against another's. . . . And what would become of life itself? If our age had not replaced the belief in the immortality of the individual person with the immortality of humanity and its civilization, we could take the prospect of nuclear death in our stride. We could even afford to look forward to the day of the great slaughter as a day on which the preparatory and vain life on this earth would come to an end for most of us and the true, eternal life in another world begin. Yet a secular age, which has lost faith in individual immortality in another world and is aware of the impending doom of the world through which it tries to perpetuate itself here and now is left without a remedy. Once it has become aware of its condition it must despair.[4]

Today, as I have mentioned, we are witnessing a revival of interest in the mystical experience, even in the most unlikely quarters. An eminent professor of psychiatry recently went to India to interview children who claimed to remember previous incarnations. Highly reputable experimental scientific psychologists are using drugs that predispose to mystical experiences in their psychotherapy. They take the drug with the patient, and do not hesitate to call the resulting experiences "sacred." This trend is probably based on acceptance of the point made by Dr. Morgenthau, that the only way of coping with the problems raised by nuclear death is to revive and cling to one's belief in a heaven, the afterlife. It may also be an indirect expression of the recognition that if there were any survivors after a nuclear war, the world for them would be even worse than for those living at the time of Dante. It would be a world of profound and unrelievable misery, which no human efforts could alleviate, and therefore without a basis for hope or morality, unless it were to be found in an afterworld.

That the mystical experience has been brought into the laboratory, as it were, is indeed a cause for rejoicing, because it opens up fascinating vistas for deeper understanding of the relationship between brain processes and subjective experiences. It does not follow, however, that because the experience *seems* true, therefore it *is* true. Many dreams seem more real than real life. What then remains for those who cannot achieve a mystical solution or believe that there is salvation in a pill? Must they really despair, as Dr. Morgenthau says, or is there still a possible consolation?

I believe there is, and that it can come unbidden to those who squarely face the prospect of death, even without belief in an afterlife. One starts with the recognition that the riddle of personal death defies the human intellect. The humanist consolation is really no more rational than the mystical one; even if society lasted for thousands of years, the individual becomes extinguished soon after his death. Both genetically and socially the contribution of any one generation is attenuated to the vanishing point in, say, two centuries. Our great-great-great-great-great-great grandparents who lived about two centuries ago are not alive today in any meaningful sense. The span of existence of any given society, or of the human race itself, is infinitesimal compared with the duration of the universe. So the consolation offered by humanistic religions, although psychologically real, is also essentially irrational. We are reminded that the human intellect, like a flashlight, illuminates a small area sharply. Around the bright spot stretch boundless realms of darkness.

Since the answer to the riddle of personal death is, I believe, beyond the grasp of the intellect, it is worthwhile to examine the actual experiences of those who have accepted the likelihood that they were going to die shortly, whether there is a rational explanation for these experiences or not.

Acceptance of the high probability of early death has its pitfalls; in fact, they are all too obvious. It predisposes to anxiety and depression. It can result in fatalism, leading to moral disintegration: the philosophy of "eat, drink, and be merry, for tomorrow we die." Or it can produce a passive resignation, which is paralyzing. On the other hand, if the danger of death can be combatted, real acceptance of it *can* be a powerful incentive to try to prevent it. Thus many who have grasped the meaning of nuclear war are strongly compelled to campaign against it. This too has its drawbacks from a personal standpoint. I am living testimony to the fact that it is hard to maintain a regular job in life and still devote a large portion of one's time to the effort to avert nuclear war. Furthermore if the outcome is really hopeless, then the whole endeavor is foolish. It would be much more sensible to go on cultivating one's garden than to expend one's strength, like Don Quixote, tilting at windmills. There is, however, always a chance that complete pessimism is unjustified, that the catastrophe can still be averted if enough people try hard enough. One would hate to die with the lingering doubt that if only one had expended a little more effort civilization could have been saved. At the worst it is better to die protesting an enormity than passively acquiescing. Even if we can accomplish nothing, we still have a choice as to *how* to die: Assenting to a vain effort to win a nuclear war, which can only destroy everything for which we are striving, or striving to promote a course of action that, though it may not save our lives, has some hope of leading to the ultimate triumph in freedom and human dignity.

Even if death is unavoidable, however, as it is in the last analysis for everyone, there are many witnesses to testify that its contemplation can enormously enrich life.

The examples I have chosen are all from persons who make no mention of an afterlife or actually reject it. The first is an article written by Senator Richard Neuberger called "When I Learned I Had Cancer."[5] He makes two points very strongly. The first is that when you think you are going to die soon, your perspective on life changes and trivial annoyances fade away. He wrote:

> Yet a change came over me which I believe is irreversible. Questions of prestige, of political success, of financial status, became all at once unimportant. In those first hours when I realized I had cancer, I never thought of my seat in the Senate, of my bank ac-

count, or of the destiny of the free world. . . . My wife and I have not had a quarrel since my illness was diagnosed. I used to scold her about squeezing the toothpaste from the top instead of the bottom, about not catering sufficiently to my fussy appetite, about making up guest lists without consulting me, about spending too much on clothes. Now I am either unaware of such matters, or they seem irrelevant.

His second point, which I want to stress, is the heightened appreciation of the joy of everyday experiences:

In their stead has come a new appreciation of things I once took for granted—eating lunch with a friend, scratching Muffet's ears and listening for his purrs, the company of my wife, reading a book or magazine in the quiet cone of my bed lamp at night, raiding the refrigerator for a glass of orange juice or slice of coffee cake. For the first time I think I actually am savoring life. I realize, finally, that I am not immortal. I shudder when I remember all the occasions that I spoiled for myself—even when I was in the best of health—by false pride, synthetic values, and fancied slights.

And here is a physician, a humanist, who had cancer of both breasts and therefore knew her outlook was pretty gloomy:

My basic attitude now is one of wanting to live as long as I can, and to enjoy everything with an appetite that does not seem to have been harmed by the long years in the shadow. It has probably been made all the keener thereby. I may be enjoying my garden in spring, for instance, for the last or next to the last time. My ever-increasing pleasure in playing the piano and in becoming a more able musician may have to be cut short. . . . Oddly enough this situation does not make me unhappy. Rather, in some strange way, it often gives me a very wonderful feeling of being in touch with the deeper currents of life and nature. I seem to understand finally that death and deterioration of the body, and even possibly of the individual mind and spirit, are only incidental to the tremendous, incomprehensible, secret progression of the manifold forces of the universe. Thus, time takes on a new meaning. And impatience vanishes. And with the withdrawal of impatience, we can relax, be content and sense to the full every miracle in the endless succession that is around and in us always.[6]

Let me give you just one more, by Professor Hans Zinsser, when he knew he was dying of leukemia. He refers to himself in the third person. You will note how strikingly similar his reactions are to those I have already cited:

In the prospect of death, life seemed to be given new meaning and fresh poignancy. It seemed, he said, from the moment, as though all that his heart felt and his senses perceived were taking on a "deep autumnal tone" and an increased vividness. From now on, instead of being saddened, he found—to his own delighted astonishment—that his sensitiveness to the simplest experiences, even for things that in other years he might hardly have noticed, was infinitely enhanced. . . . [He] felt a deeper tenderness for the people whom he loved, and a warmer sympathy and understanding for many whose friendship he had lost in one way or another. . . . Each moment of the day, every prospect on meadow or hill or sea, every change of life from dawn to dusk, excited him emotionally with an unexpected clarity of perception and a new suggestiveness of association. . . . Everything that went on about him or within him struck upon his heart and mind with a new and powerful resonance. So, on the whole, he was far from either meriting or desiring sympathy. . . . He was not, at any time, tempted to seek strength in wishful surrender to a religious faith in which far greater men than he had taken refuge just before death. . . . Indeed, he became more firm in his determination to see things out consistently along his own lines of resignation to agnostic uncertainty.[7]

The Broadway play *The Gift of Time* led me to read the book on Charles Wertenbaker's death. One little statement in it is very revealing. When he learned he had cancer, he seriously contemplated drowning himself but did not do it. Though he suffered dreadfully in the days remaining to him, he wrote in his last days that if he had carried out his intention, "I'd have drowned the best part of my life." His widow echoed this sentiment: "The good hours were the best of a lifetime."[8]

These examples of the rewards of facing the prospect of an early death raise many questions, two of which I should like to touch on. The first is how common is this experience? Must it be reserved for a fortunate few with special gifts of personality or temperament, or can most of us achieve it? I have consulted medical colleagues who have had rather extensive experience with the dying, but they had never thought of the problem in positive terms. They could only tell me that whether a person meets death courageously or fearfully is unpredictable. They never sought to inquire whether the knowledge enriched his life. They did say, however, that more persons than they would have anticipated maintained a courageous attitude. So perhaps the experiences I have quoted are not too rare. The other question is to what extent the experience of the enrichment of the present depends on relinquishing concern for the future. The examples were all persons in middle or late life, and they had achieved their major goals. It was relatively easy for them to invest themselves in the present. But what of our young people for whom life lies ahead? How much does the contemplation of distant goals add to the meaning of life? How great must the hope of attaining these goals be? These are difficult questions. At first glance the problem would seem more severe for the child, since most of his life lies ahead, than for the adults. Ultimate goals influence the meaning of their lives very little. Even the child's feelings of success or failure are determined by his current world, the reactions of his parents, teachers, and friends, and *not* by his ultimate goals. An "A" in a course may give a child the same psychological boost which a great writer or scientist receives from winning the Nobel prize. So perhaps the best way for youngsters to deal with death is simply to utilize the mechanism of denial, as they have always done, regardless of their religious beliefs. That is, it is unwise to drill the prospect of early death into our children. As the child gets older, goals of course do play a larger part in determining his present experience of life. The future goal, however, has meaning only as it is psychologically present today. The experience of striving toward the goal is what counts. As long as there is even a faint hope of a future, the incentive to continue striving will remain. The future for any individual person is always problematical, with or without nuclear war, but this is no reason for him to abandon his goals, for his pessimism may prove to be unjustified.

In any case the main lesson of the examples is the reaffirmation that it is the quality of life that counts, not its duration. Living with the prospect of death can enrich life in several ways. One is no longer bothered by petty annoyances and gains a deeper sense of solidarity with loved ones. Above all, one can hope to savor more fully the joys of life and to sense the deeper meaning of existence. Why this must be so must remain a mystery. The intellect can carry us only to a certain point. That it is so we know from reports of persons who have had the experience.

If we avert our gaze from the prospect of nuclear death, we do nothing to combat it, and so acquiesce passively in our fate. If we face it squarely, this may lead not to despair but to attainment of inner rewards and to a renewed zest in the battle to attain peace, a battle that must be won.

To end with a quotation from Felix Adler, the founder of the Ethical Movement:

> In our miserable state as human ephemerality swept across the scene of sky and land between morning and night we yet, in our intermittent moments of lucid outlook have such glimpses of grandeur as are sufficient to waken and justify the feeling that we have had our share, that there is no cause or occasion for us to revile the order of things, but rather to be grateful and hold our peace. I have been permitted, let a man say, in this poor life of mine to behold the sun and the stars and to divine the order and beauty that is beyond them. I have been permitted to look into loving eyes and to catch glimpses of the light at which they were kindled.

Notes

CHAPTER 1

1. Harris, T. A., *I'm O.K., You're O.K.: A Practical Guide to Transactional Analysis* (New York: Harper and Row, 1969); Neuman, M., and Berkowitz, B., *How To Be Your Own Best Friend* (New York: Random House, 1973).

2. Frank, J. D., Therapeutic Factors in Psychotherapy, *Am. J. Psychotherapy* 25:350–61, 1971; Frank, J. D., Psychotherapy or Psychotherapies?, pp. 13–23, in Masserman, J. H., ed., *Current Psychiatric Therapies*, vol. 13 (New York: Grune and Stratton, 1973).

3. Masserman, J. H., *A Psychiatric Odyssey* (New York: Science House, 1971).

4. Hsu, F. L. K., Kinship Is the Key, *The Center Magazine*, November/December, 1973, pp. 4–14.

5. Schutz, W. C., *Joy: Expanding Human Awareness* (New York: Grove Press, 1967).

6. Lieberman, M. A., Yalom, I. D., and Miles, M. B., *Encounter Groups: First Facts* (New York: Basic Books, 1973).

7. Pande, S. K., The Mystique of "Western" Psychotherapy: An Eastern Interpretation, *J. Nerv. Ment. Dis.* 146:425–32, 1968; Neki, J. S., Guru-Cheta Relationship: The Possibility of a Therapeutic Paradigm, *Am. J. Orthopsychiat.* 43:755–65, 1973.

8. Berne, E., *Transactional Analysis in Psychotherapy* (New York: Grove Press, 1961); Low, A., *Mental Health Through Will-Training* (Boston: Christopher Publishing House, 1950).

9. Henry, W. E., Sims, J. H., and Spray, S. L., *The Fifth Profession* (San Francisco: Jossey Bass, 1971).

10. Caplan, G., Emotional Crises, in Deutsch, A., and Fishman H., eds., *The Encyclopedia of Mental Health,* vol. 2 (New York: Franklin Watts, 1963); Rusk, T. N., Opportunity and Technique in Crisis Psychiatry, *Comp. Psychiat.* 12:249–63, 1971; Gruenberg, E. M., The Social Breakdown Syndrome—Some Origins, *Am. J. Psychiat.* 123:1481–89, 1967.

11. Sifneos, P. E., *Short-Term Psychotherapy and Emotional Crisis* (Cambridge, Mass.: Harvard University Press, 1972).

12. May, P. R. A., *Treatment of Schizophrenia: A Comparative Study of Five Treatment Methods* (New York: Science House, 1968).

13. Tyhurst, J. S., The Role of Transition States—Including Disasters—in Mental Illness, pp. 149–72 in *Symposium on Preventive and Social Psychiatry* (Washington, D.C.: Walter Reed Army Institute of Research, 1957).

14. Eysenck, H. J., The Effects of Psychotherapy, *Int. J. Psychiat.* 1:97–142, 1965; Bergin, A. E., The Evaluation of Therapeutic Outcomes, pp. 217–70 in Bergin, A. E., and Garfield, S. L., eds., *Handbook of Psychotherapy and Behavior Change: An Empirical Analysis* (New York: John Wiley and Sons, 1971).

15. Bandura, A., Psychotherapy Based Upon Modeling Principles, pp. 653–708 in Bergin, A. E., and Garfield, S. L., eds., *Handbook of Psychotherapy and Behavior Change: An Empirical Analysis* (New York: John Wiley and Sons, 1971); Paul, G. L., *Insight vs. Desensitization in Psychotherapy* (Stanford, Calif.: Stanford University Press, 1966).

16. Marks, I. M., *Fears and Phobias* (New York: Academic Press, 1969).

17. Voth, H. M., and Orth, M. H., *Psychotherapy and the Role of the Environment* (New York: Behavioral Publications, 1973).

18. Klein, M. H., Dittman, A. T., Parloff, M. R., and Gill, M. W., Behavior Therapy: Observations and Reflections, *J. Consult. Clin. Psychol.* 33:259–66, 1969.

19. Yalom, I. D., *The Theory and Practice of Group Psychotherapy* (New York: Basic Books, 1970).

20. Speck, R. V., and Rueveni, U., Network Therapy—A Developing Concept, *Family Process* 8:182, 1969.

21. Kadushin, C., *Why People Go to Psychiatrists* (New York: Atherton, 1969).

22. Henderson, A. S., Care-Eliciting Behavior in Man, *J. Nerv. Ment. Dis.* 159: 172–81, 1974.

23. Malan, D. H., *A Study of Brief Psychotherapy* (Philadelphia: Lippincott, 1963).

24. Havens, L. L., Clinical Methods in Psychiatry, *Int. J. Psychiat.* 10:7–28, 1972.

CHAPTER 2

1. See, for instance, Parsons, T., Illness and the Role of the Physician: A Sociological Perspective, *Am. J. Orthopsychiat.* 21:452–60, 1951. Sebastian DeGrazia gives a brilliant if biased analysis of cultural and other factors contributing to the psychotherapist's influence over his patients. See DeGrazia, *Errors of Psychotherapy* (New York: Doubleday, 1952).

2. Reider, N., A Type of Transference to Institutions, *J. Hillside Hosp.* 2:23–29, 1953. For an interesting account of experimental studies on the context of a situation as an important determinant of influence, see Blake, R. R., and Mouton, J. S., The Dynamics of Influence and Coercion, *Int. J. Social Psychiat.* 2:263–74, 1957.

3. Freud, S., *A General Introduction to Psychoanalysis* (New York: Liveright, 1920), p. 212.

4. Breuer, J., and Freud, S., Studies on Hysteria, in Freud, *The Complete Psychological Works* 2:3–305 (London: Hogarth Press, 1955), p. 265.

5. Schaffer, L., and Myers, J. K., Psychotherapy and Social Stratification, *Psychiat.* 17:83–93, 1954.

6. Whitehorn, J. C., and Betz, B. J., *Effective Psychotherapy with the Schizophrenic Patient* (New York: Aronson, 1975).

7. See, for instance, Winokur, G., "Brainwashing"—A Social Phenomenon of Our Time, *Human Organization* 13:16–18, 1955; and Wyatt, F., Climate of Opinion and Methods of Readjustment, *Am. Psychologist* 11:537–42, 1956.

8. Glover, E., Research Methods in Psycho-Analysis, *Int. J. Psycho-Analysis* 33:403–9, 1952.

9. Wolff, W., Fact and Value in Psychotherapy, *Am J. Psychotherapy* 8:466–86, 1954.

10. Appel, K. E., Lhamon, W. T., Myers, J. M., and Harvey, W. A., Long Term Psychotherapy, *Res. Publ. Assn. Nerv. Ment. Dis.* 31:21–34, 1951.

11. See note 9, p. 470.

12. Ellenberger, H., The Ancestry of Dynamic Psychotherapy, *Bull. Menninger Clin.* 20:288–99, p. 290, 1956.

13. Frank, J. D., Gliedman, L. H., Imber, S. D., Nash, E. H., Jr., and Stone, A. R., Why Patients Leave Psychotherapy, *AMA Arch. Neurol. and Psychiat.* 77:283–99, 1957. The results are mentioned in more detail in Imber, Frank, Gliedman, Nash, and Stone, Suggestibility, Social Class and the Acceptance of Psychotherapy, *J. Clin. Psychol.* 12:341–44, 1956, and in Imber, Nash, and Stone, Social Class and Duration of Psychotherapy, *J. Clin. Psychol.* 11:281–84, 1955.

14. See note 5.

15. Frank and others, note 13, p. 294.

16. With psychotics the suggested relation between degree of distress and willingness to trust the therapist often does not hold, because their distrust of others, especially those who seem to be offering help, is so profound. With such patients, the common core of successful psychotherapy may be the ability to break through this attitude and establish a trusting, confidential relationship. See, for example, Whitehorn, J. C., and Betz, B. J., A Comparison of Psychotherapeutic Relationships between Physicians and Schizophrenic Patients When Insulin Is Combined with Psychotherapy and When Psychotherapy Is Used Alone, *Am. J. Psychiat.* 113:901–10, 1957. This common feature may explain the equally good results claimed by advocates of apparently incompatible therapeutic approaches. See, for example, Brody, E. B., and Redlich, F. C., eds., *Psychotherapy with Schizophrenics* (New York: International Universities Press, 1952).

17. See note 9.

18. This point is interestingly discussed by B. F. Skinner in Rogers, C. R., and Skinner, B. F., Some Issues Concerning the Control of Human Behavior: A Symposium, *Science* 124:1057–66, 1956.

19. The description of brainwashing in this paper is based on: Hinkle, L. E., Jr., and Wolff, H. G., Communist Interrogation and Indoctrination of "Enemies of the State," *AMA Arch. Neurol. Psychiat.* 76: 115–74, 1956; Lifton, R. J., "Thought Reform" of Western Civilians in Chinese Communist Prisons, *Psychiat.* 19:173–95, 1956; Lifton, Chinese Communist Thought Reform, pp. 219–312, in *Group Processes: Transactions of the Third Conference* (New York: Josiah Macy, Jr. Foundation, 1957); Schein, E. H., The Chinese Indoctrination Program for Prisoners of War, *Psychiat.* 19:149–72, 1956. See also Sargant, W., *Battle for the Mind* (New York: Doubleday, 1957). He suggests that thought reform, religious revivals, and certain psychiatric treatments facilitate attitude change by producing excessive excitation, leading to emotional exhaustion and hypersuggestibility.

20. This reinforcement of certain of the prisoner's responses is analogous to operant conditioning, as will be discussed more fully in connection with psychotherapy.

21. Schein, note 19, p. 163 and footnote.

22. Ibid., pp. 162–63.

23. Lifton, *Group Processes*, note 19, p. 269.

24. Hinkle and Wolff (note 19), p. 171.

25. Goffman, E., Interpersonal Persuasion, pp. 117–93, in *Group Processes: Transactions of the Third Conference* (New York: Josiah Macy, Jr. Foundation, 1957).

26. Kubie, L. S., *Practical Aspects of Psychoanalysis* (New York: Norton, 1936), p. 140.

27. See note 26, p. 145.

28. Freud, note 3, pp. 319–21 (Freud's italics).

29. Stunkard, A., Some Interpersonal Aspects of an Oriental Religion, *Psychiat.* 14:419–31, 1951.

30. Cantril, H., *The Psychology of Social Movements* (New York: John Wiley and Sons, 1941).

31. Bordin, E. S., Ambiguity as a Therapeutic Variable, *J. Consult. Psychol.* 19:9–15, 1955.

32. For a brilliant analysis of compliance, identification, and internalization in the influencing process, see H. C. Kelman, Compliance, Identification, and Internalization: Three Processes of Attitude Change, *J. Conflict Res.* 2:51–60, 1958.

33. Hilgard, E. R., *Theories of Learning* (New York: Appleton-Century-Crofts, 1948), ch. 4, pp. 82–120.

34. Ruesch, J., Psychotherapy and Communication, pp. 180–87, in Fromm-Reichmann, F., and Moreno, J. L., eds., *Progress in Psychotherapy*, 1956 (New York: Grune and Stratton, 1956), p. 183.

35. Greenspoon, J., The Reinforcing Effect of Two Spoken Sounds on the Frequency of Two Responses, *Am. J. Psychol.* 68:409–16, 1955.

36. Salzinger, K., and Pisoni, S., Reinforcement of Affect Responses of Schizophrenics During the Clinical Interview, *J. Abnormal and Social Psychol.* 57:84–90, 1958.

37. Murray, E. J., A Content-Analysis Method for Studying Psychotherapy, *Psychological Monographs* (1956) 70, Whole No. 420. The "Herbert Bryan" protocol is in Rogers, C. R., *Counseling and Psychotherapy* (New York: Houghton Mifflin, 1942), pp. 259–437.

38. See, for instance, Kubie, note 26, Ch. 7.

39. Breuer and Freud, note 4, p. 295.

40. See Glover, note 8, p. 405, and The Therapeutic Effect of Inexact Interpretation: A Contribution to the Theory of Suggestion, *Int. J. Psycho-Analysis* 12:397–411, 1931. Other psychoanalytic writers have stressed the "hypersuggestibility" of patients in analysis, seeing in the transference an analogy to hypnotic rapport. See, for example, Macalpine, I., The Development of the Transference, *Psychoanalytic*

Quarterly 19:501–39, 1950; Nunberg, H., Transference and Reality, *Int. J. Psycho-Analysis* 32:1–9, 1951; Fisher, C., Studies on the Nature of Suggestion: Pt. 1, Experimental Induction of Dreams by Direct Suggestion, *J. Am. Psychoanalytic Assn.* 1:222–55, 1953.

41. Rogers, note 18, p. 1063.

42. Stekel, W., *Interpretation of Dreams* (New York: Liveright, 1943), quoted by Wolff, W., in Fact and Value in Psychotherapy, *Am. J. Psychotherapy* 8:466–86, 1954; p. 466.

43. Rogers, C. R., A Research Program in Client-Centered Therapy, *Res. Publ. Assn. Nerv. Ment. Dis.* 31:106–13, 1951.

44. Murray, note 37.

45. Heine, R. W., A Comparison of Patients' Reports on Psychotherapeutic Experience with Psychoanalytic, Nondirective and Adlerian Therapists, *Am. J. Psychotherapy* 7:16–23, 1953.

46. Rosenthal, D., Changes in Some Moral Values Following Psychotherapy, *J. Consult. Psychol.* 19:431–36, 1955. For historical examples of "doctrinal compliance" see Ehrenwald, J., The Telepathy Hypothesis and Doctrinal Compliance in Psychotherapy, *Am. J. Psychotherapy* 11:359–79, 1957.

47. For example, in an experimental study of psychotherapy with a schizophrenic, M. B. Parloff found that "although topic choice appeared to follow the therapist's values remarkably closely, the patient's own evaluation of these topics in some instances, moved quite independently.... This finding suggests that the patient may be superficially compliant to the unconsciously expressed expectations of the therapist, without, however, internalizing such values." Parloff, M. B., Communication of Values and Therapeutic Change, paper read at the American Psychological Association meeting, New York, 1957.

48. Bettelheim, B., Remarks on the Psychological Appeal of Totalitarianism, *Am. J. Economics and Sociology* 12:89–96, 1952. Recent experimental studies have found that inducing a person to speak overtly in favor of some position changes his private opinion in the direction of the one he had publicly stated. See Janis, I. L., and King, B. T., The Influence of Role-Playing on Opinion Change, *J. Abnormal and Social Psychol.* 49:211–18, 1954; King, B. T., and Janis, I. L., Comparison of the Effectiveness of Improvised Versus Non-Improvised Role-Playing in Producing Opinion Changes, *Human Relations* 9:177–86, 1956.

49. Verplanck, W. S., The Operant Conditioning of Human Motor Behavior, *Psychol. Bull.* 53:70–83, 1956.

50. Parloff, M. B., Kelman, H. C., and Frank, J. D., Comfort, Effectiveness, and Self-Awareness as Criteria of Improvement in Psychotherapy, *Am J. Psychiat.* 111:343–51, 1954.

51. See note 13. See also Rogers, note 43.

52. Thompson, C. *Psychoanalysis: Evolution and Development* (New York: Hermitage House, 1950), p. 235.

53. Seeman, J., quoted in Schlien, J. M., Time-Limited Psychotherapy: An Experimental Investigation of Practical Values and Theoretical Implications, *J. Counseling Psychol.* 4:318–22, 1957.

54. See, for instance, Conn, J. H., Brief Psychotherapy of the Sex Offender: A Report of a Liaison Service Between a Court and a Private Psychiatrist, *J. Clin. Psychopathol.* 10:1–26, 1949; Conn, J. H., Hypnosynthesis III: Hypnotherapy of Chronic War Neuroses with a Discussion of the Value of Abreaction, Regression, and Revivication, *J. Clin. and Experimental Hypnosis* 1:29–43, 1953.

55. Fortin, J. N., and Abse, D. W., Group Psychotherapy with Peptic Ulcer, *Int. J. Group Psychotherapy* 6:383–91, 1956, p. 385.

56. Ibid., p. 390 and following.

57. Chappell, M. N., Stefano, J. J., Rogerson, J. S., and Pike, F. H., The Value of Group Psychological Procedures in the Treatment of Peptic Ulcer, *Am. J. Dig. Dis. Nut.* 3:813–17, 1937.

58. One patient could not be located.

59. Unfortunately Fortin and Abse do not state how many of their patients had mild recurrences, and Chappell and his colleagues do not give the improvement rate at the end of a year, so the results of the two treatment programs cannot be strictly compared. Assuming that the student who hemorrhaged in the first study is equivalent to the "relapsed" patients in the second, Chappell had the same recurrence rate at the end of three years that Fortin and Abse had at the end of a year—about 10 percent in each series. On the unlikely assumption that the four patients lost to the Chappell study had relapsed, their three-year recurrence rate is about 20 percent. Including the mild recurrences, this brings the Chappell three-year relapse rate to about 50 percent. Even this figure is well below the expected recurrence rate of over 75 percent mentioned by Fortin and Abse.

60. Frank, J. D., Gliedman, L. H., Imber, S. D., Stone, A. R., and Nash, E. H., Jr., Patients' Expectancies and Relearning as Factors Determining Improvement in Psychotherapy, *Am. J. Psychiat.* 115:961–68, 1959.

61. Schlien, J. M., Mosak, H. H., and Dreikurs, R., Effect of Time Limits: A Comparison of Two Psychotherapies, *J. Counseling Psychol.* 9:31–34, 1962. According to Schlien (see note 53), patients on time-limited therapy showed changes on TAT scores in the follow-up period, which were interpreted as undesirable, despite their maintained improvement on the other indices.

62. Alexander, F., Discussion of "Aims and Limitations of

Psychotherapy," by Paul H. Hoch, pp. 82–86, in Fromm-Reichmann and Moreno, note 34, p. 82.

63. For interesting biographical vignettes of nine such converts, see Begbie, H., *Twice-Born Men* (London: Revell, 1909).

64. Weininger, B., The Interpersonal Factor in the Religious Experience, *Psychoanalysis* 3:27–44, 1955.

65. James, W., *The Varieties of Religious Experience* (New York: Modern Library, 1936), p. 200.

66. Pierre Janet's discussion of "Miraculous Healing," ch. 1 in *Psychological Healing*, vol. 1 (New York: Macmillan, 1925) is the best account of miracle cures that has come to my attention. A very good recent account is found in Cranston, R., *The Miracle of Lourdes* (New York: McGraw-Hill, 1955).

67. See, for example, Rehder's experiment, described in chapter 9 of the present volume.

68. Janet, note 66, p. 48.

69. Wolff, H., What Hope Does for Man, *Saturday Rev. Lit.*, January 8, 1957, p. 45.

70. Kurland, A. A., The Drug Placebo: Its Psychodynamic and Conditional Reflex Action, *Behavioral Science*, 2:101–10, 1957, offers a survey of knowledge as to the effects of placebos.

71. Bloch, B., Ueber die Heilung der Warzen durch Suggestion, *Klin. Wochenschr.* 6:2271–2325, 1927.

72. Volgyesi, F. A., School for Patients, Hypnosis-Therapy and Psycho-Prophylaxis, *Brit. J. Med. Hypnotism*, 5:8–17, 1954.

73. Hampson, J. L., Rosenthal, D., and Frank, J. D., A Comparative Study of the Effect of Mephenesin and Placebo on the Symptomatology of a Mixed Group of Psychiatric Outpatients, *Bull. Johns Hopkins Hosp.* 95:170–77, 1954.

74. Appel and others, see note 10.

75. See note 6.

76. Rosenthal, D., and Frank, J. D., Psychotherapy and the Placebo Effect, *Psychol. Bull.* 53:294–302, 1956. See also the editorial by Whitehorn, J. C., Psychiatric Implications of the "Placebo Effect," *Am. J. Psychiat.*, 114:662–64, 1958.

77. Gliedman, L. H., Nash, E. H., Imber, S. D., Stone, A. R., and Frank, J. D., Reduction of Symptoms by Pharmacologically Inert Substances and by Short-Term Psychotherapy, *AMA Arch. Neurol. Psychiat.* 79:345–51, 1958.

78. Lasagna, L., Mosteller, F., von Felsinger, J. M., and Beecher, H. K., A Study of the Placebo Response, *Am. J. Med.* 16:770–79, 1954.

79. See, for example, the contributions to *Progress in Psychotherapy, 1956*, note 34.

80. Frank and others, note 13.

81. Balint, M., The Doctor, His Patient, and the Illness, *Lancet* 268:683–88, 1955.

82. Modell, W., *The Relief of Symptoms* (Philadelphia: Saunders, 1955), p. 56.

83. Sydney G. Margolin advocates deliberately fostering regression of certain patients in: On Some Principles of Therapy, *Am J. Psychiat.* 114:1087–96, 1958.

84. Frank, J. D., Psychotherapeutic Aspects of Symptomatic Treatment, *Am. J. Psychiat.* 103:21–25, 1946.

85. Sandor Rado sees as one of the critical tasks in the treatment of behavior disorders, "to generate in [the patient] an emotional matrix dominated by the welfare emotions [pleasurable desire, joy, affection, love, self-respect and pride]"; see *Psychoanalysis of Behavior* (New York: Grune and Stratton, 1956), p. 253. Perhaps faith should be included in the list.

86. For a penetrating discussion of this issue, see Kris, E., Psychoanalytic Propositions, ch. 22, pp. 332–51 in Marx, M. H., ed., *Psychological Theory* (New York. Macmillan, 1951).

CHAPTER 3

1. Battle, C. C., Imber, S. D., Hoehn-Saric, R., Stone, A. R., Nash, E. H., and Frank, J. D., Target Complaints as Criteria of Improvement, *Am. J. Psychotherapy* 20:184, 1966; Weiss, J. M. A., And Schaie, K. W., The Psychiatric Evaluation Index, *Am. J. Psychotherapy* 18:3, 1964.

2. Freyhan, F. A., Rationale and Indications of Biological Treatment of Psychiatric Disorders, *Compreh. Psychiat.* 6:283, 1965.

3. Tyhurst, J. S., The Role of Transition States—Including Disasters—in Mental Illness, in *Symposium on Preventive and Social Psychiatry*, Walter Reed Army Institute of Research, Washington, D.C., 1958, pp. 149–169.

4. Haley, J., *Strategies of Psychotherapy* (New York: Grune and Stratton, 1963.

5. Blumer, D., Psychiatric Considerations in Pain, in R. R. Rothman and F. A. Simeone, eds., *The Spine* (New York: W. B. Saunders, 1975), pp. 871–906.

6. Frank, J. D., Nash, E. H., Stone, A. R., and Imber, S. D., Immediate and Long-Term Symptomatic Course of Psychiatric Outpateints, *Am. J. Psychiat.* 120:429, 1963; Stone, A. R., Frank, J. D., Nash, E. H., and Imber, S. D., An Intensive Five-Year Follow-Up

Study of Treated Psychiatric Outpatients, *J. Nerv. Ment. Dis.* 133:410, 1961.

7. Truax, C. B., and Carkhuff, R. R., Significant Developments in Psychotherapy Research, pp. 124–155, in Abt, L. E., and Reiss, B. F., eds., *Progress in Clinical Psychology*, vol. 6 (New York: Grune and Stratton, 1964).

8. Sandor Rado has used the term "adaptational" to characterize his theory of psychodynamics. See, for example, Adaptational Psychodynamics: A Basic Science in his *Psychoanalysis of Behavior* (New York: Grune and Stratton, 1956), pp. 332–46. I have chosen the term because it comes closest to describing the approach I have in mind. It is used in a purely descriptive sense and does not imply any particular body of theory.

9. Whitehorn, J. C., The Concepts of "Meaning" and "Cause" in Psychodynamics, *Am. J. Psychiat.* 104:289, 1947.

10. Ellis, A., and Harper, P. A., *A Guide to Rational Living* (Englewood Cliffs, N.J.: Prentice Hall, 1961); Berne, E., *Transactional Analysis in Psychotherapy: A Systematic Individual and Social Psychiatry* (New York: Grove Press, 1961).

11. Moreno, J. L., Sociometry in Relation to Other Social Sciences, *Sociometry* 1:206, 1937.

12. Frankl, V. E., *Man's Search for Meaning: An Introduction to Logotherapy* (New York: Touchstone Books, 1970).

13. Hoehn-Saric, R., Frank, J. D., Imber, S. D., Nash, E. H., Stone, A. R., and Battle, C. C., Systematic Preparation of Patients for Psychotherapy. I. Effects on Therapy Behavior and Outcome, *J. Psychiat. Res.* 2:267, 1964.

CHAPTER 5

1. Mason, R. C., Clark, G., Reeves, R. B., and Wagner, B., Acceptance and Healing, *J. Relig. Health* 8:123–42, 1969, p. 140.

2. Evans, F. J., Placebo Effects in Pain Reduction, *Adv. Neurol.* 4:284–96, 1974.

3. Schwartz, G. E., Biofeedback as Therapy, *Am. Psychol.* 28:666–73, 1973.

4. Carrington, P., and Ephron, H. S., Meditation as an Adjunct to Psychotherapy, in Arieti, S., and Chrzanowski, G., eds., *New Dimen-*

sions in Psychiatry: A World View (New York: John Wiley and Sons, 1975), pp. 262–91.

5. This study is described more fully in ch. 9 of this volume.

6. Grad, B., Some Biological Effects of the "Laying on of Hands": A Review of Experiments with Animals and Plants, *J. Am. Soc. Psychical Res.* 59:95–127, 1965.

7. Smith, M. J., Paranormal Effects on Enzyme Activity, *Human Dimen.* 1:15–19, 1972.

8. Terry, J. C., and Honorton, C., Psi Information Retrieval in the Ganzfeld: Two Confirmatory Studies, *J. Am. Soc. Psychical Res.* 70(2):207–17, 1976.

9. LeShan, L., *The Medium, the Mystic and the Physicist* (New York: Viking Press, 1974).

10. Shealy, N. C., *Occult Medicine Can Save Your Life* (New York: Dial Press, 1975).

11. Klein, M. H., Dittman, A. T., Parloff, M. R., and Gill, M. W., Behavior Therapy: Observations and Reflections, *J. Consult. Clin. Psychol.* 33:259–66, 1969, p. 262.

12. Malan, D. H., The Outcome Problem in Psychotherapy Research, *Arch. General Psychiat.* 29:719–29, 1973.

CHAPTER 6

1. Rovere, R., Letter from Washington, *New Yorker*, January 29, 1955, pp. 66–74.

2. Rogers, C. R., *Counseling and Psychotherapy* (Cambridge, Mass.: Houghton, Mifflin, 1942).

3. Wexler, M., The Structural Problem in Schizophrenia: The Role of the Internal Object, *Psychotherapy with Schizophrenics* (New York: International Universities Press, 1952); Mowrer, O. H., The Therapeutic Process: III: Learning Theory and the Neurotic Fallacy, *Am. J. Orthopsychiat.* 22:679–89, 1952.

4. Bach, G. R., *Intensive Group Psychotherapy* (New York: Ronald Press, 1954).

5. Foulkes, S. H., *Introduction to Group Analytic Psychotherapy* (London: Wm. Heinemann Medical Books, 1948).

6. Dreikurs, R., The Unique Social Climate Experienced in Group Psychotherapy, *Group Psychotherapy* 3:292–99, 1955.

7. Newcomb, T. M., Autistic Hostility and Social Reality, *Human Relations* 1:69–86, 1947–48.

8. Powdermaker, F., and Frank, J. D., Group Psychotherapy with Neurotics, *Am. J. Psychiat.* 105:449–55, 1948.

CHAPTER 7

1. Libo, L. M., *Measuring Group Cohesiveness* (Ann Arbor: University of Michigan, 1953), p. 5.

2. The following discussion draws heavily on Cartwright, D., and Zander, A., *Group Dynamics* (Evanston, Ill.: Row Peterson and Co., 1953); Libo, note 1; Lippitt, R., Group Dynamics: 2. Group Dynamics and Personality Dynamics, *Am. J. Orthopsychiat.* 21:18–31, 1951; Bach, G. R., *Intensive Group Psychotherapy* (New York: Ronald Press, 1954).

3. David Levy has discussed this point in a particularly stimulating way. See: The Strange Hen, *Am. J. Orthopsychiat.* 20:355–62, 1950.

4. Lindt, H. and Sherman, M. A., "Social Incognito" in Analytically Oriented Group Psychotherapy, *Int. J. Group Pscyhotherapy* 2:209, 1952.

5. See ch. 6 of this volume.

6. Cooley, C. H., The Social Foundations and Functions of Thought and Communication, in Hare, A., Borgatta, E., and Bales, R., eds., *Small Groups: Studies in Social Interaction* (New York: Alfred A. Knopf, 1955).

7. Mann, J., Some Theoretic Concepts of the Group Process, *Int. J. Group Psychotherapy* 5:235, 1955.

8. Lewin, K., Group Decision and Social Change, in Newcomb, T. M., and Hartley, E. L., eds., *Readings in Social Psychology* (New York: Holt, 1947).

9. Foulkes, S. H., *Introduction to Group-Analytic Psychotherapy* (London: Heinemann, 1948), p. 29.

10. Cartwright and Zander, p. 141; see note 2.

11. Newcomb, T. M., Autistic Hostility and Social Reality, *Human Relations* 1:69–87, 1947–48.

CHAPTER 8

1. Rome, H. P., and Foge, R. H., The Psychosomatic Manifestations of Filariasis, *JAMA* 123, December 11, 1943.
2. Benjamin, J. E., and Hoyt, R. C., Disability Following Postvaccinal (Yellow Fever) Hepatitis, *JAMA* 128:319, June 2, 1945.

CHAPTER 9

1. Friedman, M., and Rosenman, R. H., *Type A Behavior and Your Heart* (New York: Alfred A. Knopf, 1974).
2. Parkinson, C. N., *East and West* (Boston: Houghton Mifflin, 1963).
3. Kuhn, T. S., *The Structure of Scientific Revolutions* (Chicago: University of Chicago Press, 1962).
4. Malan, D. H., The Outcome Problem in Psychotherapy Research, *Arch. General Psychiat.* 29:719–29, 1973.
5. Hinkle, L. E., Jr., et al., Studies in Human Ecology: Factors Relevant to the Occurrence of Bodily Illness and Disturbances in Mood, Thought and Behavior in Three Homogeneous Population Groups, *Am. J. Psychiat.* 114:212–20, 1957.
6. Masuda, M., and Holmes, T. H., Magnitude Estimates of Social Readjustments, *J. Psychosom. Res.* 11:219–25, 1967; and Wyler, A. R., Masuda, M., and Holmes, T. H., Magnitude of Life Events and Seriousness of Illness, *Psychosom. Med.* 33:115–22, 1971.
7. Rahe, L. H., Subjects' Recent Life Changes and Their Illness Susceptibility, *Adv. Psychosom. Med.* 8:2–19, 1972.
8. Wyler and others, see note 6.
9. Selye, H., *The Stress of Life* (New York: McGraw-Hill, 1956).
10. Lazarus, R. S., A Cognitively Oriented Psychologist Looks at Biofeedback, *Am. Psychol.* 30:555–61, 1975.
11. Wolff, G., and Money, J., Relationship Between Sleep and Growth in Patients with Reversible Somatotropin Deficiency, *Psychol. Med.* 3:18–27, 1973.
12. Powell, G. F., Hopwood, N. J., and Barrett, E. S., Growth Hormone Studies Before and During Catch-up Growth in a Child with Emotional Deprivation and Short Stature. *J. Clin. Endocrinol. Metab.* 37:674–79, 1973.

13. *Editor's note:* For an example of an observational study of hospitalized patients, see ch. 8 of this volume.

14. Veterans Administration, *Rehabilitation of the Chronic Neurologic Patient* (Washington, D.C.: Veterans Administration, 1949; VA pamphlet 10-29).

15. Skipper, J. K., Jr., and Leonard, R. C., Children, Stress and Hospitalization: A Field Experiment, *J. Health Social Behav.* 9:275–87, 1968.

16. Imboden, J. B., Canter, A., Cluff, L. E., and Trevor, R. W., Brucellosis. III. Psychological Aspects of Delayed Convalescence, *Arch. Intern. Med.* 103:406–14, 1959.

17. Cluff, L. E., Canter, A., and Imboden, J., Asian Influenza: Infection, Disease and Psychological Factors, *Arch. Intern. Med.* 117:159–64, 1966.

18. Mason, R. C., Clark, G., Reeves, R. B., and Wagner, B., Acceptance and Healing, *J. Relig Health* 8:123–42, 1969.

19. Cranston, R., *The Miracle of Lourdes* (New York: McGraw-Hill, 1955).

20. Osler, W., The Faith That Heals, *Brit. Med. J.* 1:1470–72, 1910.

21. Rehder, H., Wunderheilungen: Ein Experiment, *Hippokrates* 26:577–80, 1955.

22. Evans, F. J., The Placebo Response in Pain Reduction, *Adv. Neurol.* 4:284–96, 1974.

23. Wolf, S., Effects of Suggestion and Conditioning on the Action of Chemical Agents in Human Subjects: The Pharmacology of Placebos, *J. Clin. Invest.* 29:100–109, 1950.

24. Beecher, H. K., Surgery as Placebo, *JAMA* 176:1102–07, 1961.

25. Ross, R. S., Ischemic Heart Disease: An Overview, *Am. J. Cardiol.* 36:496–505, 1975.

26. Achuff, S. C., Griffith, L. S. C., Conti, R. C., Humphries, J. O'N., Brawley, R. K., Gott, U. L., and Ross, R. S., The "Angina Producing" Myocardial Segment: An Approach to the Interpretation of Results of Coronary Artery Bypass Surgery, *Proc. 22d Annual Scient. Sess. Am. Coll. Cardiol.*, San Francisco, 1973.

27. Wittkower, E., Studies on Influence of Emotions on Functions of Organs, Including Observations in Normals and Neurotics, *J. Ment. Sci.* 81:533–682, 1935.

28. Schwartz, G. E., Biofeedback as Therapy, *Am. Psychol.* 28:666–73, 1973.

29. Engel, B. G., Nikovmanesh, P., and Shuster, M. M., Operant Conditioning of Rectosphincteric Responses in the Treatment of Fecal Incontinence, *New Eng. J. Med.* 290:646–49, 1974.

30. Blanchard, E. B., and Young, L. D., Clinical Application of Biofeedback Training, *Arch. Gen Psychiat.* 30:573–89, 1974.

31. Carrington, P., and Ephron, H. S., Meditation as an Adjunct to Psychotherapy, pp. 262–91 in Arieti, S., and Chrzanowski, G., eds., *New Dimensions in Psychiatry: A World View* (New York: Wiley, 1975).

32. Glueck, B. C., and Stroebel, C. F., Biofeedback and Meditation in the Treatment of Psychiatric Illnesses, *Compreh. Psychiat.* 16:303–21, 1975.

33. Everson, T. C., and Cole, W. H., *Spontaneous Regression of Cancer* (Philadelphia: Saunders, 1966).

34. Bahnson, M. B., and Bahnson, C. B., Ego Defenses in Cancer Patients, *Annals N.Y. Acad. Sci.* 164:546–59, 1969.

35. LeShan, L., An Emotional Life-History Pattern Associated with Neoplastic Disease, *Annals N.Y. Acad. Sci.* 125:780–93, 1965/66.

36. Thomas C. B., and Duszynski, K. R., Closeness to Parents and the Family Constellation in a Prospective Study of Five Disease States: Suicide, Mental Illness, Malignant Tumor, Hypertension and Coronary Heart Disease, *Johns Hopkins Med. J.* 134:251–70, 1974.

37. Le Shan, L., note 35.

38. Klopfer, B., Psychological Variables in Human Cancer, *J. Personality Assessment* 21:331–40, 1957.

39. Simonton, O. C., Matthews-Simonton, S., and Creighton, J., *Getting Well Again* (Los Angeles: Tarcher, 1978).

40. Abrams, H. S., Suicidal Behavior in Chronic Dialysis Patients, *Am. J. Psychiat.* 127:1194–1204, 1971.

CHAPTER 10

1. Ringer, R. J., *Winning Through Intimidation* (Los Angeles: Los Angeles Book Publishing Co., 1974), p. 22.

2. *Psychiatric News*, September 16, 1977, p. 34.

3. New York *Times* Book Review, September 25, 1977, p. 12.

4. Festinger, L., Riecken, H. W., and Schachter, S., *When Prophecy Fails: A Social and Psychological Study of a Modern Group That Predicted the Destruction of the World* (New York: Harper and Row, 1956).

5. Ortega y Gasset, J., *Revolt of the Masses* (New York: W. W. Norton, 1964).

CHAPTER 11

1. Zinsser, H., *Rats, Lice and History* (Boston: Little Brown, 1935).
2. Abelson, P. H., Air Pollution, *Science* 147:1527, 1965.
3. Burnet, F. M., Men or Molecules? A Tilt at Molecular Biology, *Lancet*, 1:38, 1966.
4. *Ibid.*, p. 39.
5. Hollister, L. E., Baltimore *Sun*, March 20, 1966.
6. Lewis, H. R., *With Every Breath You Take* (New York: Crown, 1965), p. 262.
7. *Medical World News*, October 8, 1965.
8. *AMA News*, January 10, 1966.
9. Lewis, see note 6, p. 261.
10. *Ibid.*, p. 271.
11. *Ibid.*, p. 221.
12. Wilm, H. G., New York *Times*, May 20, 1965, p. 45, col. 1.
13. Ardrey, R., *African Genesis* (New York: Atheneum, 1961).

CHAPTER 12

1. New York *Times*, October 14, 1959, pp. 20, 1.
2. Sherif, M., and Sherif, C. W., *An Outline of Social Psychology* (New York: Harper, 1956), p. 283.
3. Quoted on title page, Bryant, A. F., *Radiation and the Race* (Philadelphia: American Friends Service Committee, 1959).
4. Smith, M. B., Rationality and Social Process, presidential address, Society for the Psychological Study of Social Issues, Am. Psychological Assn., September 7, 1959.
5. Mead, M., Significance of the Individual, *What's New* 215:2-7, 1959.
6. Boffey, P. M., Nuclear War: Federation Disputes Academy on How Bad Effects Would Be, *Science* 190:248-50, 1975.
7. Federation of American Scientists, statement of November 23, 1958, New York City.
8. Baltimore *Morning Sun*, February 5, 1960, p. 1.
9. Kahn, H., The Nature and Feasibility of War and Deterrence, lecture delivered at Johns Hopkins University Applied Physics Laboratory, December, 1959.

10. Russell, B., *Common Sense and Nuclear Warfare* (New York: Simon and Schuster, 1959), p. 42.

11. Kahn, H., *The Nature and Feasibility of War and Deterrence* (Santa Monica, Calif.: Rand Corporation, 1960), p. 43.

12. Veysey, A., British-U.S. Team Controls Thors, Denver *Post*, February 17, 1960, p. 10.

13. Robinson, D., Can Your City Control "Atomic Accident"? *This Week*, May 11, 1958, pp. 10, 12, 13, 29.

14. Tynan, K., *New Yorker*, April 4, 1959, pp. 114–15.

15. Pope, A., "Essay on Man, Epistle 2," in *The Complete Poetical Works of Alexander Pope* (Boston: Houghton Mifflin, 1931), p. 144.

16. Cavers, D. F., Why Not Economic Sanctions?, unpublished manuscript.

17. *Wall Street Journal*, March 25, 1959, pp. 1, 16.

18. Joint Committee on Atomic Energy, Congress of the United States, *Biological and Environmental Effects of Nuclear War* (Washington, D.C.: Government Printing Office, August, 1959).

19. See note 2.

20. These aspects have been well outlined by Gladstone, A., The Conception of the Enemy, *J. Conflict Res.* 3:132–37, 1959.

21. Cantril, H., Perception and Interpersonal Relations, *Am. J. Psychiat.* 114:119–26, 1957.

22. Halle, L. J., The Struggle Called "Coexistence," New York *Times* Magazine, November 15, 1959, pp. 14, 110, 118; p. 110.

23. Osgood, C. E., Suggestions for Winning the Real War with Communism, *J. Conflict Res.* 3:295–325, 1959.

24. Baltimore Sunday *Sun*, November 8, 1959, p. 1.

25. Merton, R. K., *Social Theory and Social Structure* (Glencoe, Ill.: Free Press, 1957).

26. For example, the administrator of an admission ward in a naval hospital created strong group expectations that patients would not become violent and that restraint would never be necessary. Out of nearly a thousand patients admitted over a ten-month period, he did not have to order restraint or isolation of a single one. Wilmer, H. A., Toward a Definition of the Therapeutic Community, *Am. J. Psychiat.* 114:824–34, 1958.

27. The melancholy sequence of events following the downing of the U-2 plane in April, 1960, illustrates the self-fulfilling prophecy all too well. Each country takes steps, based on fear of the other's intentions, which, by heightening mutual mistrust, increase the likelihood that the other will justify its pessimistic expectation.

28. The House Appropriations Committee, in its report on the 1961 appropriations for the Department of Defense, stated: "We should

maintain our armed forces in such a way that . . . should it ever become obvious that an attack upon ourselves or our allies is imminent, we can launch an attack before the aggressor has hit either us or our allies. . . . No other form of deterrence can be fully relied upon" (House report 1561, p. 8). There is evidence that Russian leaders are also considering similar plans. It is easy to imagine what will happen if either country concludes, erroneously or otherwise, that the other is about to attack. The first would at once attempt to strike, leading the other country to do the same. Obviously a policy of mutual preemptive attack enormously heightens the risk of nuclear war through an error of judgment.

29. Baltimore *Morning Sun,* December 16, 1959, pp. 1, 8.

30. Mills, C. W., *The Causes of World War III* (New York: Simon and Schuster, 1958).

31. According to Bruce Bliven, Bernard Brodie, an able exponent of limited war, recognizes that to make this possible, "the combatants would have to agree, without consultation, to hobble the tremendous destructive power they have already mobilized and would have to indicate their self-restraining intentions unmistakably. Nothing like this has ever happened in war's history, but Dr. Brodie thinks it can be done and that doing it is the hope of the world." Bliven, B., Jr., review of Brodie, B., *Strategy in the Missile Age,* in *New Yorker,* March 12, 1960, pp. 186–95; p. 190.

32. de Madariaga, S., Disarmament? The Problem Lies Deeper, *New York Times* Magazine, October 11, 1959, pp. 17, 72–75; p. 74.

33. See note 23.

34. Proceedings of Pugwash Conference of International Scientists on Biological and Chemical Warfare, Pugwash, Nova Scotia, August 24–30, 1959, pp. 5–6.

35. For brief but comprehensive expositions of nonviolence, see: *Speak Truth to Power* (Philadelphia: American Friends Service Committee, 1955); and Hinshaw, C. E., *Nonviolent Resistance: A Nation's Way to Peace* (Wallingford, Pa.: Pendle Hill, 1956).

36. McClelland, D. C., *Psychoanalysis and Religious Mysticism* (Wallingford, Pa.: Pendle Hill, 1959), p. 13.

37. Einstein, A., and Freud, S., *Why War?* (Geneva: League of Nations, International Institute of Intellectual Cooperation, 1933), pp. 28–29.

38. D. O. Hebb and W. R. Thompson adduce interesting evidence that genuinely altruistic behavior increases as one ascends the phylogenetic scale, and that it is already prominent in the chimpanzee, The Social Significance of Animal Studies, ch. 15, pp. 532–61, in Lindzey, G., ed., *Handbook of Social Psychology,* vol. 1 (Cambridge, Mass.: Addison Wesley, 1954).

39. Allport, G. W., *The Nature of Prejudice* (Boston: Beacon Press, 1954), p. xiv.

40. Eggan, D., The General Problem of Hopi Adjustment, *Am. Anthropologist* 45:357–73, 1943; pp. 372–73.

41. Kardiner, A., and others, *The Psychological Frontiers of Society* (New York: Columbia University Press, 1945), p. 49.

42. Buck, P., quoted in Fry, A. R., comp., *Victories Without Violence* (London: Edgar G. Dunstan, 1950), pp. 69–71.

43. The successful renunciation of violence by the staff of a psychiatric admission ward illustrates both the reciprocal nature of human behavior and the power of group standards to control members of the group (see note 26). However, in that case the dominant group took the initiative, and a crucial problem is whether a similar initiative by the underdogs could also succeed.

44. Gandhi, M. K., *An Autobiography: The Study of My Experiments with Truth* (Boston: Beacon Press, 1957), p. 276.

45. Naess, A., A Systematization of Gandhian Ethics of Conflict Resolution, *J. Conflict Res.* 2:140–55, 1958, p. 144.

46. Whitehorn, J. C., Stress and Mental Health, *Northwest Medicine* 58:822–30, 1959.

47. See note 2.

48. James, W., *The Varieties of Religious Experience* (New York: Longmans, Green, 1902), p. 367.

49. "Today there are 27 Westerns and 20 whodunits on the weekly programs of the major networks. . . . All the . . . damned and doomed dregs of humanity giving an advanced course . . . in all the techniques of crime and the modes of violence." Luce, C. B., Without Portfolio, *McCall's*, March, 1960, pp. 18, 176, 178; p. 176.

50. Johnson, B. L., If Peace Were to Break Out, *Christian Century*, December 9, 1959; reprinted in *Congressional Record*, January 7, 1960, p. A-25.

51. Personal communication.

CHAPTER 13

1. Halle, L. J., The Struggle Called "Coexistence," *New York Times* Magazine, November 15, 1959, p. 110.

2. Wedge, B. M., and Muromcew, C., Psychological Factors in Soviet Disarmament Negotiations, *J. Conflict Res.* 9:18, 1965.

3. Glenn, E. S., Across the Cultural Barrier, *Key Reporter* 31:3, 1965.

4. Wedge, B. M., A Note on Soviet-American Negotiation, in Miller, M., ed., *Proceedings of the Emergency Conference on Hostility, Aggression and War* (Washington, D.C.: American Association for Social Psychiatry, 1961).

5. Blake, R. R., and Mouton, J. S., Loyalty of Representatives to Ingroup Positions during Intergroup Competition, *Sociometry* 24:177, 1961.

6. *Ibid.*

7. Blake, R. R., Psychology and the Crisis of Statesmanship, *Am. Psychologist* 14:90, 1959.

8. Blake, R. R., and Mouton, J. S., Comprehension of Own and of Outgroup Positions under Intergroup Competition, *J. Conflict Res.* 5:304, 1961.

9. Blake, R. R., and Mouton, J. S., Comprehension of Points of Communality in Competing Solutions, *Sociometry* 25:56, 1962.

10. Blake, R. R., and Mouton, J. S., Overevaluation of Own Group's Product in Intergroup Competition, *J. Abnormal Social Psychol.* 64:237, 1962.

11. Rapoport, A., Research for Peace, *Listener*, March 31, 1966, p. 455.

12. Cohen, J., Reflections on the Resolution of Conflict in International Affairs, in *Proceedings of the International Congress on Applied Psychology* (Copenhagen: I. Munksgaard, 1962).

13. Hayakawa, S., On Communication with the Soviet Union, Part 1, *Etc.: A Review of General Semantics* 17:396, 1960.

14. See note 7.

15. Coch, L., and French, J. R. P., Jr., Overcoming Resistance to Change, *Human Relations* 1:512, 1948.

16. Thorneycroft, E., *Personal Responsibility and the Law of Nations* (The Hague: Martinus Nishoff, 1961).

17. Official Statement of COSWA VII, *Bull. Atomic Scientists* 18:25, 1962.

CHAPTER 14

1. Boulding, G. K., After Civilization, What? *Bull. Atomic Scientists* 18:2–6, 1962, p. 6.

2. Kennedy, J. F., Speech at the United Nations, Sept. 25, 1961. Quoted in *SANE World*, January, 1964.

3. World Health Organization, *Health Aspects of Chemical and Biological Weapons* (Geneva: WHO, 1970).

4. Fulbright, J. W., personal communication.

5. Wedge, B. M., and Muromcew, C., Psychological Factors in Soviet Disarmament Negotiations, *J. Conflict Res.* 9:18–36, 1964.

CHAPTER 15

1. Modern totalitarian regimes have exploited this phenomenon by requiring that their citizens continually behave as if they approve the system. It is not enough to avoid open dissent: they must march, demonstrate, attend mass meetings, and otherwise publicly show their support—a striking example was the compulsory Nazi greeting "Heil Hitler." For anti-Nazis, the contrast between their enforced public behavior and secret beliefs set up strong dissonance, and sometimes the beliefs yielded. An effective component of Chinese thought reform was its insistence that its victims continually defend the communist system and express their allegiance to communism.

CHAPTER 16

1. Einstein, A., and Freud, S., *Why War?* (Geneva: League of Nations, International Institute of Intellectual Cooperation, 1933), pp. 28f.

2. *Editor's Note:* See ch. 12 for a related discussion.

CHAPTER 17

1. James, H., ed., *Letters of William James* (Boston: Atlantic Monthly Press, 1920), vol. 2, p. 211.

2. The term "humanist" is used here as defined by the American Humanist Association: "Any account of nature should pass the test of scientific evidence. . . . We find insufficient evidence for belief in the existence of a supernatural. . . . As non-theists we begin with humans, not God, nature, not deity." Humanist Manifesto II, *The Humanist*, September/October 1973, p. 5.

3. Introduction to the *Bhagavad-Gita* (New York: Mentor, 1941).

4. May, R., The Existential Approach, pp. 1348–61 in Arieti, S.,

ed., *American Handbook of Psychiatry*, vol. 2 (New York: Basic Books, 1959), p. 1354.

5. See note 1, p. 270.

6. Fischer, R., Cartography of Inner Space, pp. 197–239, in Siegel, R. K., and West, L. K., eds., *Hallucinations: Behavior, Experience and Theory* (New York: John Wiley and Sons, 1975).

7. Huxley, A., *The Doors of Perception* (New York: Harper and Row, 1963).

8. Grof, S., *Realms of the Human Unconscious: Observations from LSD Research* (New York: Viking, 1975), p. 14.

9. LeShan, L., *The Medium, the Mystic, and the Physicist* (New York: Viking, 1974).

10. Baynes, C., Introduction, to Jung, C. G., *The Secret of the Golden Flower* (London: Kegan Paul, 1931), p. viii.

CHAPTER 18

1. Lucidly expounded in the *Standard* (published by the American Ethical Union), May, 1953, by F. M. Gregg.

CHAPTER 19

1. Dante Alighieri, *The Divine Comedy*, White, L. G., trans. (New York: Pantheon, 1948), p. 182.

2. Huxley, A., *Heaven and Hell* (New York: Harper and Row, 1972).

3. Nathanson, J., Ethical Religion and the Fear of Death, address of November 23, 1958 (published by the American Ethical Union).

4. Morgenthau, H. J., Death in the Nuclear Age, *Commentary* 32:231–34, 1961; pp. 233, 234.

5. Neuberger, R. L., When I Learned I Had Cancer, *Harper's*, June 1959, pp. 42–45.

6. Quoted in ch. 16, pp. 169–77, in Pinner, M., and Miller, B. F., *When Doctors Are Patients* (New York: W. W. Norton, 1952), pp. 176–77.

7. Zinsser, H., *As I Remember Him* (Boston: Little, Brown, 1940), pp. 438–39, 440–41.

8. Wertenbaker, L. T., *Death of a Man* (New York: Random House, 1957).

Chronological List of Original Publications by Jerome D. Frank from 1931 to 1978

1. The Retroactive Effect of Pleasant and Unpleasant Odors on Learning, *Am. J. Psychol.* 43:102–08, 1931 (with E. J. Ludvigh).
2. Affective Value vs. Nature of Odors in Relation to Reproduction, *Am. J. Psychol.* 43:479–83, 1931.
3. Individual Differences in Certain Aspects of the Level of Aspiration, *Am. J. Psychol.* 47:119–28, 1935.
4. Some Psychological Determinants of the Level of Aspiration, *Am. J. Psychol.* 47:285–93, 1935.
5. The Influence of the Level of Performance in One Task on the Level of Aspiration in Another, *J. Experimental Psychol.* 18:159–71, 1935.
6. A Comparison Between Certain Properties of the Level of Aspiration and Random Guessing, *J. Psychol.* 3:43–62, 1936.
7. Level of Aspiration Test, pp. 461–71 in Murray, H. A., *Explorations in Personality*, New York: Oxford University Press, 1938.
8. Production of the Alarm Reaction in Young Rats by Transection of the Spinal Cord, *Endocrinology* 27:447–51, 1940.
9. Recent Studies of the Level of Aspiration, *Psychol. Bull.* 38:218–26, 1941.
10. The Contributions of Topological and Vector Psychology to Psychiatry, *Psychiat.* 5:15–22, 1942. Reprinted as pp. 571–81 in Tomkins, S., ed., *Contemporary Psychopathology*, Cambridge: Harvard University Press, 1943.
11. The Value of Psychology as a Premedical Study, *J. Abnormal and Social Psychol.* 37:256–59, 1942.
12. Experimental Studies of Personal Pressure and Resistance:
    I. Experimental Production of Resistance, *J. General Psychol.* 30:23–41, 1944.

II. Methods of Overcoming Resistance, *Ibid.*, 30:43–56, 1944.

III. Qualitative Analysis of Resistant Behavior, *Ibid.*, 30:57–64, 1944.

13. Emotional Reactions of American Soldiers to an Unfamiliar Disease, *Am. J. Psychiat.* 102:631–40, 1946.

14. Psychotherapeutic Aspects of Symptomatic Treatment, *Am. J. Psychiat.* 103:21–25, 1946.

15. Personal Problems Related to Army Rank, *Am. J. Psychiat.* 103:97–104, 1946.

16. Atropine Treatment of Hypoglycemic Fatigue States in Soldiers, *Psychiat. Quart.* 20:674–83, 1946.

17. Adjustment Problems of Selected Negro Soldiers, *J. Nerv. Ment. Dis.* 105:647–60, 1947.

18. *Management of Emotional Reactions in Patients with Somatic Disease*, U.S. Veterans Administration Technical Bull. TB-Med. 10–35, September 5, 1947, Washington, D.C.

19. Group Psychotherapy with Neurotics, *Am. J. Psychiat.* 105:449–55, 1948 (with F. B. Powdermaker.)

20. The Uncooperative Patient—A Therapeutic Challenge, *Medical Annals of D.C.* 17:668–72, 1948.

21. Group Psychotherapy in Relation to Research, *Group Psychotherapy* 3:197–203, 1950.

22. The Medical Patient Who Will Not Cooperate, ch. 10 in Viets, H. R., ed., *Neurology and Psychiatry in General Practice*, New York: Grune and Stratton, 1950.

23. Group Influences in Psychotherapy, *Johns Hopkins Hosp. Nurses Alumnae Assn. Mag.* 49:180–87, 1950.

24. Some Problems of Research in Group Psychotherapy, *Int. J. Group Psychotherapy* 1:59–63, 1951.

25. Corrective Emotional Experiences in Group Psychotherapy, *Am. J. Psychiat.* 108:126–31, 1951 (with Eduard Ascher).

26. Group Psychotherapy with Chronic Hospitalized Schizophrenics, pp. 216–30 in *Psychotherapy with Schizophrenics: A Symposium*, New York: International Universities Press, 1952.

27. Group Reading and Group Therapy: A Concurrent Test, *Psychiat.* 15:33–51, 1952 (with J. W. Powell and A. R. Stone).

28. Behavioral Patterns in Early Meetings of Therapeutic Groups, *Am. J. Psychiat.* 108:771–78, 1952 (with E. Ascher, J. B. Margolin, H. Nash, A. R. Stone, and E. Varon).

29. The Effects of Interpatient and Group Influences in a General Hospital, *Int. J. Group Psychotherapy* 2:127–38, 1952.

30. Group Methods in Psychotherapy, *J. Social Issues* 8:35–44, 1952.

31. Two Behavior Patterns in Therapeutic Groups and their Appar-

ent Motivation, *Human Relations* 5:289–317, 1952 (with J. B. Margolin, H. T. Nash, A. R. Stone, E. Varon, and E. Ascher).

32. Areas of Research in Group Psychotherapy, pp. 119–26 in *Psychiatric Treatment,* Proceedings of the Association for Research in Nervous and Mental Disease, Baltimore: Williams and Wilkins, 1953.

33. *Group Psychotherapy: Studies in Methodology of Research and Therapy,* Cambridge: Harvard University Press, 1953 (with F. B. Powdermaker).

34. How Do Parents Learn? *Child Study* 30:14–19, 50–51, 1953.

35. *Group Psychotherapy,* Veterans Administration Technical Bull. 10–91, June 30, 1953.

36. Group Psychotherapy with Out-Patients, *Tri-State Med. J.* February, 1954.

37. Emotional Stress in the Family and the Impact of Overt Mental Disease, *Councillor* 19:6–11, 1954.

38. The Use of "Diagnostic" Groups in a Group Therapy Program, *Int. J. Group Psychotherapy* 4:274–84, 1954 (with A. R. Stone and M. B. Parloff).

39. A Comparative Study of the Effects of Mephenesin and Placebo on the Symptomatology of a Mixed Group of Psychiatric Out-Patients, *Bull. Johns Hopkins Hosp.* 95:170–77, 1954 (with J. L. Hampson and D. Rosenthal).

40. Faith and Therapy, *Bull. Guild Cath. Psychiatrists,* 2:16–19, 1954.

41. The Self-Righteous Moralist in Early Meetings of Therapeutic Groups, *Psychiat.* 17:215–23, 1954 (with D. Rosenthal and E. H. Nash).

42. Comfort, Effectiveness, and Self-Awareness as Criteria of Improvement in Psychotherapy, *Am. J. Psychiat.* 111:343–51, 1954 (with M. B. Parloff and H. C. Kelman).

43. Conscience and Moral Law, *Standard,* published by the American Ethical Union, January–February, 1955, pp. 4–8.

44. Some Values of Conflict in Therapeutic Groups, *Group Psychotherapy* 8:142–51, 1955.

45. *Group Therapy in the Mental Hospital,* Monograph Series no. 1, American Psychiatric Association, Mental Health Service, December, 1955.

46. Therapeutic Emotional Interactions in Group Treatment, *Postgraduate Medicine* 19:36–40, 1956 (with E. Ascher).

47. Psychotherapy and the Placebo Effect, *Psychol. Bull.* 53:294–302, 1956 (with D. Rosenthal).

48. Comparison of Reserpine and Placebo in Treatment of Psychiat-

ric Out-patients, *AMA Arch. Neurol. and Psychiat.* 76:207–14, 1956 (with J. A. Meath, T. M. Feldberg, and D. Rosenthal).

49. Suggestibility, Social Class and the Acceptance of Psychotherapy, *J. Clin. Psychol.* 12:341–44, 1956 (with S. D. Imber, L. H. Gliedman, E. H. Nash, and A. R. Stone).

50. Group Therapy of Alcoholics with Concurrent Group Meetings of Their Wives, *Quarterly J. of Studies on Alcohol* 17:655–70, 1956 (with L. H. Gliedman, D. Rosenthal, and H. T. Nash).

51. Some Determinants, Manifestations, and Effects of Cohesiveness in Therapy Groups, *Int. J. Group Psychotherapy* 7:53–63, 1957.

52. Why Patients Leave Psychotherapy, *AMA Arch. Neurol. and Psychiat.* 77:283–99, 1957 (with L. H. Gliedman, S. D. Imber, E. H. Nash, and A. R. Stone).

53. Are You A Guilty Parent? *Harper's Magazine* 214:56–59, April, 1957.

54. Some Factors Related to Patients' Remaining in Group Psychotherapy, *Int. J. Group Psychotherapy* 7:264–74, 1957 (with E. H. Nash, L. H. Gliedman, S. D. Imber, and A. R. Stone).

55. Incentives for Treatment Related to Remaining or Improving in Psychotherapy, *Am. J. Psychotherapy* 11:589–98, 1957 (with L. H. Gliedman, A. R. Stone, E. H. Nash, and S. D. Imber).

56. Improvement and Amount of Therapeutic Contact: An Alternative to the Use of No-Treatment Controls in Psychotherapy, *J. Consult. Psychol.* 21:309–15, 1957 (with S. D. Imber, E. H. Nash, A. R. Stone, and L. H. Gliedman).

57. Some Aspects of Cohesiveness and Conflict in Psychiatric Out-Patient Groups, *Bull. Johns Hopkins Hosp.* 101:224–31, 1957.

58. A Psychiatrist Looks at Religion and Psychiatry, *Ethical Religion Speaks* (American Ethical Union Talk of the Month), 1957.

59. Group Psychotherapy with Psychiatric Out-Patients, *Cincinnati J. Med.* 38:56–58, 1958.

60. Reduction of Symptoms by Pharmacologically Inert Substances and by Short-Term Psychotherapy, *AMA Arch. Neurol. and Psychiat.* 79:345–51, 1958 (with L. H. Gliedman, E. H. Nash, S. D. Imber, and A. R. Stone).

61. Some Effects of Expectancy and Influence in Psychotherapy, pp. 27–43 in Masserman, J. H., and Moreno, J. L., eds., *Progress in Psychotherapy*, vol. 3, New York: Grune and Stratton, 1958.

62. Psychological Aspects of the Nuclear Arms Race, *Psychiatry* 21:221–22, 1958.

63. The Great Antagonism, *Atlantic Monthly* 202:58–62, 1958.

64. The Therapeutic Use of the Self, *Am. J. Occupational Therapy* 12:215–25, 1958.

65. The Fate of Psychiatric Clinic Outpatients Assigned to Psychotherapy, *J. Nerv. Ment. Dis.* 127:330–43, 1958 (with D. Rosenthal).

66. Problems of Controls in Psychotherapy as Exemplified by the Psychotherapy Research Project of the Phipps Psychiatric Clinic, pp. 10–26 in *Research in Psychotherapy*, Washington, D.C.: American Psychological Association, 1959.

67. Patients' Expectancies and Relearning as Factors Determining Improvement in Psychotherapy, *Am. J. Psychiat.* 115:961–68, 1959 (with L. H. Gliedman, S. D. Imber, A. R. Stone, and E. H. Nash).

68. The Dynamics of the Psychotherapeutic Relationship: Determinants and Effects of the Therapist's Influence, *Psychiat.* 22:17–39, 1959.

69. Contributor to Standal, S. W., and Corsini, R. J., eds., *Critical Incidents in Psychotherapy*, Englewood Cliffs, N.J.: Prentice-Hall, 1959.

70. The Selection of Psychiatric Outpatients for the Evaluation of Drugs, pp. 340–42 in *Psychopharmacology—Problems in Evaluation*, Washington, D.C.: National Academy of Sciences—National Research Council, 1959.

71. Arms and the Mind, *Fellowship* 25:21–23, 34–35, 1959.

72. *Group Methods in Therapy*, Public Affairs Pamphlet no. 284, New York: Public Affairs Committee, June, 1959.

73. Group Psychotherapy, pp. 1362–74 in Arieti, S., ed., *American Handbook of Psychiatry*, New York: Basic Books, 1959 (with F. B. Powdermaker).

74. Disarmament: The Imperative of Our Time, *Together* 4:32–34, 1960.

75. *Sanity and Survival—II. The Non Violent Alternative*, Berkeley, Calif.: Acts for Peace, 1960 (*Fresh Thought on War* series).

76. Breaking the Thought Barrier: Psychological Challenges of the Nuclear Age, *Psychiat.* 23:245–66, 1960.

77. Relief of Distress and Attitudinal Change, pp. 107–21 in Masserman, J. H., ed., *Science and Psychoanalysis*, vol. 4, New York: Grune and Stratton, 1960.

78. Sanity and Survival, *Clubwoman* 40:10–11, 22–24, 1960.

79. Rehabilitation of Chronically Ill Psychiatric Patients, *Rehabilitation Literature* 21:158–60, 1960 (with W. D. Wheat and R. Slaughter).

80. *Persuasion and Healing: A Comparative Study of Psychotherapy*, Baltimore: Johns Hopkins Press, 1961 (rev. ed., 1973; also paperback, New York: Schocken, 1973).

81. Emotional and Motivational Aspects of the Disarmament Problem, *J. Social Issues* 17:20–27, 1961.
82. The Role of Influence in Psychotherapy (pp. 17–41) and Therapy in a Group Setting (pp. 42–59) in Stein, Morris, I., ed., *Contemporary Psychotherapies*, Glencoe, Ill.: Free Press, 1961.
83. Atomic Arms and Pre-Atomic Man, *Bull. Atomic Scientists* 17:361–65, 1961.
84. An Intensive Five-Year Follow-up Study of Treated Psychiatric Outpatients, *J. Nerv. Ment. Dis.* 133:410–22, 1961 (with A. R. Stone, E. H. Nash, and S. D. Imber).
85. Psychological Aspects of the Disarmament Problem, pp. 112–25 in *Excerpta Medica*, International Congress Series no. 45 (Proceedings of the Sixth International Congress on Mental Health, August 30–September 5, 1961).
86. World Tensions and Disarmament, *Teachers College Record* 63:458–67, 1962.
87. Psychotherapy, pp. 721–23 in *Encyclopedia Brittanica*, vol. 18, Chicago: Encyclopedia Brittanica, 1962.
88. Human Nature and Nonviolent Resistance, pp. 192–205 in Wright, Q., Evan, W. M., and Deutsch, M., eds., *Preventing World War III: Some Proposals*, New York: Simon and Schuster, 1962.
89. Conflict without War, *Peace News*, no. 1375, November 2, 1962, p. 3.
90. Sanity and Survival, *Social Education* 26:367–74, 1962.
91. The Role of Cognitions in Illness and Healing, pp. 1–12 in Strupp, H. H., and Luborsky, L., eds., *Research in Psychotherapy*, vol 2, Washington, D.C.: American Psychological Association, 1962.
92. Negroes in Psychotherapy, *Am. J. Psychiat.* 199:456–60, 1962 (with H. Rosen).
93. The Ways to Peace—A Psychological Approach, *Liberal Context* 2:27–28, 1962.
94. Foreword, pp. ix–xi, to Goldstein, A. P., *Therapist-Patient Expectancies in Psychotherapy*, New York: Macmillan, 1962.
95. Neurosis, pp. 535–39 in Conn, H. F., ed., *Current Therapy*,1963, Philadelphia: W. B. Saunders, 1963 (pp. 549–53 in 1964 ed.).
96. How Close Are We to Accidental War? *Clubwoman* 42:19, 21–22, 34, 1963.
97. Psychological Aspects of the Disarmament Problem, pp. 82–97 in Barker C. A., coordinator, *Problems of World Disarmament*, Boston: Houghton Mifflin, 1963.
98. Group Psychotherapy, pp. 707–15 in Deutsch, A., and Fishman,

H., eds., *The Encyclopedia of Mental Health*, vol. 2, New York: Franklin Watts, 1963.

99. Psychotherapy, pp. 1728–36 in Deutsch, A., and Fishman, H., eds., *The Encyclopedia of Mental Health*, vol. 5, New York: Franklin Watts, 1963.

100. Immediate and Long-Term Symptomatic Course of Psychiatric Outpatients, *Am. J. Psychiat.* 120:429–39, 1963 (with E. H. Nash, A. R. Stone, and S. D. Imber).

101. Group Psychotherapy with Psychiatric Outpatients, *Group Psychotherapy* 16:132–40, 1963.

102. Training and Therapy, pp. 442–51 in Bradford, L. P., Gibb, J. R., and Benne, K. D., eds., *T-Group Theory and Laboratory Method*, New York: John Wiley and Sons, 1964.

103. Group Psychology and the Elimination of War, *Int. J. Group Psychotherapy* 14:41–48, 1964.

104. Selected Effects of Inert Medication on Psychiatric Outpatients, *Am. J. Psychotherapy* 18:33–48, 1964 (with E. H. Nash, S. D. Imber, and A. R. Stone).

105. Emotions and the Psychotherapeutic Process, pp. 25–34 in Masserman, J. H., ed., *Current Psychiatric Therapies*, vol. 4, New York: Grune and Stratton, 1964.

106. Psychotherapy and the Assumptive World, pp. 50–75 in *Recent Advances in the Study of Behaviour Change, Proceedings of the Academic Assembly on Clinical Psychology*, Montreal: McGill University Press, 1964.

107. Contributions of Behavioral Scientists toward a World without War, *Compreh. Psychiat.* 5:283–93, 1964.

108. Foreword, pp. vii–xxii, to Kiev, A., ed., *Magic, Faith, and Healing: Studies in Primitive Psychiatry Today*, New York: Free Press, 1964.

109. Breaking the Thought Barrier: Psychological Challenges of the Nuclear Age, *Commercial Law J.* 69:338–42, 353, 1964.

110. Systematic Preparation of Patients for Psychotherapy: I. Effects on Therapy Behavior and Outcome, *J. Psychiat. Res.* 2:267–81, 1964 (with R. Hoehn-Saric, S. D. Imber, E. H. Nash, A. R. Stone, and C. Battle).

111. The Psychology of Non-Violence, *Ramparts* 3:48–51, January–February, 1965.

112. Commitment to Peace Work: A Preliminary Study of Determinants and Sustainers of Behavior Change, *Am. J. Orthopsychiat.* 35:106–19, 1965 (with E. H. Nash).

113. *New Threats to Man: The Challenge to Ethics*, Felix Adler Lec-

ture, 1965, New York: New York Society for Ethical Culture, 1965.

114. Some Situational Factors Associated with Response to Psychotherapy, *Am. J. Orthopsychiat.* 35:682–87, 1965 (with A. R. Stone, R. Hoehn-Saric, S. D. Imber, and E. H. Nash).

115. Systematic Preparation of Patients for Short-Term Psychotherapy. II: Relation to Characteristics of Patient, Therapist and the Psychotherapeutic Process, *J. Nerv. Ment. Dis.* 140:374–83, 1965 (with E. H. Nash, R. Hoehn-Saric, C. C. Battle, A. R. Stone, and S. D. Imber).

116. Target Complaints as Criteria of Improvement, *Am. J. Psychotherapy* 20:184–92, 1966 (with C. C. Battle, S. D. Imber, R. Hoehn-Saric, A. R. Stone, and E. H. Nash).

117. Elimination of War and the Uncommitted, pp. 5–9 in *Proceedings of the Medical Association for the Prevention of War*, no. 3, London: Medical Association for the Prevention of War, 1966.

118. Discussion of "A Soviet View of Group Therapy" by N. V. Ivanov, *Int. J. Psychiat.* 2:212–14, 1966.

119. Psychotherapy and the Sense of Community, *Am. J. Psychotherapy* 20:228–34, 1966.

120. The Doctor's Job Tomorrow, *The Pharos of Alpha Omega Alpha* 29:45–48, 1966.

121. The Therapist's Contribution to Accurate Empathy, Non-Possessive Warmth, and Genuineness in Psychotherapy, *J. Clin. Psychol.* 22:331–34, 1966 (with C. B. Truax, D. G. Wargo, S. D. Imber, C. C. Battle, R. Hoehn-Saric, E. H. Nash, and A. R. Stone).

122. How Nations See Each Other, *War/Peace Report* 6:3–8, June–July, 1966

123. Treatment of the Focal Symptom: An Adaptational Approach, *Am. J. Psychotherapy* 20:564–75, 1966.

124. Galloping Technology: A New Social Disease, *J. Social Issues* 22:1–14, 1966.

125. Therapist Empathy, Genuineness, and Warmth and Patient Therapeutic Outcome, *J. Consult. Psychol.* 30:395–401, 1966 (with C. B. Truax, D. G. Wargo, S. D. Imber, R. Hoehn-Saric, E. H. Nash, A. R. Stone, and C. C. Battle).

126. The Role of Non-Specific Factors in Short-Term Psychotherapy, *Australian J. Psychol.* 18:210–17, 1966 (with A. R. Stone and S. D. Imber).

127. Commitment to Peace Work: II. A Closer Look at Determinants, *Am. J. Orthopsychiat.* 37:112–19, 1967 (with J. Schonfield).

128. Evaluation of Psychiatric Treatment, pp. 1305–9, in Freedman, A. M., and Kaplan, H. I., eds., *Comprehensive Textbook of*

Psychiatry, Baltimore: Williams and Wilkins, 1967 (2d ed.: Freedman, A. M., Kaplan, H. I., and Sadock, B. J., eds., *Comprehensive Textbook of Psychiatry,* Baltimore: Williams and Wilkins, 1975, pp. 2010–14).

129. Does Psychotherapy Work?, critical evaluation of "Some Implications of Psychotherapy Research for Therapeutic Practice" by Allen E. Bergin, *Int. J. Psychiat.* 3:153–55, 1967.

130. The Psychiatrist and International Affairs, *J. Nerv. Ment. Dis.* 144:479–84, 1967.

131. *Sanity and Survival: Psychological Aspects of War and Peace,* New York: Random House, 1967 (also paperback, New York: Vintage Books, 1967).

132. Deterrence—For How Long? *War/Peace Report* 8:3–7, 1968.

133. Recent American Research in Psychotherapy, *Brit. J. Med. Psychol.* 41:5–13, 1968.

134. Group Psychotherapy, pp. 185–89 in *International Encyclopedia of the Social Sciences,* New York: Macmillan Company and Free Press, 1968.

135. The Role of Hope in Psychotherapy, *Int. J. Psychiat.* 5:383–95, 1968.

136. A Ten-Year Follow-Up Study of Treated Psychiatric Outpatients, ch. 5 in Lesse, S., ed., *An Evaluation of the Results of the Psychotherapies,* Springfield, Ill.: Charles C Thomas, 1968 (with S. D. Imber, E. H. Nash, R. Hoehn-Saric, and A. R. Stone).

137. Focused Attitude Change in Neurotic Patients, *J. Nerv. Ment. Dis.* 147:124–33, 1968 (with R. Hoehn-Saric and B. J. Gurland).

138. The Face of the Enemy, *Psychology Today* 2:24–29, November, 1968.

139. Dynamics of Cold War Psychology, pp. 79–92 in Houghton, N. D., ed., *Struggle against History, U.S. Foreign Policy in an Age of Revolution,* New York: Washington Square Press, 1968.

140. Methods of Assessing the Results of Psychotherapy, pp. 38–53 in Porter, R., ed., *The Role of Learning in Psychotherapy,* London: J. & A. Churchill, 1968.

141. The Influence of Patients' and Therapists' Expectations on the Outcome of Psychotherapy, *Brit. J. Med. Psychol.* 41:349–56, 1968.

142. Group Dynamics of Challenge to Authority in a Changing Society, *J. Group Psychoanalysis and Process* 1:37–48, 1968.

143. Youth in Revolt—Observations by Someone over 30, *Horace Mann,* pp. 4–6, Winter, 1969.

144. Psychological Aspects of International Negotiations, *Harvard Med. Alum. Bull.* 43:10–14, Winter, 1969.

145. Common Features Account for Effectiveness, critical evaluation of "Some Empirical and Conceptual Bases for Coordinated Research in Psychotherapy" by H. H. Strupp and A. E. Bergin, *Int. J. Psychiat.* 7:122–27, 1969.

146. Prognosis in Psychoneurotic Patients, *Am. J. Psychotherapy* 23:252–59, 1969 (with R. Hoehn-Saric, A. R. Stone, and S. D. Imber).

147. Tempests of Change, *Johns Hopkins Med. J.* 124:296–304, 1969.

148. Human Group Aggression, pp. 322–31 in Sladen, B. K., and Bang, F. B., eds., *Biology of Populations*, New York: American Elsevier, 1969.

149. Sanity and Survival, *Ohio State Med. J.* 65:1101–6, 1969.

150. Psychologic Aspects of International Negotiations, *Am. J. Psychotherapy* 23:572–83, 1969.

151. Time-Focused Role Induction: Report of an Instructive Failure, *J. Nerv. Ment. Dis.* 150:27–30, 1970 (with S. D. Imber, S. K. Pande, R. Hoehn-Saric, A. R. Stone, and D. G. Wargo).

152. Pp. 159–165 in Knoll, E., and McFadden, J. N., eds., *War Crimes and the American Conscience*, New York: Holt, Rinehart and Winston, 1970.

153. The Pursuit of Peace, *Transactions* 2:4–9, August, 1970.

154. Psychotherapists Need Theories, *Int. J. Psychiat.* 9:146–49, 1970.

155. The Changing Climate of Atrocity, pp. 459–61 in Falk, R. A., Kolko, G., and Lifton, R. J., eds., *Crimes of War*, New York: Random House, 1971.

156. Can Modern Civilization Escape Self-Destruction?, pp. 236–47 in Landis, B., and Tauber, E. S., eds., *In the Name of Life: Essays in Honor of Erich Fromm*, New York: Holt, Rinehart and Winston, 1971.

157. A Commentary on the Effective Ingredients in the Patient-Therapist Interaction, pp. 280–82 in Mahrer, A. R., and Pearson, L., eds., *Creative Developments in Psychotherapy*, vol. 1, Cleveland: Press of Case Western Reserve University, 1971.

158. Psychological Aspects of International Violence, pp. 33–42 in Fawcett, J., ed., *Dynamics of Violence*, Chicago: American Medical Association, 1971.

159. Therapeutic Factors in Psychotherapy, *Am. J. Psychotherapy* 25:350–61, 1971.

160. The Psychology of Violence, pp. 89–102 in Graham, H. D., ed., *Violence: The Crisis of American Confidence*, Baltimore: Johns Hopkins Press, 1971.

161. Psychological Aspects of Nuclear Deterrence, *Proceedings of the Medical Association for Prevention of War* 2:89–99, 1971.

162. A Liveable World, pp. 21–35 in Radest, H. B., ed., *To Seek A Humane World*, London: Pemberton Books, 1971.

163. Arousal and Attitude Change in Neurotic Patients, *Arch. General Psychiat.* 26:51–56, 1972 (with R. Hoehn-Saric, B. Liberman, S. D. Imber, A. R. Stone, S. K. Pande).

164. Discussion of "The Mislabeling of Depressed Patients in New York State Hospitals" by Barry Gurland et al., pp. 29–31 in Zubin, J., and Freyhan, F. A., eds., *Disorders of Mood*, Baltimore: Johns Hopkins Press, 1972.

165. Patterns of Change in Treated Psychoneurotic Patients: A Five-Year Follow-Up Investigation of the Systematic Preparation of Patients for Psychotherapy, *J. Consult. Clin. Psychol.* 38:36–41, 1972 (with B. L. Liberman, R. Hoehn-Saric, A. R. Stone, S. D. Imber, and S. K. Pande).

166. The Structured and Scaled Interview to Assess Maladjustment (SSIAM): I. Description, Rationale, and Development, *Arch. General Psychiat.* 27:259–64, 1972 (with B. J. Gurland, N. J. Yorkston, A. R. Stone, and J. L. Fleiss).

167. Thoughts on the Control of Violence, *Friends J.* 18:418–19, August 1/15, 1972.

168. Group Perceptions and Group Relations, pp. 391–99, in Lebra, W. P., ed., *Transcultural Research in Mental Health*, Hawaii: University Press of Hawaii, 1972

169. Treatment of Homosexuals, pp. 63–68 in Livingood, J. M., ed., *National Institute of Mental Health Task Force on Homosexuality: Final Report and Background Papers*, Washington, D.C.: Government Printing Office, 1972, DHEW Publication no. (HSM) 72-9116.

170. Some Psychological Determinants of Violence and Its Control, *Australia New Zealand J. Psychiat.* 6:158–64, 1972.

171. The Bewildering World of Psychotherapy, *J. Social Issues* 28: 27–43, 1972.

172. Recent American Research on Therapeutic Attributes Shared by All Psychotherapies, *Bull. Post-Graduate Committee in Medicine, University of Sydney* 27:320–35, 1972.

173. Statement of Psychological Aspects of Foreign Aid, pp. 86–91 in *Views on Foreign Assistance Policy*, Committee on Foreign Relations, U.S. Senate, Washington, D.C.: Government Printing Office, January, 1973.

174. The Demoralized Mind, *Psychology Today* 6:22, 26, 28, 31, 100–101, April 1973.

175. Remarks on "The Treatment Process," pp. 242–44 in Chafetz, M. E., ed., *Proceedings of the Second Annual Alcoholism Conference of the National Institute on Alcohol Abuse and Alcoholism, Psychological and Social Factors in Drinking and Treatment and Treatment Evaluation*, Washington, D.C.: Government Printing Office, 1973, DHEW Publication no. (NIH) 74-676.

176. Psychiatrists and International Affairs: Pitfalls and Possibilities, *Int. J. Social Psychiat.* 18:235–38, 1972/73.

177. Psychotherapy or Psychotherapies?, pp. 13–23 in Masserman, J. H., ed., *Current Psychiatric Therapies*, vol. 13, New York: Grune and Stratton, 1973.

178. Psychotherapy and the Future of Civilization, *Voices: The Art and Science of Psychotherapy* 9:8–11, 1974.

179. Psychotherapy: The Restoration of Morale, *Am. J. Psychiat.* 131:271–74, 1974.

180. The Gift of Healing: Is It Myth or Measurable Fact? *Hosp. Physician*, January, 1974, p. 16.

181. How Psychotherapy Heals, *Henry Ford Hosp. Med. J.* 22:71–80, 1974.

182. My Philosophy of Psychotherapy, *J. Contemp. Psychotherapy* 6:115–20, 1974.

183. Attitude Change and Attribution of Arousal in Psychotherapy, *J. Nerv. Ment. Dis.* 159:234–43, 1974 (with R. Hoehn-Saric, B. Liberman, S. D. Imber, A. R. Stone, and F. D. Ribich).

184. Therapeutic Components of Psychotherapy: A 25-Year Progress Report of Research, *J. Nerv. Ment. Dis.* 159:325–42, 1974.

185. Linking Determinants of Individual and Social Violence—A Concluding Discussion, pp. 211–15 in Ben-Dak, J., ed., *The Future of Collective Violence: Societal and International Perspectives*, Lund, Sweden: Studentlitteratur, 1974.

186. Common Features of Psychotherapies and Their Patients, *Psychotherapy and Psychosomatics* 24:368–71, 1974.

187. An Overview of Psychotherapy, ch. 1, pp. 3–21 in Usdin, G., ed., *Overview of the Psychotherapies*, New York: Brunner/Mazel, 1975.

188. *Therapeutic Components of Psychotherapy*, Das Medizinische Prisma, February, 1975, Ingelheim am Rhein: C. H. Boehringer Sohn, 1975 (whole monograph).

189. Group Psychotherapy Research 25 Years Later, *Int. J. Group Psychotherapy* 25:159–62, 1975.

190. The Limits of Humanism, *Humanist*, 35:38–40, 1975.

191. The Faith That Heals, *Johns Hopkins Med. J.* 137:127–31, 1975.

192. Mind-Body Relationships in Illness and Healing, *J. Int. Acad. Preventive Med.* 2:46–59, 1975.
193. Psychotherapy of Bodily Disease: An Overview, *Psychotherapy and Psychosomatics* 26:192–202, 1975.
194. General Psychotherapy: The Restoration of Morale, pp. 117–32 in Arieti, S., ed., *American Handbook of Psychiatry*, 2d ed., vol. 5, New York: Basic Books, 1975.
195. New Therapeutic Roles, pp. 111–29 in Kaplan, B. H., Wilson, R. N., and Leighton, A. H., eds., *Further Explorations in Social Psychiatry*, New York: Basic Books, 1976.
196. The Two Faces of Psychotherapy, *Academy* 20:13–16, 1976.
197. Psychotherapy and the Sense of Mastery, pp. 47–56 in Spitzer, R. L., and Klein, D. F., eds., *Evaluation of Psychological Therapies: Psychotherapies, Behavioral Therapies, Drug Therapies and their Interactions*, Baltimore: Johns Hopkins University Press, 1976.
198. Psychological Aspects of the Nuclear Arms Race, *Bull. Atomic Scientists* 32, no. 2:22–24, April, 1976.
199. Psychological Factors in Illness and Healing, *Medical Times* 104:114–21, April, 1976.
200. Restoration of Morale and Behavior Change, pp. 73–95 in Burton, A., ed., *What Makes Behavior Change Possible?* New York: Brunner/Mazel, 1976.
201. The Two Faces of Psychotherapy, *J. Nerv. Ment. Dis.* 164:3–7, 1977.
202. Psychotherapy: The Restoration of Morale, *Weekly Psychiatry Update Series*, no. 19, Princeton, N.J.: Biomedia, 1977.
203. Nature and Functions of Belief Systems: Humanism and Transcendental Religion, *Am. Psychologist* 32:555–59, 1977.
204. Psychiatry, the Healthy Invalid, *Amer. J. Psychiat.* 134:1349–55, 1977.
205. *Effective Ingredients of Successful Psychotherapy*, New York: Brunner/Mazel, 1978 (with R. Hoehn-Saric, S. D. Imber, B. L. Liberman, and A. R. Stone).
206. Kurt Lewin in Retrospect—A Psychiatrist's View, *J. of the History of the Behavioral Sciences* 14:223–27, 1978.

Index

324